WEST AFRICAN CHURCH
HISTORY

WEST AFRICAN CHURCH HISTORY

Christian Missions and Church Foundations: 1482-1919

BY

J. KOFI AGBETI

LEIDEN
E. J. BRILL
1986

ISBN 90 04 07167 9

PRINTED IN THE NETHERLANDS BY E. J. BRILL

CONTENTS

PREFACE

History may be defined in a variety of ways.[1] But all the definitions agree that history is an unbiased story—the story of the experiences of people in their interaction with one another either as individuals or groups.

So one of the purposes for writing this book is to tell, as objectively as possible, the story of how Europeans and American Christian missionaries laid the foundations of the Church in West Africa from 1482 to 1919.

Some people may question the wisdom of this exercise when already there are many books about Christian History in West Africa. It is true that such books exist—most of them are included in the bibliography at the end of this book. But the more pertinent issue to raise about these books is the question whether or not they are histories in the sense mentioned above—unbiased stories.

It will be noticed even by a cursory reader that by 1980, most of the extant books on the subject were written between 1948 and 1968. This was the period when modern nationalism in West Africa emerged and culminated in the independence of many African countries. With the appearance of Dr. Kwame Nkrumah in Ghana in 1948 a new impetus was introduced into the political history of West Africa and Ghana in particular. The agitation for independence was intensified and hastened by the magnetism of Dr. Nkrumah. Thus Ghana's independence in 1957 was followed by that of Guinea in 1958, Mauretania, Togo, Dahomey (Benin), Senegal, Mali, Niger, Chad, Ivory Cost, Nigeria, Central African Republic and Gabon in 1960 respectively, Sierra Leone in 1961 and the Gambia in 1965.

This was the period when some African writers of modern times sought to expose only the extent to which the Colonial powers exploited their colonies. Many African Christian scholars who wrote during this period on Mission History in West Africa were also caught up with this new na-

---

[1] C. J. Renier, *History Its Purpose and Method* (George Allen & Unwin Ltd. 1950); Jan Vansina translated by H. M. Wright, *Oral Tradition. A Study in Historical Methodology* (Routledge & Kegan Paul, London 1965). G. Kitson Clark, *The Critical Historian* (Heinemann, London 1967); Gilbert J. Garraghan S. J., *A Guide to Historical Method* (Fordham University Press, New York 1946) etc. It is true however, that most histories are biased because historians are very selective in the materials they use in telling their stories. The point being made here is that the genuine historian endeavours to interpret the materials he is using as objectively as possible though it can be conceded that it is only the actor but not the observer that can be most accurately objective.

tionalism. But unlike the extreme nationalist secular historians who saw the colonial powers as only exploiters, some of the African Church Historians were more objective. Although they agreed that the imperialists eroded African values to some extent they also conceded that Christianity brought some values with it. But their approach was more of political and sociological analysis than historical.

A few examples may suffice. Professors J. F. A. Ajayi and E. A. Ayandele both Nigerians wrote in the 1960's. Ajayi's book, *Christian Mission in Nigeria 1841-1891. The Making of a New Elite* (Longmans) was published in 1965 while Ayandele's *The Missionary Impact on Modern Nigeria. 1842-1914. A Political and Social Analysis* (Longmans) came out in 1966. So these authors were more concerned with the effects rather than the story of the Missionary work in Nigeria. Thus the books lack the warmth and the vigour of a continuous and an unbiased story.

Some Western missionaries did not take kindly to the condemnation of their work by African writers. For instance, T. A. Beetham, a Methodist missionary who spent many years in Africa, especially in the Gold Coast (Ghana) in the field of education, wrote his *Christianity and the New Africa* (London) in 1967. His work is apologetic: the new African nationalists were taking the missionary and their work in Africa to task but they owed their enlightenment and education to the efforts and sacrifice of selfless missionaries.

In 1968 Prof. C. G. Baeta edited *Christianity in Tropical Africa: Studies Presented and Discussed at the Seventh International African Seminar at the University of Ghana* (Oxford). The book is not a history of Christianity in Africa. A variety of problems relating to the Christian faith and its interaction with Africans and their culture were discussed. Many papers were read by specialists in their own fields. Most of the African contributors concerned themselves mainly with the negative impact of Christianity in Africa. Any historical materials included were only incidental to the main motivation: a critical appraisal of Christianity in the African environment.

Similarly , G. O. Oosthuizen's *Post-Christianity. A Theological and Anthropological Study* (London 1968) is obviously not a history.

Other authors however wrote histories of Christianity in West Africa. But the weakness of most of them is that they were limited in scope to single denominations as they operated in particular countries. For example among Protestant Authors may be included:
F. L. Bartels, *The Roots of Ghana Methodism* (Cambridge 1965); Noel Smith, *The Presbyterian Church of Ghana 1835-1960* (Waterville Accra 1960), S. G. Williamson, *Christianity and the Akan Culture* (Accra 1965); H. W. Debrunner, *A History of Christianity in Ghana* (Accra 1967). Debrun-

ner's book is valuable as an extensive source book for historians. As a history book it is inadequate because the stories are only outlines of missionary activities in Ghana alone.

Roman Catholic historians in this group include:

M. J. Bane, *Catholic Pioneers in West Africa* (Dublin, 1956); R. M. Wiltgen, *Gold Coast Mission History, 1471-1880* (Illinois, USA. 1956); J. M. Todd, *African Mission—A Historical Study of the Society of African Missions* (London 1962); M. Pfann, *A Short History of the Catholic Church in Ghana* (Cape Coast, 1965). Although these are also histories in the proper sense of the word, they too are limited in scope—they deal only with Roman Catholic activities.

Of all the writers on Christian History in West Africa up-to-date, it is only C. P. Groves who has treated his subject with comparative satisfaction. He has told unbiased "stories" about the activities of most of the Christian missions in Africa. Between 1948 and 1958, Groves published in 4 volumes, *The Planting of Christianity in Africa* (London). The unfortunate aspect of this work is that the stories of the missions are scattered about in the four volumes and this makes it irksome when one wants to extract the history of particular missions.

The absence of one comprehensive textbook on the subject is not satisfactory because it will retard progress in the teaching and study of the subject. The point is that at the time of compiling this volume, books were very expensive to buy. Consequently, for economic reasons students who may have wished to study the subject will be hindered because it will be difficult to buy the various denominational histories. Secondly, people now-a-days want less voluminous and simplified materials to read. I think this explains why comic literature has become popular among West African students. The time has therefore come for West African Church Historians to make the subject less cumbersome by providing a textbok which treats the history of the major missions in a single volume. Unless this is done quickly and effectively, the Church may eventually lose the accurate history of its growth and expansion in West Africa. This will be tragic for the Church for without accurate facts Christians of posterity may not be able to provide proper leadership to extremist nationalist critics of Christanity whose aim may be to eliminate the Church on the grounds that the missionaries connived with the colonial powers to exploit Africa.

Another reason why such a basic textbook dealing with the history of Christianity in West Africa is necessary concerns the attitude of Advanced Level candidates in West Africa. In Cape Coast, Ghana, by 1980 there were eight Advanced Level Secondary Schools, six of which had maintained Christian influence. The Christian Religious Studies Paper

III is offered by all these schools at the Higher School Certificate/General
Certificate of Education Advanced Level Examination. The Paper is
divided into Sections A—"The History of the Christian Church in West
Africa from the Eighteenth Century to the Present Day" and Section B—
"West African Traditional Religion". Although all these secondary
schools except two as mentioned above, were established by Christian
Missionaries and were still Christian in orientation, none of them offered
Section A at the Advanced Level Examinations.

Surprisingly enough it is not only in Cape Coast that Section A was not
popular. Many schools in English Speaking West Africa did not offer the
section in question. This is confirmed by the Chief Examiner's Annual
Reports. Two examples should suffice. In the June 1976 Report it was
stated that

> Section "A" of the paper which deals with the History of the Christian
> Church in West Africa was manageable but most candidates did not at-
> tempt it.... Almost all candidates avoided questions in this Section.[2]

Two years later, in 1978 the report did not indicate any improvement.
It was recorded that:

> Only few candidates answered questions from Section A and as one can ex-
> pect, the performance is too poor (sic.). This is more so because there are
> yet few authentic textbooks to serve as standard guides. Section B is not as
> dry as Section A, as stated above, may be due to more availability of stan-
> dard reading materials.[3]

This lack of patronage of Christian History by students, most of whom
are Christians, is a serious matter. But as one of the reports above says it
is not popular due to the lack of authentic textbooks. This lack may make
the teaching uninteresting and poor. As the students are aware of this
disability they will naturally be scared away. Thus another purpose for
which this book is being written is to supply this felt need; to provide a
comprehensive "story" of the Christian Church in West Africa from
1482 to 1919. 1482 is chosen as the lowest limit because it was from that
year that definite attempts were commenced in modern times to plant
Christianity in West Africa and these attempts were conterminous with
the nineteenth century attempts. 1919 is the upper limit because after
that year ecclesiastical autonomy was thrust on some of the Mission
Churches as a result of the exigencies of World War I. It was the end of
Missionary domination and the beginning of African ecclesiastical

---

[2] *The West African Examinations Council HSC/GCE Advanced Level Examinations June 1976.
Chief Examiners' Reports.*, p. 55.
[3] *Ibid.*, June 1978, p. 40.

autonomy. The progress towards African ecclesiastical autonomy is unique in itself and should be treated separately.

The immediate audience is Religious Studies teachers and students in Secondary Schools, Seminaries, Teacher Training Colleges and Universities. Church leaders both clergy and lay in West Africa may also find it useful. Above all, Missionary Societies both in Europe and America would love to read, from the pen of an African scholar, the history of western endeavours in laying the foundation of the Christian Church in West Africa.

With this as a basic texbook, the already extant books referred to above may be used more meaningfully as reference and supplementary books.

It is true that this book also may have its limitations. For example, most of the documents used were provided by Europeans and Americans. Thus the sources are biased towards Western European and North American perspectives. Surely, African "helpers" contributed a lot to the achievements of the foreign missionaries; yet much has not been said about them by their missionary masters in the reports they sent home to the Mission Boards. This deficiency may be supplied in an anticipated volume which will deal with "Christian Missions and African Initiative 1920-1975."

The footnotes and the bibliography at the end of the book indicate the range of my indebtedness to the sources used. Locally, my thanks go to the Conferences and Researches Committee, University of Cape Coast, and the Ghana Authorship Development Fund for supplying respectively, in parts, the funds which enabled me to travel in some West African Countries to collect materials and cross check some of the secondary sources used.

Many others, Church leaders, librarians, colleagues and friends who read the manuscript and offered useful criticisms, typists etc. contributed in no small way to the production of this book. To them also I extend my indebtedness. Finally, my special thanks go to Mrs. R. E. Pearson, who read through the manuscript and polished it up for publication. Any mistakes left in it, however, are mine and mine alone.

Rev. Dr. J. Kofi Agbeti
Senior Lecturer,
Dept. of Religious Studies,
University of Cape Coast,
Cape Coast, Ghana.

PART ONE

MISSIONS FROM WESTERN EUROPE

CHAPTER ONE

INTRODUCTION: UNSUCCESSFUL MISSIONARY VENTURES
1482-1816

20th January, 1482, has been traditionally acknowledged as the date on which Christianity was first introduced to West Africa in modern times. On that day, a Portuguese expedition of 600 men, under the command of Don Diogo d'Azambuja who had landed at Elmina, near Cape Coast, in Ghana, a day before

> suspended the banner of Portugal from the bough of a lofty tree, at the foot of which they erected an altar, and the whole company assisted at the first mass that was celebrated in Guinea, and prayed for the conversion of the natives from idolatry, and (sic) the perpetual prosperity of the church which they intended to erect upon the spot.[1]

After this ritual, Diogo d'Azambuja sought audience with the Chief of Elmina and told him about the Christian faith. The immediate benefits which the chief would derive from accepting this new faith, according to d'Azambuja, were purely materialistic: the King of Portugal would make alliance with the African King and profitable trade relationship would be established between them.

Apparently, the Elmina Chief was agreeable to the transaction and granted the Portuguese a site on which a fort and a chapel were built and dedicated to St. George.

The Portuguese interest in Africa antedated their advent in Elmina in 1482. As early as 1415, they captured Ceuta through the adventures of prince Henry the Navigator. The reason for this Portuguese exploration was a reaction against the Muslim Saracens or North African Arabs who had conquered Spain and Portugal in the 8th Century A. D. After this conquest Spain and Portugal reconquered their enemies and the Portuguese resolved to follow the Moslems to their own country in North Africa. It was in pursuit of this aspiration that Prince Henry the Navigator entered Ceuta.

Using Ceuta as a springboard, the Portuguese sent more expeditions down the West Coast of Africa because they wanted to:

(a) know what lay beyond the Canary Islands and Cape Bojador and to find a route to India.

---

[1] C. P. Groves, *The Planting of Christianity in Africa* (Lond.). Vol. I, p. 123, citing R. H. Major, *The Discoveries of Prince Henry the Navigator and their Results* (1877), 2nd ed., pp. 299-300.

(b)   find a Christian population with whom profitable trade might be established.

(c)   discover the strength of the Muslim Moors who were considered enemies of Portugal.

(d)   find Christian Princes of Africa who would aid the Portuguese against the Muslim enemies, and

(e)   evangelize Africans for Christ.

In pursuit of these aims Prince Henry the Navigator made attempts to send some of his captains down the Coast beyond Cape Bojador. He did not succeed until 1434 when Gil Eannes went beyond the Cape and found land thus disproving myths about Africa that for example, Christians who travelled beyond Cape Bojador would be turned into Negroes or that the tropical sun was so hot that it poured out liquid flames which could cook sailors.[2]

Henry had hoped that the Moorish prisoners who might be sent to Portugal would be converted. Indeed, a Negro taken to Portugal made such a remarkable progress in the faith that Henry had planned to get him trained as a missionary to be sent back to his own people. This did not happen because Henry died too soon, in 1460.

The expeditions, however, continued to be sent down the coast after his death. It was one of these expeditions which landed at Elmina in 1482.

A year later, in 1483, the Portuguese at Elmina, sent an embassy into the interior reaching as far as the Mandingo capital.[3]

Farther down the coast, in Nigeria, the King of Benin requested, around 1485, that the Portuguese send misionaries to his Kingdom. Although some misionaries were sent, their work was not successful because the real motive of the King of Benin was not to obtain missionaries but Portuguese armed help. Six years later, however, it was reported that a King of Benin was baptized. Then a century later, about 1591, it was reported that the Jesuit Father Barrerius baptized another King of Benin.[4]

Spanish Friars also visited Benin about 1655 and baptized the current King. Their work had started to bear some fruit when the Portuguese nipped it in the bud by compelling the missionaries to withdraw from the field as a result of the bitter political conflict that had arisen between Portugal and Spain at the time.

To the north, in Sierra Leone, an attempt was made by some Spanish Jesuits to establish a Church from the latter part of the sixteenth century.

---

[2] Groves, *op.cit.*, Vol. 1, p. 121.

[3] H. Labouret in *Encyclopedia of Islam*, Vol.III, p. 203(b).

[4] Groves, *op. cit.*, Vol. I, p. 127.

For example, Father Barrerius won over a Chief of Sierra Leone at the beginning of the seventeenth century. The Chief agreed to divorce all his wives, except one, in order to qualify for baptism. He was Christened Philip after Philip II of Spain. He made good progress in the Christian faith leading his sons and "many people" to conversion but the wife he retained refused baptism.

After the Jesuits, the Andalusian Friars also worked in Sierra Leone in the latter part of the seventeenth century with some initial successes only.

Thus though individual Roman Catholic Christians or groups visited the West Coast of Africa to evangelize the people their labours did not bear any permanent results because

> the Negro chiefs, it is true, were dazzled by the power and magnificence of their Portuguese visitors and inclined to view their religion favourably in this reflected light, but the motive of conversion in such cases was unequal to producing in the convert any change of life.[5]

In the seventeenth century a new factor was introduced into the Christian activities along the coast. Until the end of 1617 all Christian activities in West Africa, were carried out by the Roman Catholics. But from 1618 the Protestants also entered the field. In that year, the English "Company of Adventurers of London Trading to Africa" built two forts, along the coast located one in the Gambia, and the other at Cormantine in the Gold Coast.

Following the English, the Dutch entered the field in 1637, besieging the Portuguese fort at Elmina and capturing it from its owners. From 1642 onwards the Dutch took over other Portuguese forts along the coast including Fort St. Anthony at Axim.

Later, other Europeans, French, Danes, Swedes and Brandenburghers established themselves on the Coast. The Danes built a fort at Christiansborg, near Accra in about the middle of the seventeenth century. This is the castle which became the Government house of Ghana. The Swedes and Brandenburghers also built forts, but as they withdrew from the field quite early, the Danes and the Dutch took over their forts.

The main significance of these forts, for our study, is that Chaplains were provided for each to care for the spiritual welfare of the Europeans. The work of the chaplain constituted an essential part of the daily routine of the fort. William Bossman drew attention to this fact when he recorded that

> the 'Preacher' always stands second next to the Director-General. There is also a 'Clerk of Church' though he is last but one. The Preacher enjoyed a

---

[5] *Ibid.*, p. 126.

place at the Governor's table.... We are very religious; we are obliged to go
to Church every day, on forfeiture of twenty-five styvers, except on Sundays and Thursdays, when the forfeiture for omission is doubled.[6]

The main purpose of building the forts was commercial. But the
spiritual welfare of the occupants was taken seriously. This explains why
the work of the chaplain was rated very high. The chaplains, although
their main concern was to cater for the spiritual welfare of the in-mates of
the forts, rendered services to some of the local Africans, and this
prepared the ground for later organized evangelism of the Africans. For
example, they trained deserving African boys, as prospective chaplains
for the forts. These Africans prepared the ground for the work of the
nineteenth century missionaries as the following examples illustrate.

A Dutch captain, of a trading vessel to the Gold Coast, bought a Negro
slave boy whom he gave as a present to a Dutch merchant. This merchant named the slave boy Capitein in honour of the Captain. This name
was afterwards expanded to Jacobus Elisha Johannes Capitein. He
stayed with his master on the coast for three or four years, and when he
was eleven years old, he was taken by his master to Holland for education. He worked well and at the age of twenty he was given admission to
the University of Leyden in 1737. At the end of his five years' University
work he "delivered a Latin oration on the theme that slavery is not contrary to religious liberty".[7] After this he was ordained as a minister of the
Dutch Reformed Church to become the "first African to receive Protestant ordination."[8]

After his training he was appointed Chaplain to the fort St. George
d'Elmina, in Ghana. While he was serving the Company he tried to
develop the Fanti language: he translated into Fanti the Twelve Articles
of the Apostles' Creed which was published in 1744.

He did not, however, succeed as a Chaplain because of pertinent social
problems. For example, he married a European for which the Africans
ostracized him. Above all, the Europeans to whom he was expected to
minister would not accept him because of his colour. It seems this type of
embarrassment, his utter loneliness in the midst of his own people, was
too much for him to endure and after a very short career, he died at the
age of thirty.

The Danes also took a mulatto boy, Christian Protten, to
Copenhagen. There he became a Christian and was educated. After his
education he volunteered to go to Elmina as a missionary to the Dutch
fort and settlement. His offer was accepted by the Church of the Mora-

---

[6] Groves, *ibid.*, Vol. I p. 151.
[7] *Ibid.*, p. 151.
[8] *Loc. cit.*

vian Brethren.[9] Accompanied by a Moravian brother, Henry Huckoff, he sailed in 1737 for Elmina. Huckoff died soon after their arrival. Temperamentally, Protten was not suited for missionary work for it has been suggested that he behaved as if he was "in danger of apprehension as a run-away slave".[10] Consequently, he moved back and forth to Europe. In 1756 he returned again to Africa and settled at Christiansborg, the Danish station. He stayed only for five years and returned to Europe. Between 1763 and 1769 when he died he only rendered spasmodic service at Christiansborg. Although he failed as a missionary he too tried to develop the Fanti language, succeeding in the production of a Fanti grammar in 1764 including Fanti translations of selected Bible passages.

The English people also formed two Societies during the period: in 1699 the Society for the Propagation of the Gospel (SPG) and in 1701 the Society for the Propagation of Christian Knowledge (SPCK). Their purpose was missionary; but their main concern was not the evangelization of Africans but the spiritual well being of the European traders abroad.

The Society for the Propagation of the Gospel worked in the West Indies and the Americas. In 1745 it appointed the Rev. Thomas Thompson as a missionary to New Jersey. He had resigned his post as a curate of Christ's College, Cambridge in 1744 in order to become a Missionary. While he was in New Jersey he became interested in the education of the Negroes on the American plantations and admitted some of them into his congregation. After a while he felt called to serve the Negroes in their home land in Africa. Thus in 1750 he requested the S.P.G. to grant him permission to go to Africa, particularly West Africa, "to make a trial with the Natives, and see what hopes there would be of introducing among them the Christian Religion".[11] His request was favourably considered and in 1751 he was appointed a missionary to the Gold Coast, now Ghana, on an annual salary of £ 70.00.

He sailed from New York direct to West Africa. He stopped at Fort James on the Gambia and in Sierra Leone before reaching Cape Coast where he resided at the Cape Coast Castle. From there he made contacts with the local people and began preaching to them through an interpreter. Of his first service he had this to report:

> I preached to them on the Nature and Attributes of God; his Providence; and of a Future State, having one to interpret to them. After coming to

---

[9] *Ibid.*, p. 173.

[10] *Loc. cit.*

[11] *Ibid.*, p. 174 citing T. Thompson, *An Account of Two Missionary Voyages* (1758 reprinted, 1937), p. 23.

speak upon the Christian Religion, some of them made a Motion to go away, but I desired their patience a little longer, and they sat till I had done.[12]

Initially, he had worship service for the local people only once a week because they were not prepared to meet him more often. Some of them even wanted to be given liquor, as a price for attending the services. Moreover as there was no Chaplain for the merchants in the Castle he had to add their pastoral care to his duties. The immoral life of the Europeans made his work more difficult. In spite of this difficulty Thompson was greatly encouraged by some of the mulattoes who had been christened in infancy. Thus gradually, some of the local adults were baptized.

Unfortunately, however, within four years his health failed and he had to return to England in 1756 without having established any church.

Although his brief work seemed to bear no effective results, Thompson was the first Anglican missionary to come to West Africa and to succeed "in winning the first African to receive Anglican ordination."[13] It has been recorded that in 1754, he selected three Cape Coast African boys and sent them to England to be educated at Islington. These boys made remarkable progress because, as reported by Groves, after seven weeks "one of them could say the Lord's Prayer and the Apostles' Creed, and the other two answered well".[14] Unfortunately, one of them died of tuberculosis in 1758. The surviving two asked for baptism which they received in 1759. Soon after that one of them lost his reason and died leaving only one survivor Philip Quaque.[15]

When Philip Quaque completed his studies, he was ordained into the Priesthood of the Church of England, the first non-European to do so since the Reformation, and in 1765 he was appointed by the S.P.G. "as their 'Missionary, School Master and Catechist to the Negroes on the Gold Coast'."[16] In addition, he was to be the Chaplain to the Company of Merchants.

He arrived on the Coast in 1766 and laboured for fifty years. These years did not bear any effective evangelistic results. The first problem Quaque encountered was the difficulty of social adjustment. While in England he forgot his mother tongue, Fanti, and this made it difficult for him to communicate with his own people. Consequently, in 1769, the S.P.G. had to urge him "to endeavour to recover his own language".[17]

---

[12] Thompson, *ibid.*, pp. 35-36 cited in Groves, *op.cit.*, Vol. I, p. 174.

[13] *Ibid.*, p. 175

[14] *Loc. cit.*

[15] Thompson, *op. cit.*, pp. 66-67. See also C. F. Pascoe, *Two Hundred Years of the S.P.G.* (1901) I., p. 256.

[16] Groves, *loc. cit.,* Vol.I.

[17] *Ibid.*, p. 176.

This barrier to communication rendered his evangelistic work among the local people very difficult. Thus after nine years' labours he was able to baptize only fifty-two people, including Europeans and mulatto children.

Another social difficulty was that Quaque did not have any missionary colleagues with whom to share his burdens and loneliness. Consequently, from 1774, he became so bored with the life at the castle that he started visiting other trading centres for several months at a time. This made the S.P.G. consider removing him from Cape Coast to some other part of Africa where he might be more useful.

The other major problem was moral and religious. When Thomas Thompson arrived on the Coast, the chief of Cape Coast complained about the immoral lives of the Europeans who professed the Christian faith. The problem was still there during the time of Philip Quaque. The lives of most of the European traders on the Coast were unworthy examples of the Christian ideal that he preached. It has been even reported that "one Governor openly ridiculed religion, public worship was sometimes suspended for nearly a year, and in general the effect was to offer the Negro the white man's vices rather than his religion".[18] Even in 1791 the Governor ordered Philip Quaque "to attend him to Anomabu to take up arms in defence of the fort".[19] When Quaque refused to obey the order, because it was contrary to his Christian conviction, he was suspended as chaplain; "but on appeal to the African Company he was reinstated with an increased salary".[20]

Finally, he had severe economic handicaps. It seems he was inadequately remunerated. Consequently, he diverted his attention to trade. It seems that it was true that he had "quite deviated from the Intentions of the Society, and his proper line of Duty by paying more Attention to the Purposes of Trade than of Religion"[21] because by the time he died in 1816 he had not drawn his salary from the Society for five years.

Thus it is clear that even though individuals and some Christian groups were concerned about introducing Christianity to West Africa during this period, their efforts were not successful in the sense that no effective and permanent mission stations and Churches were established. This was because the Africans trained for the purpose, as seen above, were not temperamentally suited for the evangelistic work, the traditional African political environment was not stable enough to enable the castle Chaplains to reach out among the people without fear and the majority of the Europeans on the Coast, the merchants, did not encourage the Mis-

---

[18] *Loc. cit.*
[19] *Loc. cit.*
[20] *Loc. cit.*
[21] *Loc. cit.*

sionaries in their work because trade, not evangelism, was the main purpose of the Europeans who invaded West Africa during this period.[22]

Towards the end of this period, however, there was a general change in
the Western European attitude to Christianity and the Christian Faith
became alive again. This led to the emergence of the Evangelical Revival
and the reawakening of missionary zeal in Western Europe and America.
The sponsors of this revival chose Africa and Asia as their immediate
spheres of operation. The stories which follow are accounts of how the
major Missionary Societies who laboured in English-speaking West
Africa from the nineteenth century until World War I endeavoured to
bring the Christian faith to the Africans in West Africa.

---

[22] See S. K. Odamtten, *The Missionary Factor in Ghana's Development (1820-1880)* (Accra,
1978), pp. 11-29, for a fuller discussion relating to the reasons for the failure of the missionary work.

CHAPTER TWO

THE ROOTS IN EUROPE AND AMERICA

The Missionary Societies which founded the Church in English-speaking West Africa came from Western Europe and America. The circumstances which led to their formation are described below.

Church History has often been divided into epochs such as the Apostolic Age, the Early Church, the Dark Ages, the Middle Ages, the Reformation and the Modern Times.

The Apostolic Age deals with the period and work of the surviving Twelve Disciples (the Apostles) after the Resurrection and the Ascension of Jesus until the death of the last of their number John, the Divine, on the Island of Patmos between AD 98 and 117.

This period was followed by that of the Early Church, during which the young Christians continued to build the Church and suffer opposition and persecution mainly from the Emperors. But Constantine who became Emperor in 313 A.D., put an end to the persecutions, proclaimed Sunday, a public holiday in 321 A.D. and "Christianity was officially commended, emperor worship was forbidden and some pagan temples were destroyed."[1]

As the Christians began to enjoy political peace, they turned their attention to the development of their faith. They struggled to work out an acceptable doctrine about the relation between God and the Son: they wanted to know whether or not the Son was *Equal* with the Father and the kind of relation which existed between the two natures in Jesus. That is they wanted to know if the Incarnate Christ (Jesus on earth) had both the Divine and Human Natures in Him at once or whether He had only *One* Nature.

It was not easy for the theologians such as Tertullian, Arius, Athanasius, the Cappadocian Fathers, Nestorius, Cyril of Alexandria, the Antiochene Christologists and others to resolve these problems amicably. Their impatience with one another, their pride and lack of love for their opponents led to many divisions within the Church.

Many Councils were convened at various times to heal the divisions, but without much success. In 451 A.D., however, there was a partial settlement of some of the theological problems at Chalcedon. It was only

---

[1] Wilfred W. Biggs, *An Introduction to the History of the Christian Church* (London, Edward and Arnold, 1965), p. 21

a partial solution because the Christians from the Eastern section of the Roman Empire, led by the Antiochene theologians, were not satisfied with the Chalcedonian decision that the Incarnate Christ had *Two Natures* (human and divine) as taught by the Alexandrian theologians led by Cyril.

As Rome lent very strong support to the Alexandrian (Western) view against the Antiochene (Eastern) view that the Incarnate Christ had only *One Nature*, the Antiochene theologians felt that they had lost the battle. As a result, the Eastern Christendom, especially in the Byzantine Empire, refused to accept the decision of Chalcedon. Thus Christendom became divided into two geographical areas: Western Christendom with Headquarters in Rome and Eastern Christendom with Headquarters in Constantinople.

At this point we shall omit the history of Eastern Christendom and concentrate on the life of Western Christendom because it is there that the roots of the Churches in West Africa are found.

The next five hundred years in Western Christendom, from about 451 A.D. to 950 A.D., are referred to as the Dark Ages. This was the period when barbarian tribes from north-eastern Europe and Arabs invaded the Roman Empire causing it to capitulate in 476 A.D.[2] Conditions remained unstable until 950 A.D., when the Western Christians reconquered the barbarians and reestablished the "true" Christian faith.[3] But where the Arabs conquered, the loss to the Christian faith was decisive.

The next epoch, known as the Middle Ages, from about 950 A.D. to 1500 A.D., was an era of vigorous Christian expansion in Western Christendom. During the period, the power of the Pope increased as the church advanced until he wielded supreme authority over Western Christendom. Unfortunately, however, geographical expansion did not match with spiritual maturity and growth in the Church. Rather, morals declined considerably in the fourteenth century A.D. The few righteous people left in the Church did not sit unconcerned. Men like John Wyclif (1320-1384) and John Huss (1366-1415) raised opposition against the falling morals in the Church. These initial calls for reform within the Church were, however, brutally silenced by the Church leaders who executed some of these early reformers.

---

[2] The invasion was very extensive. For example the Visigoths were in Spain, Ostragoths in Italy, Burgundians in Southern France, Vandals in North Africa, Anglo-Saxons in Britain and the Franks in Northern France —these were all Teutonic tribes. The Arabs invaded Southern Europe.

[3] It should be noted that the Teutonic invaders were tribes from heretical Christian areas.

From 1500 A.D. we enter the period of the Modern Church. With the emergence of the Modern Church came the decline of the Papal authority. During the period the whole of Western Europe was becoming nationally and politically conscious. Socially, communications were improving and an agricultural economy began to emerge. As a result cooperatives were formed through feudal ties. As commerce grew and cities were built some of the kingdoms in Europe became powerful, and some of the Kings began to interfere politically with the authority of the Pope. They found his influence with their domains untenable. They desired to have, for example, ecclesiastical control in their lands. As a result of the growth of nationalism some of the Christians themselves now preferred political leadership and security to Papal authority in these matters.

At the same time the renaissance set people's minds free to examine events critically. So the evils that had been existing within the Church were now questioned more openly. Thus Erasmus in Rome in 1509 and Luther in Germany in 1511 were so much appalled by the corruption they saw among the Bishops and the Priests in the Churches in these places that they could not hold their peace. They demanded reformation. It should be noted that this was not the first time that the few righteous people left in the corrupt Church demanded reform—Wyclif, Huss and others had lost their lives in previous centuries for demanding reform in the Church. But now the Church leaders could no longer nip this call for reform in the bud. The demand now was more potent because of people's awareness of the defects in the Church. Moreover now there was the possibility of remedy because the Pope's authority had been decreased by the secular changes taking place in Western Europe and the reformers of the period could look to secular governments for help when necessary. For example, if the Pope and Bishops refused to show interest in the call for reform, the monarch could now order them to take the required action or be deposed.

In this new setting Erasmus and Luther inspired the educated men of their time, who longed for the purity of life in the Church, to rise up against the corrupt Ecclesiastical order. Erasmus himself attacked the traditionalism and the orthodoxy of the Church in Rome. Though he did not live to see the cleansing of the Church actually done, his work was brought to fruition by Martin Luther whose activities actually brought the Protestant Reformation into being in Germany from 1515 A.D.

It is true that Luther and the other Reformers such as Zwingli (1484-1531) in Switzerland and Calvin (1509-1564) in Geneva raised the moral standard of their Churches and eventually compelled the Roman Catholic authorities to execute a self-reexamination at Trent between 1545 and 1563. Unfortunately, however, the Reformation also split the

Western Christendom into two: the Protestant and Roman Catholic denominations. Worst of all, the Protestant group itself became further and further sub-divided, as time went on, into other smaller Protestant denominations.

We cannot end a summary of the Reformation Movement in Western Europe without looking also at what happened in Britain. From the Continent of Europe the Reformation spirit spread to Great Britain. In Scotland, John Knox (1505-1572) opposed the Catholic Church and as a result of his Reformation activities, the Presbyterian form of Church organization developed in Scotland around 1560. From Scotland the Presbyterian form of Church Government spread to France where they were known as the Hugenots; they co-existed with the Roman Catholics.

In England, at the beginning of the sixteenth century, the ordinary people, the academics and the educated, were also dissatisfied with the Ecclesiastical Order. But unlike the academics and the educated people of mainland Europe, the English scholars were not in a position to do anything about the corruptions in the Church. So in England the Reformation was due to a factor other than the agitation of the scholars: it was largely due to the person of King Henry VIII. Through the King's marital manœuvres, the authority of the Pope as the Ecclesiastical Head of the Church in England was questioned. Thus between 1530 and 1534, Thomas Cranmer (1489-1556), a lecturer at the University of Cambridge and the chief advisor of King Henry VIII, progressively led the Church in England to proclaim its independence of Rome. Nationalistic feeling in England lent support to the King's opposition to Rome and, gradually, the King replaced the Pope as the Head of the Church by definition.

Henry's Reformation was not as doctrinal as the Protestant Reformation in general. It was only a political reformation; accordingly, the English schism from Rome was without heresy as such. Henry remained a fervent Roman Catholic and he suppressed Protestantism during his time. Thus the Church of England remained a new Roman Catholic Church—the Anglo-Catholic Church (Anglican Church).

But during the reign of Henry's successors, there was violent reaction in England against the Reformation; this opposition reached its climax during the reign of Queen Mary.

Two centuries later, in the eighteenth century, John Wesley, a deacon of the Anglo-Catholic Church, became unhappy about the spiritual slumber within the Church. The Church authorities, however, opposed his call for and activities towards reform. Gradually, John was so discouraged by the leaders of the church that he was compelled to break away and form the Wesleyan Methodist Connexion in 1744 taking with him his followers.

The Evangelical Revival which John Wesley initiated in England in the eighteenth century, was a reaction against Deism. This secular philosophy stood for a system which believed that God could be known only through nature and not through revealed religion or Biblical Revelation. This way of looking at existence had begun in the seventeenth century. At that time certain groups of scholars became convinced that:

> The Universe was subject, not to arbitrary action, divine or other but to immutable law, and men began to look upon the world in which they lived, not as the centre of the universe, but as a moving speck in the great stream of being.[4]

The immediate result was that the scholars began questioning seriously fundamental Christian belief. Descartes (1596-1650), for example, began by doubting everything of set purpose and regarding clearness as the sole test of truth.[5] This means, in the words of Wilfred W. Biggs, that Descartes "[reduced] truth to the certainty of self-knowledge, and [enthroned] doubt as an important element in human enquiry".[6] Although Descartes retained his Christian faith, he did not employ it in his enquiries. This kind of attitude developed gradually among the scholars until in 1679 Hobbes said that "the scripture itself must be subject to human reason."[7] It was this type of argument and methodology which led people to reject revealed religion, and to accept and rely on natural religion (Deism).

Those who held this view (Deists), during the period, came to believe that Christianity was not a fit subject of enquiry: it was fictitious since it could not be subjected to the Baconian method of observation and inductive experiment.

So towards the end of the seventeenth century and by the beginning of the eighteenth, natural religion (religion based on the natural observable facts in the world) had almost replaced revealed religion (religion based on revelation) and the Christian faith declined considerably again. As a result, Christian and social behaviour were at a very low ebb.

In this distressing situation, like-minded Christians discovered one another; their common aspiration was the need for spiritual revival. They struggled to seek and discover the spiritual purpose for life. This, they believed, could be found through the quickening influence of the Christian revelation.

It was at this juncture that John Wesley and his Oxford friends and later followers set themselves the task of revival. Their aim was to lead

---

[4] J. W. C. Wand, *A History of the Modern Church from 1500 A.D.* (Lond. 1952), p. 172.
[5] *Ibid.*, p. 173.
[6] Biggs, *op. cit.*, p. 182.
[7] Wand, *op. cit.*, p. 175.

people away from spiritual slavery by guiding and teaching them to turn their attention to a diligent and prayerful study of the Bible. This new spirit of Biblical enquiry, in search for spiritual freedom, culminated, at the beginning of the nineteenth century, in the formation of the anti-slavery movements.

The actual Evangelical group which fanned the antislavery agitation is referred to in history as the Clapham sect. John Venn caught the evangelical spirit and when he became rector of Clapham in 1785 he formed an Evangelical group. This fellowship met often in the house of Henry Thornton (1760-1815), a wealthy banker at Clapham Common, West London. Other members included Granville Sharp (1735-1813) who, greatly interested in the welfare of slaves, had influenced the British Parliament in 1772 to give a ruling against the forcible detention of slaves, James Stephen (1758-1832) a barrister and William Wilberforce (1759-1833) MP. At their meetings they discussed the Christian faith and the slave trade. They took up seriously Sharp's concern for the freedom of the slaves and through their agitation slavery became illegal not only in the British Isles but throughout the British Empire. But this created a problem: what should happen to the freed slaves? After some considera-tion Parliament decided that the slaves should be repatriated to the conti-nent from which they had been purchased. Upon the recommendation of Dr. Henry Smeathman, a naturalist, who had been to Sierra Leone, that country was chosen as their new home and Granville Sharp put in charge of the operation. Smeathman had presented a memorandum "strongly advocating Sierra Leone as a suitable and salubrious locality for a settle-ment".[8] He did not think that the climatic conditions in Sierra Leone would pose any difficulties to the slaves.

So in 1787, after the Clapham Sect and the Quakers had succeeded in forming a Society for the Abolition of the Slave Trade in order to educate the English people, the first batch[9] of freed slaves was despatched to Sierra Leone. It was hoped that eventually Sierra Leone might be made a centre of civilization and Christianity. This expedition, however, met with disaster because the rainy season during which they arrived was not conducive to good health, and the leaders were ignorant of the character of the settlers. Granville Sharp had assumed that they were self-disciplined but this was not so.

The venture, however, was not abandoned. Later the Sierra Leone Company was formed and approved by the British Government. Its

---

[8] C. P. Groves, *The Planting of Christianity in Africa* Vol. I (London, 1964), p. 184. See also Chapter III below, p. 19.

[9] *Loc. cit.*, the batch comprised 411 people including "sixty women of ill repute, without Grandville Sharp's knowledge".

motive was philanthropic and it aimed to abolish the slave trade completely, educate the freed slaves, set them up in agricultural work and promote good government amongst them.

In 1807, the bill to abolish the slave trade was passed in the British Parliament. Between 1808 and 1832, the bill was operative but slavery continued. So, in 1833, the bill to prohibit slavery was introduced and passed. In the following year, 1834, this bill was operative throughout the British Dominion.

From all this struggle, two important facts emerged. First, those Evangelicals of Clapham demonstrated a genuine Christian desire to preserve the freedom of men, both spiritually and materially. Second, Evangelism would be meaningless to slaves. Thus the abolition of the slave trade and of slavery was necessary for the Evangelism of Africa.

These points were practically demonstrated, before the Prohibition Bill, in the formation of most of the Missionary Societies whose sole purpose was to evangelize Africa and Asia.[10]

Briefly, Dr. Coke tried to form, in 1784, an undenominational society, *"the Society for the Establishment of Missions among the Heathens"*. His aim was, first, to educate the missionaries at home in the local language of the proposed mission field before sending them out and, second, to print the Holy Scriptures for the use of prospective converts. These plans did not succeed because they met with little support.

In 1792 the *Baptist Missionary Society* was formed by William Carey who went to India and was supported by the evangelicals in England. Three years after that in 1795 the *London Missionary Society* was formed in response to letters received from Sierra Leone and India. This was an Inter-denominational society. Its centre of activity was South Africa. Various others were also formed after this as follows:

1796 - *Edinburgh and Glasgow Missionary Societies*—both of which were inter-denominational.

1799 - *Church Missionary Society*—The Claphamites were its active counsellors. It was sanctioned by the Archbishop of Canterbury in 1800. Its First field of activity was Sierra Leone.

1804 - *The British and Foreign Bible Society* came into being. The Claphamites were associated with this also. It aimed at a wide distribution of the Bible without commentary in order that the converts might learn from the source of preaching.

---

[10] It is debatable whether Evangelism was the primary and sole aim of the Missionary societies or exploitation. Readers may begin to debate this now. A full comment will be made in Part III.

1810 -   Meanwhile, *American Missionary Societies* were being formed from
         1810. Their immediate target was the Congo. In English speak-
         ing areas they worked mainly in Sierra Leone, Liberia and
         Nigeria.

1813 -   *The Wesleyan Methodist Missionary Society* was born and directed by
         the Wesleyan Methodist Conference. It began its work in West
         Africa, in the Gambia, in 1821.

1815 -   *The Basel Missionary Society* was formed. This society initially
         opened a Training Centre for the training of Missionaries in
         Basel. Its first missionaries came to West Africa in 1828.

1836 -   *The Northern German Missionary Society* came into being and it
         began its work in West Africa, at Peki, in 1847, in Eweland.

1856 -   *The Society of African Missions*, (Societas Missionum ad Afros) was
         founded by Bishop Marion Bresillac. His intention was to form a
         society of young missionaries, who would devote their lives to the
         conversion of Africans. The missionaries were to spend their
         whole life in the mission field among the converts. The Society
         started its work in Sierra Leone in 1859, Benin (Dahomey) in
         1860, Nigeria in 1867 and Ghana in 1880.

It will be seen that the nature of the Church in West Africa, after it had
been founded—a divided Church—happened to be so because its roots in
Western Europe and America had been divided by the Reformation. The
denominations which emerged from the Reformation developed different
kinds of doctrine, church organization and liturgy. Thus the Missionary
Societies, which built the West African Churches imposed their respec-
tive denominational practices and differences on the new converts in the
mission fields, the first of which was Sierra Leone.

CHAPTER THREE

CHURCH MISSIONARY SOCIETY: THE BEGINNINGS IN SIERRA LEONE, 1804 - 1914

The Church Missionary Society, the principal missionary society formed by the Church of England, in 1799, selected Sierra Leone as its first mission field.[1]

The historical reason why Sierra Leone was chosen may be stated briefly as follows: between 1771 and 1774, Henry Smeathman, an amateur botanist, spent three years in Sierra Leone, on the Banana Islands, off the coast, and collected botanical specimens for Sir Joseph Banks at Kew Gardens in England. Feeling he knew the area, when the problem of resettling the freed slaves arose,[2] Smeathman urged the "Committee for Relieving the Black Poor" to select Sierra Leone. This counsel was one of the cogent reasons which encouraged the English Government to send the freed slaves to Sierra Leone. Consequently, from 1787 three batches were despatched: the first group arrived in Freetown from England in 1787. The Temne Chief, King Tom sold a 20 mile square piece of land to the immigrants and the village which they developed was named Granville Town.

The settlers met with very serious problems which jeopardized the future of the colony. In the first place, the climate was not conducive to their health and many became sick. Secondly, the local population was antagonistic to them. In 1789 the settlers were attacked by King Jimmy (King Tom's successor) and Granville Town was burnt down. As a result, the settlers were dispersed but the experiment did not collapse completely. Some English benefactors intervened. They formed the St. George's Bay Association and received a charter in 1791 as the Sierra Leone Company. The company sent one Mr. Falconbridge as an agent to reorganize a new site near the former one. When he got to Granville Town, Mr. Falconbridge gathered about 50 of the settlers and a new Granville Town was built at Fourah Bay (later known as Cline Bay).

The second batch of settlers arrived in 1792 from Nova Scotia. These were slaves who fought on the side of their British masters during the American War of Independence. After the war, they were taken to Canada by their masters, freed and settled at Nova Scotia. The climate in

---

[1] Chapter II p. 16.
[2] See also Chapter XI below.

Canada was unbearably cold for them. The Sierra Leone Company heard about their plight and gave them asylum in Sierra Leone. About 1,200 of them were taken there at the expense of the British Government. They founded a new settlement on the old site of Granville Town and named it Freetown.

The third group of settlers, consisted initially of 550 Maroons. These were slaves who had escaped from their masters and settled in the mountains of Jamaica. After some time, they were exiled from Jamaica and went to settle in Nova Scotia. Later they were permitted to join the Sierra Leone group. They arrived in Freetown in 1800.

The fourth group was made up of liberated slaves who had been set free from captured slave ships and settled by the British in Sierra Leone.

The African settlers from Britain, Canada and America to the settlement were Christians. They belonged to a variety of denominations comprising the Countess of Huntingdon's Connexion, Baptist, Wesleyan, Anapatist etc. This implies that before the Church Missionary Society started work in Sierra Leone, Christianity had already been introduced to the country. But since the liberated slaves mentioned in group four above were not Christians, missionary work among the settlers was still necessary.

In addition to the concern for evangelizing the liberated slaves the C.M.S. chose Sierra Leone and its neighbourhood as its first missionary field because the founders of the Society, the Claphamites, had hoped that civilization and Christianity might eventually be carried to the rest of Africa, using Sierra Leone as the radiating centre.[3]

Another reason for the choice of Sierra Leone was that a number of the shareholders in the Sierra Leone Company were members of the C.M.S. committee. Fourthly, Zachary Macaulay, retiring from the governorship of Sierra Leone in 1799 took 25 Sierra Leonean children (21 boys and 4 girls) with him to England. They were sent to school and the good progress they made aroused the C.M.S. committee's interest in the future of Sierra Leone. The committee became convinced that when the youths returned home after their education, they would teach the same truths of scripture history they had learnt to their country men. Finally and above all Macaulay's knowledge of Sierra Leone and its environs and his painful disappointment when the initial attempt to settle the freed slaves failed made him encourage the C.M.S. to take up the work in Sierra Leone.

The pioneer C.M.S. Missionaries who went to Sierra Leone were German not English. Three main reasons have been recorded to explain this. Firstly, no Church of England Clergy offered for service in the Sierra

---

[3] C. P. Groves, *Planting of Christianity in Africa* (London) Vol. I, p. 205.

Leone Mission field. Secondly, the Bishops were not willing to ordain men for the society's service. Thirdly, the plan to send lay catechists failed. This lack of interest was due to the fact that the English were apprehensive of the devastating climate along the West Coast of Africa, especially Sierra Leone, and that the Evangelicals in the C.M.S. were not missionary minded enough.[4] This does not mean that individual Anglican ministers were not missionary minded. Far from it. As early as 1792 Melville Horne, an Anglican Clergyman was in Sierra Leone as Chaplain to the immigrant settlers. He had a burning zeal for evangelism. He had intended to carry the good news to the local people in addition to his chaplaincy work. He became disappointed when this missionary zeal could not be satisfied as a result of crowded chaplaincy duties. He left Freetown for England and recommended the field for serious consideration to prospective Christian workers who would go to Sierra Leone.

As missionaries were not available in Britain, the C.M.S. turned its attention to the Berlin Missionary Seminary. This seminary was established as a result of the Missionary Awakening on the continent, to train missionaries for the London Missionary Society which was an International Organization.

Two of the Students, Melchior Renner and Peter Hartwig, responded to the appeal of the C.M.S. and in 1802, were accepted as missionary catechists for work in the Susu country. They were sent to London where they received training in the use of the English and Susu languages in the African Academy at Clapham. After the training, they returned to Germany in 1803, where they received Lutheran ordination. In January 1804 they were consecrated as missionaries and on 14th April, the same year, they arrived in Freetown.

The policy they were to follow was outlined in the valedictory charge given them before their departure thus:

> You will take all prudent occasions of weaning the Native Chiefs from this traffic (slave-Trade) by depicting its criminality, the miseries which it occasions to Africa.[5]

During the first two years of their arrival on the mission field, Renner and Hartwig remained in the Colony and worked as Chaplains. The C.M.S. was reluctant to approve that they should advance immediately among the indigenous people because, in the first place, one Peter Greig had been murdered outside the Colony.[6] In the second place, the Slave

---

[4] See the note on the ''18th Century Missionary Attempts,'' Groves. Vol. I, p. 184 ff.

[5] *Ibid.*, p. 214.

[6] *Ibid.*, p. 211-212. The Glasgow and Edinburgh Societies sent missionaries to Sierra Leone in 1795. Peter Greig belonged to the Edinburgh society. He and his colleague Henry Brunton were sent by Macaulay to Rio Pongas. There Greig was murdered by Fulani traders because probably they coveted his personal belongings.

Trade had not died out completely at Rio Pongas one of the principal Slave Trading Centres in the Susu country which was earmarked as a prospective mission station. It was only after the Abolition Act was passed in 1807 that the way was opened for an advance into the interior.

In 1806, three new missionaries Gustavus Nylander, John Prasse and Leopold Butscher were recruited from Berlin. Two of them, Butscher and Nylander plus one of the pioneers, Renner, were the first C.M.S. missionaries to work among the Susu. They moved from Freetown to Rio Pongas and opened the first C.M.S. mission at Bassai in 1808. The other pioneer, Hartwig had defected and accepted secular employment in Freetown. The third new recruit, John Prasse alone remained as the chaplain in the colony.

Before the Missionaries entered Bassai, John Grey, a former government official had lived and died there. After his death, a trader, Mr. Curtis bought his house and property. When the Missionaries arrived there, Mr. Curtis rented the house free to them.

As soon as they got settled down the missionaries made rules for themselves. They agreed to: (a) hold divine service on the Lord's Day, (b) have no trade transaction whatever with the people on that day, (c) have family prayers morning and evening at seven o'clock, and require atttendance by all persons connected with them who understood English, (d) hold a meeting for prayer in the German language, as being more familiar to them, on the first Monday of every month and (e) receive the children of all European traders who wished to send them for tuition, provided that their parents find them food and apparel.[7]

Between 1808 and 1812, practically nothing was achieved apart from the education and preaching given to some of the local children. The main reason why only children were catered for, during the period, was that the chiefs showed more interest in receiving Western type of education for their children than in evangelization. This was because of the Muslim influence in the area.

The pupils at first were made up of children of liberated slaves. Initially, the missionaries had redeemed some children. These were taught in English because the missionaries felt that it would be a decade before they could complete their linguistic work on the Susu language and thus enable the Susu to read in their own tongue. In 1811, six more children of liberated slaves were handed to the C.M.S. by the Court of Vice-Admiralty.[8] These children were also sent to the school at Rio Pongas.

---

    [7] T. S. Johnson, *The Story of a Mission. The Sierra Leone Church: First Daughter of C.M.S.* (London S.P.C.K., 1953), p. 24.
    [8] A court of Vice-Admiralty was appointed to sit in Freetown to deal with the captured slave cargoes landing in Sierra Leone. See Groves, *op. cit.*, Vol. 1., p. 216, fn. 17.

The school made encouraging progress and by 1812 there were 120 pupils on the roll including about 20 children of the chiefs.

Thus from 1804 to 1812 the C.M.S. made no progress in evangelizing the Sierra Leoneans: they built no chapel, no proper public worship was organized, no itinerant preaching was carried out; no local people were admitted as communicant members and even the classrooms used were unsuitable—cramped and confined. But the C.M.S. was not discouraged.

Between 1812 and 1823 however, the missionary staff was increased. The first lay German missionary artisans who had been resident in England were recruited for work in Sierra Leone. Their aim was to encourage "the Africans to aspire to a civilized life."[9] Secondly, an Afro-American, who knew many African languages, joined the teaching staff in 1814. Prasse relinquished his chaplaincy work in Freetown and began missionary work on the Bullom shore, across the estuary north of Freetown. He had learnt the local language, produced a grammar and vocabulary of Bullom and translated some chapters of St. Matthew's Gospel.

Unfortunately, however, at the end of the Napoleonic war in 1815, France claimed that five years would elapse before the slave trade could be ended in her possessions. This persistence of the slave trade led to the increase of liberated slaves in Sierra Leone. By 1814 it was estimated that there were 10,000 liberated Africans in Sierra Leone of whom 1,000 were children.[10]

The population of Sierra Leone, especially in Freetown, no longer consisted mainly of settlers from Europe and America alone. It now included "Africans recently torn from family and clan and deposited, friendless and destitute, on Africa's soil certainly, but far from home."[11] These were different from the earlier settlers in their religion—they were not Christians. Consequently, the Governor of the Colony, Colonel Maxwell, drew the C.M.S.'s attention to this opportunity, because the new situation created social problems for the Government. Thus the C.M.S., already at work, was called upon to play a major part in socialising the increased motley crowd that poured in from the slave boats.

The C.M.S. took advantage of the new situation and in 1815 decided to take stock of the previous attempts they had made in Sierra Leone. Edward Bickersteth, a Norwich solicitor, was invited to visit Sierra Leone to review the work to-date. He accepted the invitation, received ordina-

---

[9] *Ibid.*, p. 216.
[10] *Ibid.*, p. 217.
[11] *Ibid.*, p. 218.

tion and sailed for Sierra Leone on 7th March 1816. The result of his visit has been summarized thus:

> Bickersteth's visit was greatly blessed of God. It corrected many evils; it initiated many new plans; it gave a fresh impetus to the whole work; it proved the real starting-point of the permanent Sierra Leone Mission.[12]

Bickersteth recommended that the Missionary priority should be evangelism and directed that this should be done mainly among the liberated Africans. As a result of these recommendations, Governor Sir Charles McCarthy (1814-1823) informed the Colonial Secretary, Mr Bathurst, of Bickersteth's proposals. Consequently, the Home Government gave permission that the liberated slaves might be properly organized. Thus between 1816 and 1819 the liberated Africans were organized into 9 villages—Gloucester, Leopold, Bathurst, Charlotte, Wellington, Waterloo, Hastings, York and Kent. Furthermore the Colony itself was divided, in 1817, into twelve parishes, each having a minister and a school master.[13] The staff was to be provided by the C.M.S. and their maintenance funded by the Government.

In response to the new challenge, two new missionaries, During and Johnson, both of German origin, were recruited to work exclusively among the liberated Africans in Freetown. Due to the urgency of the new demand in Freetown, the advance into the interior was partially suspended until 1854 when work in the Susu country was revived at Fallansia by Mr. Leacock and his colleagues sponsored by a Christian Association based in the West Indies.

In Freetown, William Auguste Bernard Johnson was assigned to Regents Town, one of the freed-slave villages. Though Johnson was only a lay missionary, he did very good work there, serving as school master and Government Superintendent. In 1816, the first year of his arrival, he concerned himself with the spiritual welfare of the people. As a result of his enquiries about their souls' condition together with his spiritual counsel, 21 adults, one boy and a number of infants, all captured Africans, were baptized by Butscher whom he had invited from Leicester Mountains for that purpose. By January, 1817, the membership had grown to 41 communicants. In recognition of his tenacity of purpose and the sincerity of his vocation, he was ordained by his German colleagues, into the Lutheran Ministry, in March 1817.

The conscientious manner in which he conducted his work led him into conflict with the Governor, Sir Charles McCarthy. One cause of

---

[12] *Ibid.* p. 275, citing Stock, *History of the Church Missionary Society* (1899), I, pp. 159 and 160.

[13] Johnson, *loc. cit.*

disagreement was baptism. Johnson handled baptism very carefully; he thoroughly trained the catechumens in the faith and publicly examined them before baptism. Only those who showed evidence of spiritual concern were baptized. The Governor thought that Johnson was too strict and advised the missionary to relax the standard required for baptism. Johnson did not find it necessary to lower standards. The Governor, therefore, reported him to the Secretaries of the Society who, in turn, wrote to Johnson to say that they thought he was too strict. In spite of his strictness Johnson won more communicants than workers in any of the other seven villages. The nineth village was not yet organized in 1817. Out of 603 communicants for the eight villages, 410 came from Regent Town alone.

In the area of education also, Johnson did marvellously. In 1817, there were 172 boys and 87 girls in the day school and 99 men and boys and 28 women who were taught trades such as masonry and brickmaking. By the end of his tour in March 1823, there were a total of 1,079 people in the night school and 710 adults could read. Enrolment in the day school had increased to 251 boys and 230 girls.

In the area of social welfare, Johnson was revolutionary. He established a "Benefit Society" where each communicant member paid a halfpenny a week. From this fund, support was given in time of sickness or distress. In matters of road transportation too Johnson was helpful. He diverted the old road and had a new road to Freetown engineered with the help of the members of his Church.

These achievements at Regent Town are only a representative account of the overall improvement of the lot of the liberated Africans in all the villages—Charlotte, Bathurst, Kissy, Wellington, Waterloo, Benquema, Campbell Town, Tomboo, York, Kent, Russel and Banana Islands.[14]

All these notable achievements were not scored without problems. Firstly, the beginning of work among the liberated slaves was difficult. The settlers did not initially show interest in the Gospel—they did not trust the missionaries because they suspected that they might resell them. Secondly, the missionaries suffered from diseases and died in great numbers: of the 26 missionaries who had been sent by 1816, 16 had died.[15]

The commonest causes of death usually given include: the missionaries' lack of knowledge of tropical sanitation; their lack of caution and over exertion in their evangelistic and other pursuits; their remaining for too long a period on the Coast without regular furloughs home, (for

[14] The liberated villages had increased from 8 to 13.
[15] Johnson, op.cit., p. 2.

example, out of the 26 missionaries sent out between 1804 and 1816 only two had visited home); and finally, the yellow fever epidemic of 1823.

These bitter experiences could be very disheartening to the missionary committee; but Johnson has reported that at one of their meetings when the story of the deaths was recounted to the committee,

> They gazed at one another's face across the table; then they knelt together at the footstool of Divine mercy ... and one leading member rose and said in a tone of deep feeling and deep resolve 'we must not abandon West Africa'.[16]

It was this tenacity of purpose exhibited by the C.M.S. Committee during this period of bitter experiences, that kept the missionary zeal for West Africa ablaze.

Apart from the planting of Churches in these villages, a few city churches were also developed at Padema Road and Kissy Road. The C.M.S. work in Freetown was started in these two places—Padema Road on the West, and Kissy Road in the East of Freetown. The other important city church was St. George's Church, the colonial Church in Freetown. Its foundation stone was laid on 9th January, 1817.

Between 1824 and 1839 there was progress on all fronts: St. George's Cathedral was completed in 1828; Holy Trinity Church was built to replace Gibraltar Town Church which had been destroyed by a tornado. Its foundation stone was laid on 2nd January, 1839.

The steady growth of the work now gave a lot of encourgement to the C.M.S. Thus from 1840 onwards they reaffirmed their avowed missionary policy to make Sierra Leone "the centre from which light and truth were to penetrate the continent".[17] By 1840, the C.M.S. reported a numerical strength of 1,500 communicants, a Christian community of 7,000 and fifty schools with 6,000 pupils in Sierra Leone. The nucleus had indeed been formed and the radiating centre could now be guided to send out its light and truth beyond its boundaries.

The development of the missionary work from 1824 onwards followed very distinct strategies. The first was in the field of education. At the time that the new parishes were being formed between 1817 and 1823, it was felt that a central residential school would be needed to serve the villages. Thus, after the death of the missionary W. A. B. Johnson at the end of 1823, a Christian Institution was established on Leicester Mountain near Freetown. Its aims were not realised, so in 1827 Fourah Bay College was set up in its place. A new Grammar School was established in 1845 to prepare suitable candidates for recruitment by Fourah Bay College. The

---

16 *Loc. cit.*
17 Groves, *op. cit.*, Vol. II, p. 16

students were to be offered "a sound religious and general education."[18] Those with vocation—those who inclined toward the Christian ministry—would pass on to Fourah Bay College, while the others, without vocation, would enter life to "leaven the social life of the community."[19]

The pioneer students of the new Grammar School were 30 in number. They were very ambitious and demanded that classical education might be given them. As a result, Latin and Greek were offered to the most advanced students. In the first four years 94 passed out, 8 as schoolmasters. 15 had passed on to Fourah Bay and the rest entered life.[20]

To cater for the girls, a Female Institution was opened in 1845, the same year as the Grammar School, at Regent Town. Later it was transferred to Freetown. It trained schoolmistresses and equipped them to educate Christian mothers whom the missionaries considered to be the true backbone to the "establishment of any Native-Christian Church."[21]

The second strategy was the development of language. In 1847, Sigismund Wilhelm Koelle, a German, was recruited for the C.M.S. from Basel. After training at Islington, he was ordained for work in Sierra Leone where he arrived on 3rd November 1847. He took an appointment as a tutor at the Fourah Bay Institution and as a research student in African Languages. He travelled extensively, reaching as far as Bornu near Lake Chad. He studied the Bornu language with the purpose of using that area as the base for radiating Christianity to the near-by Muslim areas. He also visited the region near Cape Mount in Liberia and made a study of the Vai language. Before his arrival there, an indigenous man, about 40 years old, had developed some alphabets of the Vai language.[22] Koelle was so encouraged by the initiative of that man that he opened schools in the area. Unfortunately, however, the whole project proved a fiasco because of tribal wars. But before he left the Vai towns for good Koelle published a Grammar book of the language: S. W. Koelle, *Outlines of a Grammar of the Via Language (1854)*. His principal contribution to linguistics, however, was his *Polyglotta Africana* (Lond. 1854).

Koelle did not study languages just because of his liguistic interests; he studied them as a means to an end—the carrying of the Christian Gospel to the non-Christian world.[23]

---

[18] *Ibid.*, p. 17.
[19] *Loc.cit.*
[20] *Loc.cit.*, citing the *Proceedings of the C.M.S.* (1850), p. LXIV
[21] Groves, *loc.cit*; Vol. II.
[22] *Ibid.*, p. 21
[23] *Ibid.*, p. 21

In spite of the contacts that Koelle made in the interior, the C.M.S.
did not succeed in establishing permanent missions there at this time.
The reason was that an African who had been appointed to Gallinhas,
near Cape Mount, as the British Agent, was found murdered. When the
Chiefs were questioned they refused to hand over the criminals for
punishment and the British Government destroyed the principal towns
thus creating enmity between the local people and Europeans.

The third strategy was directed towards local devolution. The impetus
was provided by Henry Venn, the secretary of the C.M.S. at the time. In
1851, he wrote and circulated a paper: "Minute upon the Employment
and Ordination of Native Teachers among the Missionaries of the Society". The policy he advocated was this:

> Regarding the ultimate object of a Mission, viewed under its ecclesiastical result, to
> be the settlement of a Native Church under Native Pastors upon a self supporting
> system, it should be borne in mind that the progress of a Mission mainly depends
> upon the training up and the location of Native Pastors; and that, as it has been hap-
> pily expressed the 'euthanasia of Mission' takes place when a missionary, surround-
> ed by well trained Native congregations under Native Pastors, is able to resign all
> Pastoral work into their hands, and gradually relax his superintendence over the
> pastors themselves, till it insensibly ceases; and so the mission passes into a settled
> Christian community. Then the missionary and all missionary agency should be
> transferred to the regions beyond.[24]

The C.M.S. recognized that before Venn's ideas could be properly implemented, Sierra Leone should be created into a Diocese. Since the
commencement of Missionary work there, for nearly half a century,
1804-1851, no Bishop had been appointed. Because of this all those who
had been baptized were not confirmed and men could not be ordained
and the Churches and cemeteries could not be consecrated. Thus in 1852
the Diocese of Sierra Leone was erected, "in communion with the
Church of England, and constituted the Bishopric of Sierra Leone, a
body corporated with perpetual succession."[25] This Diocese comprised
Sierra Leone, the Gambia, the Gold Coast (now Ghana), Lagos,
Madeira and the Canary Islands with Mauritania and Morocco.

The first Bishop was the Rev. Owen Emeric Vidal. After his consecration in Britain, in 1852, he sailed for Sierra Leone. He arrived in
Freetown on 27th December the same year, 1852, accompanied by six
new missionaries.

The missionaries in the field, together with their congregations, were
very much encouraged by the presence of the new-comers for obvious
reasons which include the following: among the six new missionaries was

---

[24] *Ibid.*, p. 217 and also Stock, *History*, II, *op cit.*, (1899), p. 415.
[25] Johnson, *op.cit.*, p. 60.

one named J. U. Graff. The Rev. Graff had laboured earlier in Hastings as a Missionary. But now he had returned, elevated in status, as the new Archdeacon of the Diocese. It has just been mentioned that because no Bishop had been appointed to Sierra Leone since the beginning of the Missionary enterprise, certain Episcopal duties had been left undone. The new Bishop tackled some of these problems soon after his arrival. For instance on 20th January 1853, only three weeks after his arrival in the Diocese, the Bishop celebrated his first ordination in St. George's Cathedral in Freetown. The ordinands were three expatriates: E. Dicker who was ordained to the priesthood and Gerate Kefer and Maser who were made deacons. Finally, 800 confirmation candidates from Freetown, Kissy and Wellington were confirmed in the same Cathedral on 18th March, 1853.

After these functions, Bishop Vidal travelled to Lagos in Nigeria. On his return voyage from Lagos he had an attack of fever and died at sea on 24th December 1853. A year elapsed before a successor, Bishop J. W. Weeks, was appointed. He arrived in Sierra Leone in 1855. Very unfortunately, he also died, within two years, in 1857. He has been remembered as the first Bishop to ordain African Anglican Clergy, in Sierra Leone, to pastor their own kith and kin. The men he ordained were eight in number. J. C. Taylor, Jacob Cole, John Josiah Thomas, Joseph Wilson, J. C. Taylor II, James Quaker, S. Wiltshire and J. Cambell.

Because of the short time that they spent in Sierra Leone, Bishops Vidal and Weeks could not immediately implement Venn's local devolution policy. That responsibility was left for the next Bishop, E. H. Beckles to execute. He arrived in Sierra Leone in 1860 and set up a "Native Pastorate". First, under him, a Constitution of the Church suited to local conditions was promulgated.[26] This abrogated the British ecclesiastical constitution which had been applied to the Sierra Leonean Church. The general principles to govern the constitution of the "Native Pastorate" were drawn by the C.M.S. secretary in London and the Bishop of Sierra Leone. They stated

> That the charge and superintendence of native pastors and Christian congregations which have been or may hereafter be raised through the instrumentality of the Society's mission in Sierra Leone, be placed under the Bishop of Sierra Leone assisted by a Council and by a Church Committee and that arrangements be proposed for providing the native pastors with a suitable income from local resources and also, for giving them a status assimilated to that of incumbent at home (e.g. England).[27]

---

[26] *Ibid.*, p. 62.
[27] *Loc. cit.*

The members of the Council and the Church Commitee respectively were to be nominated partly by the Bishop of Sierra Leone and the C.M.S. and partly elected by the Clergy in Sierra Leone. The preliminary arrangements having been completed, the "Native Pastorate" was formed in 1860 consisting of a Council and a Church Committee.

The Council's functions were mainly administrative. It assisted the Bishop in the Ecclesiastical administration of the see, formed Ecclesiastical districts, appointed pastors to their stations and heard complaints against pastors and so on.

The Church Committee was responsible for the collection and disbursement of Church funds. For example, it should pay the stipends of pastors and repair or build chapels, parsonages and other church related building projects.

The educational institutions and the parishes which were still stations for Missionaries (mission stations) remained directly under the C.M.S.

The foundation parishes which constituted the "Native Pastorate" were Kissy, Wellington and Hastings. In 1861, to commemorate the formation of the "Native Pastorate" and the institution of giving financial support to the African pastors raised from local sources, the "Native Pastorate" Auxiliary Association was formed and in 1862, other stations were included in the "Native Pastorate."

In 1869 Bishop Beckles left Sierra Leone and was succeeded by Bishop H. Cheetham in 1870. He developed the system. He left the Diocese in 1881 and was succeeded by Bishop Ingham (1883-1897). It was during his tenure of office that in 1890 the "Native Pastorate" constitution was replaced by a more elaborate one. When this new constitution was introduced, five of the African priests refused to give assent to it. They maintained that it was against their consciences to accept the change and that they could not be forced to give their assent to the new constitution *against their will*.[28] After a fruitless persuation their licences were withdrawn. This led to litigation. However, the court exonerated the five priests on the grounds that "they had not in any way either *expressly* or by *implication* given their assent to it."[29] However, for the preservation of peace in the church, the five priests relinguished their parsonages. With the formation of the "Native Pastorate" the missionary expansion into the interior became a permanent endeavour of the Church. It will be recalled that earlier attempts into the interior had not been very successful. For example, work in the Susu country between 1808 and 1815

---

[28] *Ibid.*, p. 65.
[29] *Ibid.*, p.66 (It is not exactly clear what this statement meant)

had not yielded much. The Rev. C. L. T. Hansel had worked among the Temne tribes between 1833 and 1834 but unfortunately no mission station was established before he was forced to leave on health grounds. After his departure the work was not continued until 1840 when a new attempt was commenced at Port Lokkoh. Even though this was a very important trading centre no progress was made because the population was predominantly Muslim and the Sierra Leonean traders there were not missionary minded. It was only at Magbele, about 60 miles from Freetown and 24 miles north of river Rokelle, where the inhabitants were mainly "pagan", that mission premises were erected in 1853.

The Bullom to the north of the Temne and the Sherbro to the south also received some attention. But the missions in these areas were suspended in 1875 because the African agents there could not remain at their posts because of the plundering habits of the inhabitants.

But after the introduction of the new constitution of the "Native Pastorate" in 1890, the Anglican Church in Sierra Leone began to expand geographically. In 1897 the mission on the Bullom shore was reactivated, in 1898 the Sherbro mission was revived and by 1907 the Sherbro mission became the growing point of the Mende mission. It was from that year, 1907, that the Sierra Leone church began raising £1000 each year for the Mende Mission.[30]

Also in 1897 a pioneer mission was opened in the Yalunka country at Sinkunia about 210 miles north-east of Freetown. From Sinkunia, Falaba, 18 miles beyond, was opened and the Rev. T. E. Alvazez, the pioneer missionary to the Yalunka country, travelled to about within 30 miles from the Niger. A station was also opened in the Limba country between the Temne and the Yalunka in 1900. All these outposts were mission stations, that is, they were manned by European missionaries.

In 1908, however, these European outposts were transferred to the Sierra Leone church, the "Native Pastorate", because illness and death prevented the European Missionaries from staying at their posts continually. By 1914 the Church Missionary Society's responsibility was limited to the institutions of higher education.

Earlier in 1913, during the Jubilee celebration of the establishment of the Sierra Leone "Native Pastorate", the hinterland Churches were constituted into a separate Archdeaconry and the Rev. E. T. Cole, M. A., was appointed the first Archdeacon of the Protectorate. Thus by 1914, when World War I was declared, after roughly a century of Missionary activity of the Church Missionary Society in West Africa, Anglican Christianity began to take root among the indigenous people in the interior. It was from this Sierra Leone base that Anglican Christianity spread to other parts of English-speaking West Africa.

---

[30] *Proceedings of the Church Missionary Society* (1908), p. 27.

CHAPTER FOUR

CHURCH MISSIONARY SOCIETY: OUTREACH FROM SIERRA LEONE

The Anglican Church in Sierra Leone was a real missionary church. From it Anglicanism reached the Gambia and Nigeria. Firstly, let us treat THE GAMBIA.

The Anglican church in the Gambia emerged out of the British garrison of West Indian soldiers quartered in Bathurst (now Banjul) during the first quarter of the nineteenth century. A padre or Chaplain of the Church of England persuasion, was attached to the army. He held Sunday services in the officers' mess for the soldiers and other British officials.

Around the same period, the Gambian Civil Service and the Police Force were being formed. Most of the pioneer African employees were recruited from Sierra Leone, especially from Freetown. Many of them were Anglicans. Thus on their arrival in Banjul, they joined the soldiers at the mess-room service on Sundays because the Padre and his little barracks congregation had been placed by the C.M.S. in London under the supervision of the Church in Sierra Leone.

As time went on, the regiment was disbanded, but the nucleus Christian community remained active. It was composed mainly of the Sierra Leonean civil servants and police men together with a few Gambians. They appreciated the services of the Padre so much so that when news reached them that the regiment was being disbanded, they sent a petition to the church in Sierra Leone to permit the Padre to remain in Bathurst and take charge of the little Christian community. The petitioners agreed to provide a parsonage and the stipend of the chaplain. The request was granted in 1836. Meanwhile the little flock continued to hold their Sunday devotion in the mess-room and during the week days the same room was used as a day school known as the garrison school.

This little Christian community made quick progress in numbers due to the immigration of freed slave-settlers from America and the resettlement of the liberated slaves in Bathurst. By 1885, the garrison school had developed into a well-founded and continuing institution called the Anglican School of St. Mary.

Between 1899 and 1910 the present chapel of St. Mary was built by the members when the Rev. Samuel Hughes, a Sierra Leonean priest, was in charge. It was opened and dedicated in 1910 to the Glory of God by the

Lord Bishop of Sierra Leone. Hughes was followed by priests from Sierra Leone and Britain until World War I in 1914.

During the period under discussion the Anglican Church in the Gambia did not do any appreciable out-reach work beyond the Bathurst (Banjul) area.

This lack of missionary zeal of the Anglican Church in the Gambia may be attributed to a variety of reasons. In the first place, the presence of the Muslim population in the Gambia was a serious handicap. Throughout history it has not been easy to proselytise Muslims to the Christian faith because the core of the Christian faith, the belief that Jesus Christ is God, conflicts with the Islamic teaching that Jesus was only one of the prophets. Secondly, language was also a barrier to evangelism. The people in the Gambia speak either Mandinka, Wollof or Fula. The missionaries who built the church in Bathurst, the Sierra Leonean priests and European missionaries, did not learn and use any of these languages for the purpose of winning the indigenous population.

The priests who came from Sierra Leone belonged to the freed slave extraction. They and the European missionaries used English in worship. The liberated Africans at home, however, used "Creole or Aku—a patois evolved by the liberated Africans with a grammatical structure which is largely African, and a vocabulary which is a mixture of English with a few Portuguese or Yoruba and other African words."[1] Even though a good many of the liberated Africans spoke a local language in addition to Aku and English, the missionaries insisted that worship should be conducted in English. Consequently, the membership of the congregation remained predominantly of liberated Africans and their descendants with whom the missionaries could easily communicate. There was almost no study of other local languages, or planning to evangelize villages beyond Bathurst.

Thirdly, the presence of the immigrant Africans was a hinderance to expansion. When they settled in their new home, they became inward-looking. They adopted an attitude of superiority and so found it difficult to condescend to evangelize the local people during the period of this investigation. As a result, little attention was paid to the conversion, at least, of the non-Muslims whose religion was African Traditional Religion.

The *NIGERIAN* story was different from that of the Gambia. While the Anglican Church in the Gambia was inward-looking that in Nigeria was outward-looking.

---

[1] Barbara Prickett, *Island Base* (Meth. Church Gambia n.d.), p. 7.

As early as 1841, the Church Missionary Society made an attempt to evangelize the interior of Africa by way of Upper Niger. In that year the Rev. W. C. Thomson of the Temne mission in Sierra Leone was seconded to lead a Government reconciliation embassy to the Fula. He established friendly relations with the Fula chiefs in the regions visited, and intended to send missionaries there and later to open schools. But the bright prospects he anticipated were frustrated by civil disturbances in the Fula Kingdom and his death in those regions in 1843. The hopes of evangelizing the interior from Sierra Leone by way of Upper Niger faded out of missionary strategy.

Earlier, in 1838, some of the liberated slaves in Sierra Leone serving on a trading ship reached Lagos. They recognized the port as the place where they had been shipped away by the slave dealers. They disembarked and went inland to Abeokuta, their home town. Soon afterwards other liberated Yoruba in Sierra Leone migrated home. Within three years it was estimated that more than five hundred liberated slaves had returned home to Abeokuta.[2]

These immigrants had been converted to Christianity in Sierra Leone, and on their return to Abeokuta, they missed very much the spiritual care they had enjoyed at their former abode. The missionary bodies in Sierra Leone, then, also became concerned about the spiritual welfare of their members who had migrated to Nigeria. Consequently, Henry Townsend, a Church Missionary Society missionary in Sierra Leone, was appointed to survey the situation in Yorubaland.

He landed at Badagry on 19th December, 1842, having been conveyed free of charge by an African who owned the trading vessel, *Wilberforce*. He arrived at Abeokuta on 4th January, 1843 and was cordially welcomed by Shodeke in appreciation of the British efforts in the emancipation of the slaves. The King also gave assurance that he would welcome, both missionary and merchant white men, in his country. Townsends report to the home committee was so favourable that the C.M.S. decided to establish a mission in Yorubaland with Abeokuta as its pioneer station. As a sign of encouragement to the Abeokuta Christians, one Andrew Welhelm from Sierra Leone was left in charge.

On his return home to England Townsend, who had been teaching as a schooolmaster in Sierra Leone, was ordained priest by the Bishop of London and sent back, together with Samuel Crowther and C. A. Gollmer (a German Missionary, trained in Basel), to the new station at Abeokuta. They arrived together at Badagry with their wives and four African teachers in January, 1845 and established the *Yoruba Mission*.

---

[2] Groves, *op.cit.*, vol. II, p. 46.

They were delayed there for eight months, because the Shodeke who had previously welcomed them had died and the King of Dahomey had seized the Egba fortified post on the road to Badagry thus cutting communications with the interior. Townsend and Crowther however advanced to Abeokuta when the opportunity came, arriving there in August 1846 but Gollmer was left at Badagry to take charge of that station.

The political situation in Yorubaland at the time, different from that of Sierra Leone, hindered the work at Abeokuta. Whereas there was effective British control in Sierra Leone, Yorubaland was entirely under African political authority. This made the beginning of the missionary enterprise among the Yoruba hazardous. The reason was that the kings and their subjects did not always have the same mind on some serious critical questions, and differences of opinion led to internal and external disruptions and political instability.[3]

Despite this problem, the C.M.S. made considerable progress for the following reasons.

In the first place, the local people were very much impressed by the British efforts in the liberation movement. The relatives remaining at home had not hoped to meet their enslaved brethren again. When reunions took place pleasant emotional feelings of gratitude were aroused.[4] This favourable attitude was an advantage which the missionaries considered to be a solid foundation upon which the gospel could be easily propagated.

Secondly, British naval commanders endorsed the mission because they were active in the liberation movement and the British squadron in Lagos had a genuine regard for the missionaries and their endeavours. The officers regarded their work as a preparation of the ground for a positive contribution of Christianity in Africa. Thus whenever the Commodore made treaties with the local people he saw to it that provision was included for the operation of missionaries.

Thirdly, the Abeokuta elders tolerated religious liberty. For example, Crowther recorded the case of a man who refused to worship an Ifa god. When he was arraigned before the elders, they declared that he was at liberty to do as he pleased with his religion.[5]

Finally, the attitude of the chiefs to European presence in their domain also promoted the work of the pioneer missionaries. The chiefs felt that the presence of a white man in their towns was prestigious. Consequently, it was easy for the missionaries to remain in a station, without

---

[3] *Ibid.*, p. 51.

[4] J. Page, *The Black Bishop* (1908), pp. 95-6, cited by Groves, *loc.cit.*, Vol. II.

[5] *Ibid.*, p. 52 citing the *Proceedings of the CMS* (1848), p. IXV.

molestation, and to teach, even though the chiefs were suspicious of their purpose. This is why, when the chief of Ijaye asked Townsend in 1852 to send him a missionary he made it clear that he would protect the missionary's person, but not his purpose, from molestation. It should, however, be noted that there were other, more liberal, chiefs who also sincerely appreciated the missionary purpose. For example the chief of Ketu was so opposed to slavery that when he was visited by Crowther, the chief told him to send him forty missionaries whom he would welcome and protect.

These assets were to some extent short lived because, "as the early glow of gratitude" expired, the Christian standard imposed on the new converts became irksome. In addition to this interpretation, there were real and serious disabilities too which hindered missionary activities of those early days.

The first of these was the attitude of the slave-dealers. Naturally, the Western slave-dealers, including the local chiefs who traded in slaves, resented and opposed the young mission. They were determined to crush it at Badagry to prevent expansion of Christianity to Abeokuta. Thus these enemies of the faith, using Lagos in the east, and Porto Novo on the west, endeavoured to isolate Badagry from Abeokuta. At the onset, the threat caused anxiety for the young mission but eventually it ceased to worry them because "in 1851, Consul Beecroft intervened with good effect, strengthening the hands of the well-disposed chiefs and enheartening the Christian workers."[6]

Secondly, opposition came from the local traditional believers. The new converts refused to conform to the traditional beliefs of the Yoruba religion and this aroused the antagonism of the traditional priesthood to whose prestige and livelihood the attitude of the new converts was inimical.

Thirdly and politically, the external relations of Abeokuta with Dahomey were not cordial because Dahomey had been an enemy of the Egba of Abeokuta. In 1850 it was evident that Dahomey planned to attack Abeokuta. To prevent any such confrontation Consul Beecroft and Commander Forbes R.N. jointly visited Gezo, the chief of Dahomey, to dissuade him from attacking the Egba. Gezo refused to heed their counsel and in March 1851 the war was waged. To the surprise of Gezo the Egba won the battle because the Commodore of the navy sent naval protection to Dadagry. Dahomean losses were great, about 3,000 casualties, while the Egba lost only between 200 and 300 people.

---

[6] *Ibid.*, p. 53, fn. 2.

This latter disability, ultimately, became an asset to the expansion of Christianity for, in the first place, the missionaries intervened and secured an exchange of the war prisoners with Dahomey. Hitherto captives had been regarded as the private property of their captors. But their release now, due to missionary intervention, was considered by some of the Yoruba people as representing an important principle of Christianity. In the second place, the victory was ascribed by most people to the presence of the Christians among the Egba and the assistance of the God of the Christians. Consequently, most of the important Egba chiefs sent their children to the mission schools and the persecutions of the Christians came to an end. (Note that the interpretation of military victory as a sign of divine favour can arouse much ethical consideration which we are not concerned with here.)

A fourth serious disability hindering the activities of the missionaries was the staffing problem. Malaria depleted the Euopean staff so much in those early years that it was difficult to maintain an effective staff. In 1853 alone, for example, out of the seven missionaries who arrived from Europe, three died during the year and a fourth was invalided home. But Townsend, Gollmer and Hinderer were spared many years of continuous service and together with Samuel Ajayi Crowther formed an impregnable nucleus.

The last enemy was Kosoko who in 1845 exiled his uncle, Akitoye, the ruler of Lagos, and usurped the chief's post. Kosoko, a stubborn slave-trader, disliked the British because they restrained the trade. He hated the missionaries because, by converting the chiefs to Christianity, they also won them (the chiefs of Abeokuta especially) away from the trade.

Kosoko, however, did not last long on the stool. Akitoye, who was residing in Badagry, was still recognized by the other chiefs of Abeokuta as the lawful ruler of Lagos. That he might put an end to Kosoko's further attempts to destroy Badagry, Akitoye petitioned the naval commander for support and Queen Victoria to take possession of Lagos in order to preserve peace in the area.[7]

In response, Consul Beecroft was instructed by Palmerston, the Secretary of State for the Colonies, to conclude an agreement with Kosoko to desist from the slave-trade. The first attempt failed. The British therefore undertook naval operation against Kosoko. It was a severe battle which eventually ended in the self-exile of Kosoko and the reinstatement of Akitoye in December 1851.

---

[7] See A. Burns, *History of Nigeria* (London. 1969), 7th ed., pp. 118-119 for texts of the letter Akitoye sent to the Commander and the Queen.

The results of this victory were far reaching: the slave-trade in that area was utterly paralysed; Dahomey lost her most powerful ally, Lagos, and Abeokuta had strong protection. The treaty made immediately by the Commodore with Akitoye and the chiefs of Lagos explicitly safeguarded the missionaries and their work. The relevant article reads:

> Complete protection shall be afforded to Missionaries or Ministers of the Gospel, of whatever nation or country, following their vocation of spreading the knowledge and doctrines of Christianity, and extending the benefits and civilization ... nor shall any subject of the King and chiefs of Lagos who may embrace the Christian faith be, on that account, or on account of the teaching or exercise thereof, molested or troubled in any manner whatsoever.[8]

Finally, Lagos, which had been closed to missionary activity was open and the C.M.S. decided to move its staff there from Badagry. From Lagos, due to the existence of the River Ogun, it would be easier to reach Abeokuta by water transport. So Gollmer and his wife were sent to Lagos to initiate a mission there.

In 1853, however, Kosoko returned and temporarily attacked Lagos with 1,500 men. The attack was foiled by men from a man-of-war and Kosoko fled again. During the fighting Gollmer exhibited "perfect devotion and no small degree of moral courage."[9]

Shortly after the war Akitoye died and was succeeded by his son Dosumu. Eight years afterwards, in 1861 Lagos was annexed to the British Dependencies and the slave-trade completely suppressed.

Though these pioneer years were a trying period for the *Yoruba Mission*, positive progress was made. On 6th February, 1848 when the first Christian Baptisms in Abeokuta were celebrated, there had already been a congregation of about 250 people. On that same day two men and three women including Samuel A. Crowther's mother were enrolled as members of the Christian church. Thereafter, people were enrolled for instruction until by 1857 there were 827 Anglican communicant members in Yorubaland. These members sincerely believed in our Lord Jesus Christ but the missionaries stated that they found it difficult to abide by Christian morals. Townsend believed that the Sierra Leonean repatriates taught the new converts "to think lightly of their sin, before or after the fact."[10]

Another important development during this first decade was the appointment of O. E. Vidal in 1852 as the Bishop of Sierra Leone. The

---

[8] Groves, *op.cit.*, Vol. II, p. 56, see Burns, *op.cit.*, pp. 317-18, Article VIII.
[9] Groves, *op.cit.*, Vol. II, p. 57.
[10] *Ibid.*, p. 57-58 citing *Proceedings of the CMS* (1854) pp. 40-1.

Yoruba mission was part of the Bishop's jurisdiction because, as we have seen earlier, the mission had originated from Sierra Leone. After Vidal had settled down in Sierra Leone, he visited the Lagos and Abeokuta missions in 1854, confirming 500 to 600 converts and admitting to the deacon's orders the first two Africans as the first stage towards their ordination into holy orders. Unfortunately, this was the last visit of the Bishop because he died at sea on his return voyage to Sierra Leone.

He was succeeded in 1855 by J. W. Weeks. He also visited Lagos and Abeokuta, confirmed converts, ordained three Africans into the full priesthood of the Anglican Church and introduced important disciplinary regulations. Like his predecessor he also died when he was returning to Sierra Leone in 1857. John Bowen was consecrated in September 1857 to succeed Weeks. He remained in the diocese for two years and died after working with the *Yoruba Mission* and visiting as far as the Delta of the Niger.[11]

In addition to Evangelism, the *Yoruba Mission* promoted other policies which were formulated to improve the social welfare of the people. These policies included the introduction of improved methods of agriculture. From the very beginning of the Mission at Badagry, Samuel Adjayi Crowther sought to encourage agriculture. He introduced to the people the use of the plough and instituted prizes for the best farms. He also introduced the use of a steel cornmill.

At Abeokuta too a healthy external trade in local products was introduced and the River Ogun from Lagos was opened to ''lawful'' commerce. Goods such as palm-oil, beniseed, ivory, gum, spice, bales of cotton were exported from Lagos to England.[12] The success of this policy has been expressed in a testimony received by Crowther in these words:

> These head chiefs could not help confessing to me, that they, aged persons, never remembered any time of the slave-trade that so much wealth was brought to their country as has been since the commencement of the palm-oil trade the last four years; that they were perfectly satisfied with legitimate trade, and with the proceedings of the British Government.[13]

In order to diversify the trade, an Industrial Institution was established by the Mission to help the Egba Chiefs in preparing their cotton for exportation. In the Institution, the students were taught how to clean and pack cotton and how to repair the machinery. As a result of the success of this Institution, when a central training institution for teachers was established in 1856, agriculture, carpentry and printing were included in the curriculum.

---

[11] Groves, *op.cit.*, Vol. II, p. 59.
[12] Groves, *loc.cit.*, Fn.3 citing C. A. Gollmer, *Proceedings of the CMS* (1855), p. 46
[13] Groves, *loc.cit.*, citing *Proceedings of the CMS* (1857), p. 38.

From a small beginning, Abeokuta became an important radiating centre whence the work of the *Yoruba Mission* expanded during the pioneer decades. From Abeokuta, Ibadan station was opened by David and Anna Hinderer in 1853. As a result of the Hinderer's first visit to Ibadan in 1851, the Oni of Ife, the acknowledged Head of the Yoruba, invited the missionaries to go and teach him "the new way of happiness." Ijaye was opened by A. C. Mann, a Wurttemberger, in the year 1853 when the Hinderers settled at Ibadan. This was followed by opening the Oyo station in 1856 by Townsend. Oyo was the political headquarters of the Yoruba people. From there extensions were made, in the same year, to Ogbomosho and Illorin on the frontier of Hausaland by A. C. Mann, thus bringing Christianity to the frontiers of the Moslems.

These achievements were possible because the Christian pioneers of Abeokuta had impressed the chiefs and people of Yorubaland tremendously. For example, in 1855, the traders in Lagos sent a petition to England to restrain the CMS from asking Townsend and Gollmer, then on furlough, to return to the coast. But the Alake of Abeokuta protested vehemently in a lengthy letter, part of which reads:

> Now, although I myself am still a heathen, yet I am not blind to facts. The first is, that the present state of Abeokuta is not what it was ten years ago, for instead of war there is peace. The second is, that Christianity is a really powerful religion, for its effects upon the minds of my people are so well marked that we all admire it. And thirdly, that the Oyibos (missionaries), although a small and weak body, observing them outwardly, yet they are stronger than any of my mighty men in the country. One instance of this will suffice. In the case of the Adu war....
>
> Who were those that pitched tents of conciliation in a most dangerous spot, between the camps of two savage and hostile people? They were the two missionaries, Messrs. Townsend and Crowther. In a few days after, to my great astonishment, these Oyibos actually brought the warriors home.... One last point ... the liberty we now enjoy. Within six years back the roads to Ijaye, Ibadan, Ketu, and Jebu were very dangerous; a caravan of fifty could not pass them with safety. Kidnappers made these roads their homes, and the chiefs and rulers of these several towns countenanced the actions of these men-stealers. But observe the contrast. At present, a single female could travel three days' journey without any fear of danger, for where there is no danger there is also no cause for fear. Little boys and girls can go eight, nine, ten miles beyond the walls of Abeokuta safely, no one daring to touch them. Is this not really a cause of much thanks to you for sending us such men? ... It is their peace we now enjoy. The absence of these missionaries, therefore, from us has made us, chilly. We pray you to send them to us again, and many others like them.[14]

---

[14] Groves *op. cit.*, Vol. II, p. 63. An account of the achievement of the missionaries as peacemakers during the Adu war has been preserved in the *Proceedings of the CMS* (1854), pp. 43-44. Groves had recorded that the letter was dictated by the Alake in Yoruba and

It was because of the favourable impact made in Abeokuta by the initial missionary work that, the chiefs of the other large Yoruba towns decided, at the end of 1855 to give up the practice of kidnapping and to encourage amicable relationships among themselves. As a practical demonstration of their sincerity, Ibadan returned to Abeokuta prisoners captured just before the agreement was reached.

Here then was evidence that the missionaries were realizing their aim of evangelizing Africa.

Unfortunately, however, missionary activities were suspended in 1860 as a result of an outbreak of civil war between the Egba of Abeokuta and the people of Ibadan. Abeokuta at that time was economically prosperous. In her attempt to monopolize the trade in those regions, Abeokuta did not allow the people of Ibadan to use the route through the city to Lagos for their trading. This naturally produced a state of war.

This situation was made more complex in 1861 when the British annexed Lagos. The Egba considered this a threat to their independence and withdrew their friendship with the British. The complexity of the situation has been summarised in these words by John Hawley Glover to the Secretary of State:

> The exasperation of Abeokuta at the check given to the slave-trade by the occupation of Lagos, the wish of this Government for another road to and from the interior, (besides that of Abeokuta), the non-rendering of slaves who sought protection in this settlement, their rejection of Her Majesty's Vice-Consul, and the murders and robberies committed by them on the person and properties of British subjects, their reverses in the war with Ibadan, and our refusal to allow them to destroy the town of Ikorodu—all these were causes sufficient in themselves to prevent any relations of close friendship existing between them and ourserves.[15]

The wars which followed, until 1867, humiliated Abeokuta considerably, because the British supported the people of Ibadan against them. In 1865 there was a brief cessation of hostilities but in ''1867 the Egba chiefs suddenly turned on the missionaries: mission premises were looted and destroyed, and all missionaries, Anglican, Wesleyan and Baptist were expelled with nothing but the clothes in which they stood.''[16]

Eugene Stock analysed the reasons behind this sudden attack on the missionaries as being:

---

translated into English by one of the Sierra Leone teachers for transmission to London unknown to the European missionary left at the station. For the full text, see *Proceedings of the CMS* (1856), pp. 111-115.

[15] Groves, *op.cit.*, Vol. II, pp. 234-235 citing Lady Glover, *Life of Sir John Hawley Glover* (1897), p. 93.

[16] Groves, *op.cit.*, Vol. II p. 235.

the resentment at the blockade imposed by the Lagos Government; the
failure to elect a successor to the deceased Alake with the result that some of
the wilder spirits among the chiefs had seized control; the subversive influence of certain Sierra Leone men who were interested in the slave-trade;
and the growing influence of Islam in the city.[17]

Although the expelled missionaries were confident that they would be
recalled early, their hopes were not fulfilled until 1880.

There was much to lament about during this disturbing period: the
bright hopes wich the missionaries had anticipated for the *Yoruba Mission*
as the "Sunrise of the Tropics", were drastically menaced. But out of it
all, the church survived, still supported by a small trickle of a faithful
remnant who continued to witness to the Christian truth. For example,
although the people of Abeokuta and Ibadan were still on unfriendly
terms, the remaining Christians in each of these cities pledged their troth
that:

> However great misunderstandings may be among the Heathen of Abeokuta
> and Ibadan, let unity and peace be among us Christians of the two rival
> cities, for we are the followers of the Prince of Peace.[18]

Thus when the missionaries returned in 1880, the work had not died
out completely. They settled down quickly and revived the stations.
From 1886, the Yoruba Mission made unprecedented expansion from
Abeokuta to the land of the Ijebu. From Ijebu the work spread like wild
fire. By 1899 Illorin near the Islamic border in the north was visited by
missionaries from both the Yoruba and the Niger Missions.

The Niger Mission had been established on 25th July, 1857 in the following manner. When A. C. Mann visited Illorin in 1856, he was well
received by the Muslims and the people of the Northern regions. This encouraged the CMS to commission Samuel Ajayi Crowther to collect
materials for the Igbo language and J. F. Schon to revise his Hausa New
Testament translation for the press: David Hinderer was instructed to
move into Hausaland and from there, travel by land route to the Niger.
(The earlier attempt to reach the interior by way of the river aborted in
1841). Hinderer's journey was not however made because internal disturbances made the north inaccessible at the time.

A decision was therefore taken by the CMS to begin a *Niger Mission*: It
happened that in 1854 the British Government had sent another expedition to explore the River Niger. This journey had been successful in that
there had been no deaths caused by malaria or other factors. Samuel
Crowther had been released by the Society to accompany this expedition

---

[17] *Loc.cit.*
[18] *Ibid.*, p. 236, citing Stock, *op.cit.*, Vol. II, p. 444.

and in his report to the CMS he emphasised the great missionary opportunities that lay along the banks of the river.

> The reception we met with from the kings and chiefs of the countries was beyond expectation. I believe the time has fully come when Christianity must be introduced on the banks of the Niger. God has provided instruments to begin the work among the liberated Africans of Sierra Leone who are natives of the Niger territories.[19]

Consequently, when in 1857 another Government expedition was organized to go up the river again and the CMS invited to participate, the invitation was warmly received. Samuel A. Crowther and J. C. Taylor, an Igbo ordained in Sierra Leone, were appointed by the Society to accompany the expedition and they were charged to take steps to establish a *Niger Mission*.

The expedition started in the Dayspring from Liverpool, on 7th May 1857. Crowther and Taylor joined the steamer at Fernando Po. They left Fernando Po on 29th June, 1857 and sailed towards the Niger Delta. As usual this expedition had no more luck than that of 1841, for at a distance of 175 miles north of Lokoja, the steamer met a disastrous end when it struck rocks at Jebba and sank. The crew were rescued by friendly inhabitants of the area. Crowther took advantage of the disaster and spent about a year in the area visiting the many neighbouring villages along the river. It is also believed that during this year Crowther studied the Nupe languages.[20]

In spite of the disaster, the expedition was successful from the missionary point of view, because, firstly, when the expedition arrived at Onitsha, on 25th July 1857, before the disaster, the first permanent station of the proposed *Niger Mission* was established. Secondly, "the message of Christ was given opportunity to reach the people all along that part of the Niger River by the mouth of a Nigerian."[21]

J. C. Taylor was left as the first missionary of the Onitsha station where he worked for twenty months. In addition to Onitsha, Crowther selected a few strategic mission sites such as Rabba. It was his hope that when these eventually became mission stations, they "would be a connecting link between the Yoruba and the Hausa, and a stride into Mohammedan country, under a direct Mohammedan government."[22]

---

[19] John B. Grimley & Gordon E. Robinson, *Church Growth in Central and Southern Nigeria* (1960), pp. 37-38 citing Stock, *op.cit.*, Vol. II p. 121.

[20] F. Deaville Walker, *The Romance of the Black River* (London: CMS, 1930), p. 94.

[21] Grimley & Robinson, *op.cit.*, p. 38.

[22] Groves, *op.cit.*, Vol. II, p. 77.

Though Rabba had seemed promising, the work there lapsed and its outpost at Nupe was abandoned because of "the jealousy of the Muslim Mallams rather than the unwillingness of the secular rulers...".[23]

The Home Committee, however, took the whole *Niger Mission* so seriously that in 1859 five new missionaries were recruited for the Mission. Unfortunately, none of these reached their destination: Sierra Leone and Abeokuta claimed three of them; of the remaining two one was invalided home and the other died in Lagos.

Despite all these difficulties, the promise of the *Niger Mission* remained ablaze. The main concern then was the question how the promise might be fulfilled. Happily, during the 1860's when the missionaries were being persecuted in Yorubaland (see above), the *Niger Mission* began to expand. Samuel Adjayi Crowther opened stations at Brass and Bonny in the Oil Rivers in 1864. He was invited there by the Bishop of London. The reason was that William Pepple, King of Bonny, had been exiled to England in 1854. He had become a Christian during his exile and on his return home, sent message to the Bishop of London to send him a missionary. As a result, Crowther was advised by the Bishop to go to Bonny at the end of 1864. Cowther's son took charge of Bonny in 1871. In 1875 there was persecution there also and the first Christian was martyred. But two years later, in 1877, the principal persecutor among the chiefs, captain Hart, granted religious liberty and before his death in 1878 he ordered the destruction of the family idols. At Brass, also, a leading chief was converted in 1875 and in 1877 the King of Brass himself renounced idolatry.[24]

The period 1878 to 1914 was one of extension, in both the Yoruba and the Niger Missions, from the coast to the hinterland. With the exception of the war between the Egba and the Ijebu against the Ibadan which ended in 1886, there was unprecedented missionary expansion.

As had happened to the Yorubaland Mission, the *Niger Mission* also expanded. Although the expansion in this Mission was general, the main work of expansion was done by the *Lower Niger Mission* with Onitsha as the base. From there the work was extended to the east of the Niger, into Igbo hinterland. This was possibly because, on 23rd March 1902,[25] the power of the Aro, a branch of the Igbo noted for a spiritual science called Long Juju of Arochuku, was destroyed by the British Government. This

---

[23] *Ibid.*, p. 79.

[24] Stock, *op.cit.*, Vol. II, pp. 460-4. See also W. N. M. Geary, *Nigeria Under British Rule* (1927), pp. 86-7.

[25] Donald M. McFarlan, *Calabar, the Church of Scotland Mission, Founded 1846* (London), p. 108.

incident opened a new era for missionary work because one of the strongest opponents of the new faith had been destroyed.

In 1906, four years after the fall of Arochuku, T. J. Dennis opened a station at Owerri which became a very important Igbo station. Dennis did not live there, but at Ebu, only four miles from Owerri. He translated the Bible into Igbo. Earlier, in 1905 it had been decided that as the Igbo spoke many dialects the translation should be produced in a composite language accessible to all. In pursuance of this, Dennis developed a Union Igbo language. The whole work of making an Igbo Bible was completed in 1913. The missionary work continued to advance, and by 1914 the *Niger Mission* had extended from the River Niger to the Cross River with an important institution for the training of evangelists at Awka.

This unprecedented missionary advance both in the Yoruba and Niger missions was aided by the building of a railway line from Lagos to Abeokuta in 1899 and to Benin City in 1903. During the period, having taken political control over the country, the British maintained an atmosphere of stability and security. These two factors safeguarded the missionaries and evangelists in their journeys.

However, the primary factor contributing to the general success of the missions was that the indigenous people began to see that Christianity was a powerful religion and they appreciated the civilising effects it had begun to make on their minds.[26]

It was during this period of general advance in Nigeria that the Anglican work in *GHANA* was revived. In 1904, Bishop N. T. Hamlyn, the Assistant Bishop to Bishop Tugwell of Western Equatorial Africa, was asked to leave Lagos for the Gold Coast (Ghana). He was charged with reviving the abandoned Anglican missionary work there.[27]

On his arrival he was stationed at Sekondi because a Yoruba Anglican group had settled there. After five years' work the Diocese of Accra was erected in 1909 and the Headquarters of the mission was then transferred to Accra the capital town of the Gold Coast (Ghana).

The period, 1904 to 1914, just a decade, is almost negligeable when compared with the long period covered by the Anglican Church in Sierra Leone and Nigeria. In spite of that Anglican congregations in Ghana

---

[26] See the Alake of Abeokuta's letter sent to the CMS, quoted above.

[27] See the Introduction above as regards the earlier S.P.G. attempt to evangelize Ghana between 1750 and 1816. After the death of Philip Quaque in 1815 there was no attempt to Evangelize Ghana by the Anglicans. But a thin thread of Anglicanism was kept alive in the country through an Anglican Chaplaincy, "paid for by the Committee of Merchants or, in the Crown Colony framework, paid for out of Public funds" (Paul Jenkins, "The Anglican Church in Ghana, 1905-24 (1)". *Transactions of the Historical Society of Ghana.*

could be found scattered throughout the Colony, Southern Ashanti and the Northern Territories during this decade. The explanation makes very interesting reading and it illustrates the predominant African initiative which had operated in the Anglican evangelical work in Ghana.

When Hamlyn arrived in the country in 1904, he found four already existing Anglican congregations:— "There were the two Colonial Chaplaincy congregations at Cape Coast and Accra, a congregation started in Axim in the 1890's by the African legal and commercial community, and a small Yoruba Anglican group in Sekondi dating from 1902."[28]

As these pioneer congregations came into being without any Missionary supervision so also had other congregations developed. Jenkins describes four examples.[29]

The first group was organized by individuals. For example, John Swatson, from 1914, began to organize congregations at Sefwi Bodi, Dunkwa and in some coastal towns. Swatson had been converted by a wandering evangelist, Prophet Harris, from Ivory Coast. He had become an evangelist like Harris and made converts. While Harris encouraged his converts to join existing mission churches, Swatson tried to link his work with the Anglican Mission. He first formed his own church organization, "with a few Nzima teacher-catechists each responsible for a handful of congregations, by whom they were to be supported."[30] It was out of such an organization that "Christ Church Beyin" emerged and was handed over by Swatson to the Anglican Diocese of Accra in 1909.

The second group was formed by the Yoruba who had come to Ghana in search of employment and trade in the mining areas especially in the Western Region and Southern Ashanti. They lived in villages near Tarkwa, Prestea and Obuasi. Those of their number who had been Christians in Nigeria, carried their faith with them. They built their own churches and provided their own Lay Readers and catechists. They regarded themselves as Anglicans because probably they came from CMS regions in Yorubaland. When they were discovered, Mr. E. D. Martinson became their catechist and he continued to supervise them after his ordination in 1916.

The third group came into being at Domi Bipposu in Ashanti. Some

---

[28] *Ibid.*, p. 24. It appears that it was because the group at Axim applied to the Church Missionary Society in the late 1890s for missionary support that the CMS eventually decided to revive the SPCK work in Ghana.

[29] *Ibid.*, pp. 25-28.

[30] *Ibid.*, p. 25.

people from this village went to Dunkwa for employment. While there, some of them were evangelized by the Anglican brethren. They established a church when they returned to their village. This did not seem to make much progress. But the churches established by Jachie and Nkawie villages survived. The initiative in these villages came from the royal family, the chiefs being attracted by European education and the church.

The fourth type of group was composed, mainly, of literates who had either seceded from other existing denominations or had migrated from the old coastal towns in Ghana and "from Sierra Leone into the growing commercial centres of the interior as employees of both commercial firms and government."[31] Those of their number who were Anglicans started Anglican churches. Such groups existed in Kumasi, Nsawam and Cape Coast.[32]

Even, in the far north, at Tamale, a non-missionary congregation had existed before 1909 and the Chief Commissioner, Watherston used to conduct an Anglican service on Sundays. It is not clear who formed the congregation at Tamale; but it is possible that by 1900, the literates from Southern Ghana who went to work there started an Anglican Christian fellowship to which the Chief Commissioner lent his support.

The existence of these congregations posed their own problems for Bishop Hamlyn. There was the need for adequate number of missionaries to cater for them and open new grounds. The most realistic way in which Bishop Hamlyn dealt with the problem was that he opened a Grammar School on 4th January 1910. It was to serve as "a nursing ground for the future school teachers, catechists and African Clergy."[33] In 1914, however, the catechist and ministerial students were separated for training in Kumasi. This was done because the second Missionary, Rev. Gresham Winter Morrison who was to train them was stationed in Kumasi as the priest-in-charge.[34]

Thus by World War I, the second attempt of Anglican Missionary work in Ghana was just beginning to be reorganized. The Bishop was visiting the scattered local congregations, a Grammar School had started producing good results at Cape Coast, Kumasi had its first resident missionary and two African catechists, Messrs. E. D. Martinson and W. Hutton - Mensah, were being trained as ordinands. It was after World

---

[31] *Ibid.*, p. 26.

[32] This was not an exlcusive Anglican method of expansion. Christians from other denominations also migrated with their religion wherever they went. See Bartels, *The Roots of Ghana Methodism*, (1965), p. 37, where Methodist migrants from the coast began a Methodist movement in Kumasi before a missionary was sent there.

[33] *S.P.G. Reports* (London: 1914), p. 133.

[34] See my other book, *Christian Missions and Theological Training in West Africa.*

War I that the Anglican Church Ghana, took its major strides towards expansion and that period falls outside the limits of the present study.

About a quarter of a century after the CMS had started its missionary work in West Africa, other Missionary societies also entered the field as shown in the next chapter.

CHAPTER FIVE

WESLEYAN METHODIST MISSIONARY SOCIETY

Methodist influence in Sierra Leone started with the advent of the settlers from Nova Scotia in Freetown in 1792. It was not, at that stage, an organized missionary venture. It just happened that most of the settlers there were Christians of protestant persuasion including Methodists. The various denominations travelled with their Afro-American preachers and remained on their own during the early years of the settlement.

In 1796, four years after the settlers had arrived in Freetown, Dr. Coke, of the Wesleyan Methodist Society in England, sent a team to Sierra Leone, to civilize the Fulani. The team was to carry out community development work among them. The project, however, did not succeed because the members of the team found the work more than they could bear and so resigned. But they had established contact with the Nova Scotia Methodists before their return to Britain.

This encouraged the Wesleyan Methodist interest in Sierra Leone. Consequently, they continued to send missionaries from Britain unofficially to share fellowship with the Methodists from Nova Scotia and to offer them encouragement and assistance. So in 1804 the little congregation in Freetown was ministered to by three local preachers, two English and one Afro-American and in 1811 Dr. Coke sent a Superintendent minister, the Rev. George Warren, and three schoolmasters to Freetown to cater for the little flock. Warren survived only eight months, thus becoming the first Wesleyan Methodist missionary casualty in West Africa. One of the school masters was invalided home leaving Healey and Hirst. William Davies was sent to replace Warren, and the three, Davies Healey and Hirst began to lay the foundation of a permanent British Wesleyan Methodist work on the West Coast of Africa.

This was the position when the Wesleyan Methodist Missionary Society was formed in 1813. The society continued the informal work started earlier by sending missionaries to the colony until 1858.

Prior to that time all the Methodists who had arrived from the United States of America as colonists constituted themselves into an independent Christian community in Sierra Leone known as "the West African Methodist". They numbered about 2,300 and were drawn from fourteen congregations in Sierra Leone.

In 1858 they sent an application to the United Free Churches of Great Britain for admission into the British Methodist Fellowship. The application was approved in 1859 and the Rev. Joseph New was appointed to superintend them. He worked for nearly three years and died in 1862. He was succeeded by M. Micklethwaite who served as superintendent for twelve years.

During these twelve years the work showed steady progress despite the fact that there was shortage of European staff and the grants from the home society were restricted. The explanation for this handicap is that at that time there was agitation for reform within the Methodist Church in Britain and it appears that the call for reform absorbed so much interest and energy that less attention was paid to the mission field in spite of the fact that increased demands for men and money were pouring in from all the fields overseas.

The Society, however, preserved its aspirations for the promotion of the Sierra Leonean work irrespective of these problems. Thus in 1866 it was agreed not to despair because Sierra Leone was

> advancing beyond a mere mission to the position of a Church, in a great measure self-supporting, though for the present assisted by grants from the Mission House Fund.[1]

During the troubled days of the Methodist Church in Britain the few missionaries left in Sierra Leone were effectively assisted by African helpers and the work was satisfactorily maintained. So by 1880 the membership grew to 6,000 and advances were made into the protectorate. By 1896 stations were opened at Sherbro, Temne and Limba. These three stations constituted threefold radiating centres from which the interior was penetrated.

The advance was disrupted in 1898 when the Wesleyans in the Sherbro area were raided and African agents and about 200 communicants were killed. The membership there at the end of the year, fell from 442 to 124.[2] The mission suffered losses also at some Temne stations such as Massanka and Mabang. In spite of all these distressing experiences the Society never despaired; rather from 1900, after the hostilities had ended it started penetrating the Mende population.

From this time until the end of World War I the Wesleyan Methodist Missionary work in Sierra Leone advanced with leaps and bounds.

North West of Sierra Leone lies the Republic of *THE GAMBIA*. Its present capital town Banjul was formerly known as Bathurst. This city

---

[1] Groves, *op.cit.*, Vol. II, p. 219, citing Findlay and Holdsworth, *The History of Wesleyan Methodist Misionary Society*. Vol.IV (Five Vols.) (London, 1922), pp. 92, 97-98 & 102.
[2] See Chapter XIII for the circumstances leading to the massacre.

was founded in 1816 just three years after the formation of the Wesleyan Methodist Missionary Society. In 1821, five years after the city's foundation the W.M.M.S. sent missionaries there.

The initiative for WMMS work in Bathurst came from a Charles Grant and Governor McCarthy. Charles Grant was an English man who lived at Goree (a small island opposite Dakar). At the end of the Napoleonic wars in 1815 Goree became French by treaty and from 1816 most of the British subjects there, including Grant, began to move to Bathurst (Banjul). Grant being a devoted Christian formed a small congregation at this new station and read prayers each Sunday morning.[3] He and governor McCarthy felt the need for a minister of religion to be stationed in Bathurst to serve the little Christian group there and also to reach out beyond Bathurst where they believed the fields were ripe for harvest.

In 1820 Governor Charles McCarthy went on leave to England and appealed to the W.M.M.S. to establish a mission in the Gambia. The appeal was favourably received and in the following year 1821 the pioneer W.M.M.S. missionaries were despatched.

The first of them, the Rev. John Morgan arrived at Bathurst on 8th February, 1821. He was later joined, the same year, by John Baker who had been working down the coast, in Sierra Leone. They were initially charged to open a station at Tendaba up River but this was not feasible because of the "disturbed state of the country and a number of other circumstances."[4] Some of these circumstances Morgan has listed very clearly:[5] firstly, Tendaba was a very important slave market and the missionaries felt that they would never be allowed to stay there because the gospel message opposed slavery. Secondly, the liberated Africans at St. Mary's island were very well disposed to Christianity. Some of them who had migrated from Sierra Leone, recognized Baker when he arrived at Bathurst from Sierra Leone. Their enthusiasm towards the missionaries and their request that the missionaries should preach more sermons for their edification naturally encouraged Morgan and Baker to leave Tendaba and concentrate on Bathurst.

But the first station was not opened at Bathurst because in the south, the King of Kombo offered a piece of land to the missionaries at Mandinari where with the help of the local people, Morgan and Baker built a temporary shelter and opened the first station. Unfortunately Mandinari proved unsuitable: the water was bad and the inhabitants were not well

---

[3] W. Fox, *A Brief History of the Wesleyan Mission in West Coast of Africa* (London 1950), p. 202.

[4] J. M. Gray, *History of the Gambia* (Frank Cass & Co. Ltd.), p. 313.

[5] Barbara Prickett, *Island Base* (Meth. Church, Gambia n.d.), p. 20.

disposed to Christianity because of Muslim influence. Consequently, the missionaries turned to Bathurst where a school had been established in 1822 and opened the first permanent Wesleyan Methodist Mission station there in 1823. The climate at Bathurst was conducive to the preaching of the Gospel: the inhabitants comprised the Wollof and liberated Africans. The Wollof (Jolloff) were well disposed to Christianity because they were little influenced by Islam at that time; the liberated Africans had already been Christianized while they were in exile in America or Sierra Leone.

Between 1824 and 1844 the work in the Gambia showed concrete marks of growth. The Rev. and Mrs. Robert Hawkins arrived there in 1824. They were followed by Richard Marshall in 1828, William Moister 1831, William Fox and Thomas Dove in 1833.

The Society of Friends (Quakers) had opened a Girls' School at St. Mary's island before the Hawkins arrived. But illness forced the missionaries of the Society of Friends to leave the Gambia and before their departure their Girls' School was handed over to Mrs. Hawkins to run.

In 1825, just a year after the arrival of the Hawkins, a Mission House and a school building were put up in Bathurst. Other gains during the period 1824-1844 consisted of opening more stations at McCarthy Island, Barra, Morocunda, Jillifree, Fattatenda and Kaur. It was also during the period that St. Mary's and McCarthy Islands were given circuit status respectively and Robert Maxwell McBrair translated the Gospel of St. Matthew into Mandinka, compiled a Mandinka grammar and started work among the Fula. Many Wollof assistants were also trained by the missionaries during this period of consolidation.[6]

The next period 1844-1919 was that of expansion. The work in Bathurst, St. Mary's and McCarthy Islands, was firmly established. The District Synod was organized into Pastoral and Representative sessions; a High School was opened on 13th September 1875 followed by an Industrial/Technical school in 1901 and a Girls' High School was started in 1915 by Mrs. Toye. By the end of the period Church membership grew from 6 in 1821 to 250 in 1834, 678 in 1894 and 863 in 1914.

This steady but slow progress did not come without its attendant problems. The usual difficulties, sickness and death of the missionaries disrupted the work. Between 1821 and 1834, ten missionaries and six missionary wives arrived. Three missionaries, three missionary wives and two missionary children died while some of the adults were invalided home.

---

[6] *Ibid.*, p. 25.

The inexperience of some of the missionaries retarded the progress of the work. This disrupted the personal relationships between some of the African members of the church and the European missionaries. For example, the way Godman abolished the practice of sponsorship during infant baptism led to enmity between him and some of the African members of the church; his insistence that members must not marry unbelievers led to dissatisfaction among the members and so on.

There are other instances where the relationship among the missionaries themselves was not cordial. For example, Fox clashed with his junior colleagues, English and Crowley and there was disagreement between Henry Hirst and his colleagues. All these had negative effects on the growth of the church. Apart from the possibility of splitting the church internally, due to members taking sides, the quarrels led to the resignation of some of the African members from the Methodist congregation. During the periods of dissension no revivals were recorded in the congregations. Where membership increased during the quarrels, as it did in 1840, it was due merely to chance and not to any evangelization by the missionaries. For instance, in 1840, when Fox and his colleagues were quarrelling, many new members entered the church. The reason was that in that year many more liberated Africans arrived in Bathurst. These people had been separated completely from their tribes and once settled most of them were eager to attach themselves to the Christian community, if only because they had no other to which they could belong.[7] In the Church they believed they would have a sense of belonging and obtain a new family and security.

Later, when the quarrels stopped and cordial relationship existed among the missionaries, between Bridgart and Cooper, between Cooper and Peet, between Peet and Daw and Daw and Southern in the 1850's and 1860's there was internal revival. There was not much geographical expansion but the church in Bathurst showed concrete signs of healthier spiritual growth: the leaders took their duties more seriously, paying pastoral visits to those members who did not attend class meetings; the people voluntarily repaired the Mission House, built a chapel at Bakkaw Kunko and erected a new Mission House at McCarthy's Island. Indeed

there was a life and warmth about the church in the period from Bridgart's arrival (1854) to Southern's departure (1864) which appears in all the letters of the period and cannot be totally separated from the good relationships that prevailed.[8]

---

[7] *Ibid.*, p. 97.
[8] *Ibid.*, pp. 98-99.

In spite of the warmth of the church, the liberated Africans constituted a problem of their own. These and their descendants formed the bulk of the membership of the church in Bathurst (Banjul). The Misionaries concentrated mainly on ministering to them. As new liberated Africans poured in so also did the church membership increase.

The immigrants themselves adopted an air of superiority over the indigenous people, became settled and so inward-looking that they found it difficult to condescend to evangelize the local people. Consequently, little attention was paid to the conversion of the African Traditional worshippers and the Muslims. This seems to explain why the membership roll of the Church remained static after the end of the Slave Trade when ship loads of liberated Africans were no longer disembarked there.

Fourteen years from the commencement of Methodist work in the Gambia a similar enterprise was started in *GHANA*. The circumstances which led the W.M.M.S. to send their missionaries there were a demonstration of the role which African initiative played in the establishment of Methodist work in Ghana.

When Charles McCarthy, the Governor of Sierra Leone was asked to supervise the British forts in Ghana at the end of 1821 he accepted this responsibility and immediately opened a school at Cape Coast castle. The purpose was to train brilliant African boys for employment in the colonial administration.

The African head teacher of the School Mr. Joseph Smith, being a sincere Christian, introduced on his own initiative, Bible reading as part of the curriculum. His aim was to acquaint his pupils with an accurate knowledge of the Bible. Because of this he insisted that no comment on the reading should be made. But one of his pupils William de Graft disagreed with him. He thought that without commenting on the passages read it would be difficult to understand them fully. Smith vehemently disagreed with de Graft and this led to the emergence of two parties among the students with Smith and de Graft as leaders. de Graft called his group "A Meeting or Society for Promoting Christian Knowledge".

At their first meeting which was held on 1st October, 1831,

> they adopted for their guidance the following rule, which is copied literally from the minutes of their proceedings: 'That, as the word of God is the best rule a Christian ought to observe, it is herein avoided framing other rules to enforce good conduct; but that the Scriptures must be carefully studied through which, by the help of the Holy Spirit and Faith in Christ Jesus, our minds will be enlightened and find the way to eternal salvation'.[9]

---

[9] F. L. Bartels, *The Roots of Ghana Methodists* (Cambridge, 1965), p. 8, citing John Beecham, *Ashantee and the Gold Coast* (London, 1841), p. 260. See also Groves, *op.cit.*, Vol. I, p. 302.

The pioneer members of the "Meeting" were George Blankson, John Sam, Henry Brew, John Smith, Brown, Neizer, Aggrey, Sackey Kwobina Mensa and Insaidu. They were very systematic in their Bible study. After some time, Joseph Smith reported the "Meeting" to the Governor George Maclean on the grounds that it was a heretical and dangerous movement.

Without proper investigation the Governor imposed a fine on the group and caused the imprisonment of William de Graft the leader and John Sam, probably the secretary. This punishment automatically excluded de Graft and Sam from ever joining the civil service. It has been said that their evangelical zeal and joy while they were in prison caused the conversion of one of the prisoners.

When eventually they were released William de Graft went and settled at Dixcove. He maintained communication with the member students of his band at Cape Coast. As the membership increased, the students sent a request to de Graft to send them more Bibles.

At that time there was an English sailor, Captain Potter, on the coast. He was known to be a good Christian and so de Graft asked him to secure the Bibles from Britain for the students. He was so impressed by the request made by the members of the "Meeting" or band that he decided, if possible, to bring the Bibles and a missionary.

As Potter was a Methodist he carried the story of the band to the W.M.M.S. in London and "offered to take out at his own expense any missionary the committee might appoint."[10] The W.M.M.S. was so satisfied with the initiative shown by the African boys that they recruited their first missionary, Joseph Dunwell, for Ghana.

Dunwell arrived at Cape Coast on 1st January 1835. He lived only for six months and died on 24th June the same year. During his short stay at Cape Coast Dunwell achieved much: he reconciled the two Bible bands and their leaders who were both very helpful to him. Joseph Smith was his interpreter and "de Graft was an invaluable lieutenant".[11] He also sought out two Ashanti princes who were waiting at Cape Coast for a ship to take them to England to be educated. When he found them he was able to lead them to accept Jesus Christ before their departure for England.

The next two missionaries and their wives Rev. & Mrs. George Wrigley and the Rev. & Mrs. Peter Harrop who had arrived on 15th September 1836 and 15th January, 1837 died before they had served a

---

[10] Groves, *Ibid.*, Vol.I, pp. 302-303.
[11] *Ibid.*, p. 303.

year. These losses were tragic not only for the W.M.M.S. but also for the local Christian nucleus at Cape Coast, the fellowship of the Bible band.

The W.M.M.S., however, did not give up the enterprise. They decided wisely to send a missionary of African descent who they hoped would be able to endure the rigours of the tropical climate and the dangers of tropical diseases. Consequently, Thomas Birch Freeman, the son of an African father and an English mother, was recruited. He arrived at Cape Coast in January 1838 with his wife and Joseph Smith the Headmaster of the Castle School and Dunwell's interpreter who had been on a visit to England.

Mrs. Freeman survived only the first six months. Freeman was left alone. Naturally, he was distressed but not dismayed. He settled down after a period of ill-health and rendered untiring service to the building up of the Methodist Church in Ghana with the help of devoted African helpers.

The results of his first two years' work in the country were extraordinary as compared with the Basel missionary enterprise in the Eastern section of the country: he entered Kumasi, the Ashanti capital, on 1st April, 1839; he opened 14 more stations[12] in addition to the three pioneer stations opened by his predecessors at Cape Coast, Anomabu and Winneba; he trained a team of convinced local workers, one of whom was a candidate for the Christian ministry. During those two years the total enrolment of membership was 100 and there were five schools. Methodist men continued to labour hard in the Castle School at Cape Coast to produce Christian students some of whom became teachers for the Methodist schools being opened by Freeman.

The work was maintained, when Freeman went on furlough in 1840, by other missionary colleagues, the Rev. Robert Brooking and Rev. and Mrs. Mycock assisted by local agents. When he returned from England, Freeman continued to extend his activities in all directions. He had the second visit to Kumasi between 1841 and 1842 and succeeded in opening a mission there during that visit.

In Kumasi also, there had developed a small Methodist nucleus organized by James Hayford, a Fanti Methodist who had been living in Kumasi as the British representative appointed by Governor Maclean. He had been holding services of worship for the Fanti living in Kumasi and for the Ashanti who cared to attend. This was the actual beginning of Methodist work in Kumasi and it was with this group that Freeman opened his mission in Ashanti.

_____

[12] Bartels: *op.cit.*, p. 40.

From his base in Cape Coast Freeman travelled extensively reaching as far as Abomey (Agbome) Badagry and Abeokuta and left William de Graft as an agent at Badagry towards the end of 1842.

In spite of these enterprising adventures, Freeman incurred the displeasure of the Home Committee over matters of financial administration. It was not that he misappropriated the funds but rather he promoted ambitious building and agricultural projects which brought financial strain upon the young societies, and though his accounts did not balance he did not halt the projects or curtail them. So in 1856 the Home Committee relieved him of his financial responsibilities. Thus in the following year, 1857, feeling that he had lost the confidence of the Home Committee, Freeman retired as a missionary, after twenty years of magnificent service and took up a civil appointment at Christiansborg in Accra. He remained in the civil service for about fifteen years and returned to full-time mission work in 1873.[13]

During Freeman's retirement the missionary work was continued by other missionary colleagues and African helpers. Indeed, the period 1852-1900 was one that saw rapid expansion of Methodism in Ghana. Kumasi had been established and the work there advanced so satisfactorily that by 1900 it could be said that "Kumasi now had an enlarged mission house and a European missionary."[14]

The main reason for the rapid expansion of Methodist work during the period was that from the very beginning the European missionaries made good use of the indigenous converts as evangelists. In 1885 for example, there were only three European missionaries; but there were 15 African ministers and 126 catechists and evangelists. It was this band of faithful African helpers who kept the work alive even when the European staff was not adequate.

Secondly, as we have noticed already in this chapter, and elsewhere in this book, the converted Christians carried their new faith wherever they went. In their new settlements they established their little places of worship and later applied to the headquarters for a supply of full-time evangelistic workers.

All along, the Methodists concentrated their efforts in the Southern section of the country. But in 1911, the Rev. W. R. Griffin, the General Superintendent of the Wesleyan Mission, paid an exploratory visit to the Northern Territories (Northern Ghana) in response to the Chief Commissioner Watherston's invitation in 1908 to the Protestant missions

---

[13] *Ibid.*, p. 98.
[14] *Ibid.*, p. 154.

working in Southern Ghana to extend their work to the north also.[15] Griffin acquired a piece of land at Tamale and Wa from the Acting Chief Commissioner, Major Irvine. Soon after he returned to Accra, Griffin appointed the Rev. H. G. Martin as resident Methodist missionary to Tamale. No progress was made, however, and in 1915 the mission was reluctantly closed down because the Chief Commissioner, who succeeded Watherston, Cecil Hamilton Armitage placed difficult restrictions on the movements of the Methodist missionaries sent to the north.

Armitage had the impression that Protestants were difficult to control while Roman Catholics were "much more amenable and Law abiding...".[16] Accordingly, he determined to limit the evangelization of the Northern Territories to the Roman Catholics. Secondly, Armitage argued "that Wa had a considerable Muslim population which it would be unwise to disturb and suggested that the Wesleyans should first set their house in order in the south before they could undertake missionary work in the north."[17]

Naturally this created friction between the Wesleyan Mission and the Chief Commissioner. Armitage refused to allow the Methodists to use the land Griffin had acquired; he did not permit the Methodists the use of any government building for worship; he refused to give official recognition to the Rev. Martin as the representative of the Methodist mission; he accused Rev. Martin of using school boys in his house without permission; he complained that Martin was spreading malicious gossip and interfering in personal matters outside his competence; and he did not allow Martin to give religious instruction to the children either in or out of school.

All these led to a serious rift between the Chief Commissioner and Martin and the Chief Commissioner gave a damaging report about Martin to the Governor of the Gold Coast, Mr. Clifford. Clifford was so displeased with the tone and language used by Armitage that Armitage

> was told that the Government had no power to prevent the establishment of a mission in the Northern Territories and that the Secretary of State had expressed his approval of the Wesleyan Mission being established at Tamale.[18]

---

[15] Benedict Der. "Church State Relations in Northern Ghana, 1906-1940". *Transactions of the Historical Society of Ghana, Vol.XV(i), 1977*, p. 45. Watherston invited the Protestants because according to Der "his point of view was that the Catholics should not be allowed to control missionary work in the Northern Territories."

[16] *Ibid.*, p. 45.

[17] *Loc.cit.*

[18] *Ibid.*, p. 46.

In consequence the Wesleyan Methodists were officially permitted in 1913 to open their mission in Tamale. For obvious reasons Martin was transferred from the North and was replaced by Rev. J. M. Stormonth.

Even though the Chief Commissioner expressed a preference for Stormonth over Martin, he soon picked up a quarrel with Stormonth also. The reason was that Armitage did not give up his exclusion policy against the Protestants. He took advantage of a clause in the permission granted to the Wesleyan Methodists to establish themselves in the north and unreasonably restricted the movements of Stormonth.

The clause stated that "owing to political conditions it would be necessary for the Agent of the Society to be guided by the reasonable requirements of the Chief Commissoner as to the localities ... in which their operations are to be carried out."[19] Because of this, Armitage required Stormonth to give him advance notice of his itinerary, especially if he intended to go North-West, to the Wa area. Stormonth was required to give three week's advance notice.

Stormonth raised objections to the Chief Commissioner's demands because as Der aptly observes:-

> To require that the Wesleyan missionaries should give long advance notices before they could undertake preaching tours was not only irksome; it was not in order. Furthermore, long notices restricted the liberty of the missionaries in relation to their freedom of movement.

That was exactly what Armitage wanted. His aim was to restrict the movement of the missionaries in such a way that the Wesleyan work in the Northern Territories would fail. This policy was such a hinderance to the missionaries and their work that no progress had been made since the Methodist advent in the Northern Territories in 1911. This was the reason why they had to abandon the Northern part of Ghana in 1915.

In the South including Ashanti, however, the Methodists continued to expand and by 1919 they were scattered all over Southern Ghana from Peki in the Volta Region to Axim and its environs in the West and from Kumasi in Ashanti to Sunyani in Brong Ahafo.

Meanwhile, in *NIGERIA* the work started by Thomas Birch Freeman and William de Graft in 1842 continued to show progress. When Freeman was going to Yorubaland in 1842 he was accompanied by William de Graft who at that time had offered for ordination and was received as a probationer (minister preparing for full ordination). The welcome they received at Badagry and Abeokuta from the Sierra Leone immigrants and Shodeke of Abeokuta was very encouraging.

---

[19] *Ibid.*, p. 47, citing ADM 56/1/33, Irvine to Martin, 24th April, 1913.

When Shodeke of Abeokuta heard about Freeman and de Graft he invited representatives of the major religious groups then at Abeokuta: the African Traditional, the Muslim and the Christian groups. His purpose was that each of the representatives should state their case before him to enable him to choose the true religion. After listening to the three groups Shodeke chose Freeman's religion, Christianity, as the true one.[20] Consequently, Freeman and his colleague stayed with Shodeke for ten days in Abeokuta before they returned to Badagry on 24th December, 1842. On Christmas day Freeman's party joined with the Anglican missionary Townsend, who had arrived there on a similar mission[21] and they organized a united service.

As a result of the warm reception these pioneer Wesleyan missionaries enjoyed in Yorubaland William de Graft did not return to Ghana with Freeman. He was stationed in Badagry as the Wesleyan missionary to pastor the Methodist immigrants from Sierra Leone.

The expansion of the work was very slow in spite of the existence of an immigrant nucleus because of the tribal wars during that period culminating in the expulsion of the missionaries in 1867 already referred to in Chapter III. Despite this problem the work was kept alive by converted traders. These people carried their new faith with them to their villages and witnessed to their people. Even in the face of local persecutions they held firm to their new found faith. For instance in 1912 when the General Superintendent of the Methodist Church in Nigeria went to Shagamu, an area new to the mission, he found "the nucleus of a strong African Church already existing."[22]

This was the result of expansion through lay evangelism. It was this method which helped the Methodist and Christian expansion in Western Nigeria until 1910 especially around Lagos, Ibadan and Ilesha.

The Methodists, like the Anglicans and Roman Catholics, were comparatively late in entering *Eastern Nigeria*. The initiative did not come from the Wesleyans but from the Primitive Methodists, originally a sect which broke away from the Wesleyans between 1807 and 1810 because the sect members believed that the Wesleyan Methodists had lost the Wesleys' evangelical enthusiasm.

At first their missionaries established themselves on the Spanish Island of Fernando Po. Initially they were met with two problems: lack of adequate space for expansion and the Spanish Government's policy restricting their movement. As a result the missionaries were considerably

---

[20] Groves, *op.cit.*, Vol. II, p. 48.
[21] See Chapter III above.
[22] Groves, *op.cit.*, Vol. III, p. 215.

restricted in their activities on the Island. Spain was Roman Catholic and it appeared that the Government regarded the Protestant presence on the Island as a threat to the Roman Catholic faith.

While the missionaries were considering the possibility of abandoning Fernando Po they had an invitation from JaJa of Opobo in the Oil Rivers, south-eastern Nigeria, asking them to enter Opobo.

The invitation was communicated to the Home Missionary Committee who after careful consideration accepted it in 1892 and asked the missionaries in Fernando Po to move into Opobo. But when they left Fernando Po they occupied Rio del Rey, a territory on the borders of Cameroons and Southern Nigeria. The reason seems to be that at the time the missionaries left Fernando Po all the Opobo chiefs did not subscribe to missionary invasion of their territory.

So in 1893 the first Primitive Methodist station was opened at Archibongon the bank of the River Akwayafe with the Rev. Marcus Brown as the minister-in-charge.

Brown was later succeeded by the Rev. Thomas Stones. During the time of Stones, in February 1896, the Chief of Obio Utan or Jamestown invited the Primitive Methodists, to cross to the west bank of the Cross River estuary to open a mission in his town.

Stones accepted the invitation because he considered Jamestown, where the chief, out of his own initiative, had built a school, to be a strategic spring-board from which the mission could advance into the North. Following the opening of Jamestown the mission advanced rapidly from Oron on the Cross River northwards, and in two decades the interior of Igboland was occupied.

The reason for this rapid growth is obvious. Early in the twentieth century bituminous coal was discovered at Udi in the District of Enugu. Consequently, a railroad was built by the Colonial Government linking Enugu and Port Harcourt in 1913.

The missionaries took advantage of this improved means of communition and in five years they advanced from Ihube and Ndoro reaching as far as Bendel by road. They occupied railroad junctions such as Orim, Agbani, Uzuakoli, Umuahia and Aba. The farthest north they could reach by 1918 was the Idoma district in the south-eastern corner of NorthernNigeria.

Thus though the Primitive Methodists had anticipated that from Jamestown they could easily reach Northern Nigeria this dream was not realised during the period under discussion. It was after 1919 that the Methodists both the Wesleyans and Primitives invaded Northern Nigeria.

CHAPTER SIX

BASEL MISSIONARY SOCIETY

The Danes remained in Ghana, the then Gold Coast, until about 1850. Their principal fort was at Christiansborg near Accra. The Danish Governor in 1825 was Major de Richelieu. When he first arrived on the Coast around 1824 he found that the chaplain's post at the castle had been vacant for 15 years. He also observed that the religious and moral life of the colony was at a very low ebb. To rectify this situation he revived public worship which he conducted himself, established a school in which he taught and his enthusiasm and concern for the good life compelled him to baptize about 150 of the pupils in his school. These initial activities so impressed the people of Christiansborg that, when he was going to Denmark on leave in 1826, they requested him to bring them a minister on his return.

Richelieu reported the request to Mr. Ronne who represented the interests of the Basel Mission in Denmark. Mr. Ronne in turn contacted the Crown Prince (one of his former pupils) about the possibility of allowing the Basel Mission to open a field in the Gold Coast. He pointed out to the Prince that if official permission was granted, the Basel Mission would be prepared to support the work. When the Prince conveyed the matter to the King of Denmark he warmly gave approval, "remarking that it was appropriate a new mission should begin on Danish soil when they were celebrating the thousandth anniversary of the baptism of Harald, the first Danish Christian King."[1] Under these propitious circumstances, the Basel Committee did not hesitate in agreeing to initiate a mission in the Gold Coast under the protection of the Danes.

It was not, however, as simple as all that. There was the question of how the Basel missionaries would be related to the State Church of Denmark. At that time, Ghana was under the Danish ecclesiastical jurisdiction of the Bishop of Zealand. The Bishop, Bishop Mürter, was implored to permit the Basel Missionary Society to send some of their missionaries to open the new mission. He gave approval on condition that he be permitted to ordain the missionaries and that the missionaries be under his ecclesiastical control.

The Basel Committee raised no objections because they did not like missionaries to be so independent that they could be controlled by no

---

[1] Groves, *op.cit.*, Vol. I, p. 299.

ecclesiastical body. Secondly, the Basel men thought that they were only preparing the way for a Danish mission. As a result of these negotiations, the first four pioneer Basel missionaries were selected. They were K. F. Salbach, J. G. Schmidt, G. Holzwarth and J. P. Henke. After studying Danish at Copenhagen they landed at Christiansborg in December, 1828. They started work among the people with enthusiasm. Two of them concentrated on Christiansborg while the other two moved along the coast towards the east. Unfortunately, however, three of them Holzwarth, Salbach and Schmidt died in August, 1829. Henke who was left alone, was overwhelmed but he was not dismayed. His distress was worsened by the lax moral and religious life of some of the Europeans and Africans in the coastal settlements. Though appalled, he "continued to deliver his Christian message in the hope that some seed sown might find favourable soil, though all appearances were contrary".[2] He too died on 22nd November, 1831 in his loneliness. Thus within three years, the four pioneers had passed away into eternity without having a single convert.

It was a disappointing venture; but the Basel Committee despatched another band of three missionaries: Revs. P. P. Jager, Andreas Riis and C. F. Heinze a medical doctor. They arrived at Christiansborg in March 1833. Within four months Heinze and Jager were dead. Riis became ill but was saved by an African traditional medicineman. For three years, Riis was compelled by the Danish chaplain at Christiansborg to restrict his activities to the coast to help improve the immoral life of the people. Fortunately, when the chaplain was replaced Riis was allowed by the new chaplain to reach other Africans beyond the coast because it appeared Riis could not do much about the immoral life on the coast. Accordingly, in 1836 he and a Danish merchant, George Lutterodt, entered Akropong in Akwapim and established a new station there. This transfer was a turning-point in the life of the Basel mission for the following reasons. Akropong is a hilly area and Riis enjoyed better health there than on the coastal plains around Christiansborg. The sphere of work was now taken to rural people who offered more hope "than the sophisticated and demoralized population of a coast town."[3] Finally, Akropong was at a strategic point. It was on the way to Kumasi, the capital of the great Ashanti Kingdom. To establish a mission there became Riis's main objective.

From 1837 the prospects brightened if only temporarily. There was a reinforcement of two missionaries, I. Mürdter and A. Stanger with Miss Anna Wolters the fiancee of Riis. But within a year Stanger died, and

---

[2] *Ibid.*, p. 300.
[3] *Loc. cit.*

was followed by Mürdter in 1838. Once again Riis was left without his missionary colleagues; but this time he had the company of a wife. From 1838 Riis did a lot of exploration work. Before Mürdter's death Riis and he travelled to the Volta Region and in 1839 Riis alone travelled westwards reaching Kumasi in 1840 seeking unsuccessfully to be given an audience by the Asantehene. When later, during 1840, he went home on furlough he reported to the Basel Committee that the time was not yet ripe to open a station in Ashanti.

Twelve years had passed since work was begun. Out of nine missionaries sent out only one survived and only one convert was bapetized at Christiansborg in 1839. The Basel Committee was faced with the question whether or not the work should be continued in Ghana. Losses had been heavy. But this great price, encouraged the Basel Mission to continue the work. Moreover Riis was prepared, in spite of everything, to return to the Gold Coast mission field. The committee therefore resolved to persevere until a church was built. It then resolved to transplant into the Gold Coast Christian Negroes from a Danish territory where some people of African descent had become Christians. Two reasons inspired this policiy: first, it was felt that the immigrant Negroes would be employed to do manual labour and thus relieve the missionaries from menial work hopefully thus saving them from frequent sickness, invalidings and death. In the second place it was believed that the presence of Negro Christians and their Christian conduct would demonstrate to the local African Community that Christianity is not only a white man's religion.

The champion of the policy was Inspector Hoffmann of the Basel Mission. In pursuance of this strategy the Basel Mission turned its attention to the West Indies for the recruitment of Christian Negroes for the Mission field in Ghana. So while he was on furlough between 1840 and 1843, Riis sailed with two other colleagues from London in May 1842 to Jamaica in the West Indies where twenty-four immigrants comprising six families were recruited for Ghana.

An agreement was entered upon by the Mission and the Jamaican Presbytery. The terms were that:

> The Mission would be responsible for the emigrants' support on the Gold Coast for the first two years. Land and houses would be assigned to them on arrival, and free time allowed for cultivation. After two years their time would be their own save that the Mission would expect their services to be available when required at reasonable recompense. At the end of five years the society would defray their return passage to Jamaica provided their moral record had been satisfactory.[4]

---

[4] *Ibid.*, p. 25.

After sixty-eight days' journey from Jamaica (8th February to 17th April 1843), the party arrived in West Africa. Soon after their arrival missionary reinforcements were sent from Basel. This marked the beginning of the second stage of the Basel Missionary enterprise in Ghana when the work began to bear concrete fruits.

On their arrival, the West Indians were all attached to the Akropong station. In 1847, when the Aburi station was opened two of the immigrant families were transferred there. At first the local people both at Akropong and Aburi were very enthusiastic but they lost some of this when they discovered that the missionaries would not supply them with brandy. Eventually they did not co-operate with the Jamaicans. So the anticipated hope of the missionaries and the Home Board began to decline again.

Thus one of the initial reasons for transplanting the West Indian Christians—the hope that they would attract the indigenous Africans to Christianity seemed to be floundering. Though they were black the Jamaicans did not understand the vernacular of the local people because they had lost their mother tongue and used only English as their language. Thus language remained a barrier for them just as it was for the European missionaries. But it was not merely a barrier to communication; the use of the English language made the Jamaicans look down upon the indigenous Africans and this attitude kept them aloof from the people they were recruited to serve. The effect was that the Africans who were interested in Christianity turned more to the European missionaries than to the West Indian Christians.[5]

In the matter of manual labour the West Indians discharged their duties satisfactorily. After the expiry of the five years of the original agreement those who were not at home on the mission field returned to Jamaica. Three or four of the families remained at Akropong and eventually formed the nucleus of the little community there. For example in 1851 out of a total Christian community of 31 at Akropong, 25 were West Indian.

In the main the project was a disappointment and the Basel Missionary Society confirmed this acknowledging "that the ideal of 'a colony of heaven' was not realized by the West Indian emigrants."[5]

In spite of all this, the decade 1840-1850 brought a lot of confidence into the work as evidenced by Carl Reindorf in these words:

> The annual report of 1848, relates that at last the wilderness and solitary places were beginning to rejoice, and the fruits were to be seen. About 40

---

[5] *Ibid.*, p. 26. See pp. 70-71 below for some practical and positive contributions of the Jamaicans to Ghana's economic development.

native Christians besides the 20 West Indians were gathered in Christ's fold, both at Akropong and at Christiansborg, and at least 300 children received regular teaching. Between 1838 and 1848 only one missionary, Sebald, died at Akropong on December 7th 1845.[6]

The rest of the story from 1851 to 1914 was that of progress and expansion. There were four areas where the achievements of this period were concentrated; a scholarly development of the Twi and the Ga languages, the gradual extension of evangelical work in the Ga, Akwapim and Krobo districts, a careful training of indigenous personnel, and the development of agriculture and trade.

As regards evangelical activities, Osu station established in 1845 was difficult to evangelize, because the belief in the indigenous religion and customs was so strong that the inhabitants did not pay much heed to Christian preaching. Between 1828 and 1850 there were only fourteen adult baptisms. This did not deter the missionaries; they centred their hopes mainly on the schools and remained at their posts. The political situation in 1854 at Christiansborg[7] compelled Zimmerman to move the station from Christiansborg to Abokobi, a large village twelve miles north of Christiansborg. With A. Steinhauser, Zimmerman built a small Christian community at Abokobi.

Here the people were very receptive to the Christian religion and steadily Christianity began to supersede the indigenous religion. This was possible because the Christians who migrated from Christiansborg gave encouragement to the people of Abokobi. More specifically, however, the conversion of a local Fetish Priest in 1857 was the most powerful event which turned the people away from the indigenous religion to Christianity. This Fetish Priest was baptized, Paul Mohenu at the age of sixty. "He learned to read, became an itinerant preacher, and over a period of almost twenty years helped to found and build up congregations in Odumase, Ada and in many small vilages on the Accra plains."[8]

Earlier in 1855 Zimmerman and Locher entered the Krobo district further east of Abokobi and in 1859 a station was permanently established at Odumase, the paramount town of the area. The Chief Odonkor Azu, was very friendly with the missionaries. He offered one of his one sons, the twelve-year-old Tei, to Zimmerman to be trained as a Christian and he attended baptism instructions with some of his subjects. The signs

---

[6] Carl C. Reindorf, *The History of the Gold Coast and Asante 1500-1800* (Switzerland, 1951), 2nd ed., p. 220.

[7] See my *Christian Missions and Theological Training* and the other references there about the Poll Tax Ordinance Controversy of 1856.

[8] Noel Smith, *The Presbyterian Church of Ghana, 1835-1960* (Ghana Universities Press, Accra, 1966), p. 47.

were so propitious that the missionaries thought that the whole tribe was going to be converted. This, however, did not happen because the Chief refused to be baptized. Probably, the pressure of the old religion, the ancestral regal customs and his fidelity to the oath of office proved too great. Presumably, his subjects were waiting for him to be baptized first and they would follow. Thus as their leader refused baptism so most of them refused to declare themselves Christians. Consequently, the great initial promise, high attendance at the baptism instruction and much hearing of the Gospel message, produced only very few baptisms. In spite of this, by 1870 there were ninety Christians, a girls boarding school with twelve pupils, twenty-three children in a day school and two outstations at Sra and Ada supervised by catechists.

Akropong still remained the nerve centre of the Basel Mission on the Gold Coast. During the period it was strongly manned by Johannes Maier, Pauline Walker (Mrs. J. J. Walker), Jacob Klass, and J. Geo Widmann. These also extended the work from Akropong. The Christian quarters at Akropong slowly increased in size; a larger chapel was dedicated in 1868 and buildings were put up for schools and a seminary. In 1853 the first five females were baptized and the first Christian marriage was celebrated between two African Christians. Up to 1859 seven other such marriages were celebrated and slowly but surely an indigenous congregation began to emerge.

The new Christian community developed on the Salem pattern whereby the new converts were completely uprooted from among their own people and resettled on the Mission area in order to preserve them from falling back to non-Christian practices.

In 1856, William Oforiba and Theophilus Opoku, members of the Stool family of Akropong were baptized as well as Kwaku Sai, the first head of an *abusua* (clan). One would have thought that as these were influential personalities, their baptism would have attracted more people to the church. But this was not so; it was rather from the schools that the students were groomed to become Christians: comparatively very few adults joined the Christian community at Akropong. The chief and his elders were ready to listen to the Gospel and they appreciated the efforts of the missionaries in educational work, but they could not break with the ancestral religion and were unwilling to break the social solidarity upon which their whole philosophy of life depended—family solidarity. In any case from the schools and the few adults who had become Christians, by 1867 there were 369 Christians at Akropong and about 300 baptized Christians in the other outstations in the district.

At Aburi, seventeen young men were baptized in 1856 and by 1869 there were 368 Christians in the Aburi district comprising Mamfe and Adukrom.

All these places were manned by African workers who were trained in the Seminaries. In the Akwapim district for example, Theophilus Opoku, Nathanael Date, Joseph Mpere laboured at Aburi, Mamfe and Adukrom respectively. In the Ga-Adangme districts, Paul Mohenu, Carl Reindorf, Adolf Brandt, Carl Quist and others preached to and cared for the new congregations. Thus it will be seen "that Africans themselves played a notable part"[9] from the very early days of the Church's growth.

From Akropong also, Simon Süss opened a station at Gyadam in the Akim area in 1853 and in 1857 the first converts were baptized. Tribal wars between Akim Abuakwa and Akim Kotoku led to the destruction of Gyadam. This failure at Gyadam led the missionaries to open a station at Kibi spearheaded by a Württemberger, David Eisenschmidt. At Kibi the missionaries were faced with two major problems. First, the climate was unhealthy and this led to sickness and constant changes of missionary personnel. And second, the chief of Kibi, Amoako Atta I, was very hostile to missionary work in his domain. Despite these difficulties some beginning was made, and by 1869 there were fifty-eight converts and a school which was poorly attended because the inhabitants were not willing to send their children to school.

Anum was the farthest east penetrated by the missionaries in 1864. Its location was strategic. It was situated at the east bank of the Volta which Zimmermann regarded as the waterway to the interior. Already, Akuse, south of the river, has been opened as a mission trading-post. These two advantages made the prospects of the new Anum station look very bright. Unfortunately, however, the people were not responsive to the Gospel. Owing to tribal wars and quarrels the mission station was destroyed in 1869 by the Ashanti and the missionaries the Revs. & Mrs. Ramseyer and Kühne were taken prisoners to Kumasi.

The extension and future consolidation of the Basel work was assisted very much by the development of the Twi and Ga languages. Johannes Gottlieb Christaller was sent to Ghana by the Home Board to devote himself solely to the study of the Twi language. He arrived at Akropong in 1853. He worked assiduously and six years after his arrival in the country, in 1859, he was able to publish the four Gospels and the Acts of the Apostles in the Twi language. He also prepared other devotional materials in Twi, translated some hymns and some passages from the catechism into Twi for use in the schools. Later in 1865, when he moved from Akropong to Kibi he also studied the Akim dialect. In 1868 he completed the translation of the whole Bible into Twi and the manuscript was published in 1871. He followed this work by publishing, in 1875, a com-

---

[9] Smith, *ibid.*, p. 52.

prehensive Twi Grammar and in 1881 completed his monumental Twi
Dictionary which has been described as "a veritable encyclopaedia of
Akan life, thought and custom still authoritative after the lapse of eighty
years".[10]

The achievement of Christaller's vernacular work has been summarised by Smith as follows:

> It raised the Twi language to a literary level and provided the basis of all
> later work in the language; it gave the real insight into Akan religious social
> and moral ideas; and it welded the expression of Akan Christian worship to
> the native tongue.[11]

In the Ga-speaking areas Johannes Zimmerman too developed the Ga
language in addition to his normal missionary activities in the Ga-
Adangme area. For example, he translated the four Gospels in 1855 and
completed his Ga-Grammar and Dictionary in 1857. Similarly, the whole
Bible was translated; a Ga Hymn book started by Steinhauser was completed, Luther's smaller Catechism, the Wurttemberg Confirmation
Book, and Bible stories were all translated into Ga-Adangme.

The emphasis laid on the use of the vernacular in the Church, became
a marked feature of the Basel Missionary work in Ghana. (Generally, the
Methodist missionaries, did not learn the vernacular in the Fanti area
where they worked. Thus the Methodist Churches, even at the time of
writing this book have kept the nineteenth century "Englishness" of the
Church along the West African Coast.)

The educational activities of the missionaries also assisted the growth
of the church. Schools were opened on all the main mission stations and
as catechist-teachers were trained schools were opened on the smaller stations too. The aims of the missionaries were that through education, a
Christian community should emerge, the African should be offered the
full measure of Christian civilization and be enabled to read the Bible for
himself in order to make the word of God the basis of his life. They also
aimed to train the future leaders of the Church.

The philosophy of the period in Western Europe was "that proper
commerce was one of the best means of promoting civilization and Christianity in Africa".[12] In pursuance of this the Basel Mission engaged in
agricultural, commercial and industrial activities. One aim was that
trade in agricultural products (legitimate trade) should replace the slave
trade and as a result the Basel Mission developed a very large trading

---

[10] *Ibid.*, p. 55.
[11] *Loc. cit.*
[12] *Loc. cit.*

enterprise which undertook research into cash-crops and also trained artisans.

The Basel Mission Trading Factory (later CTL and UTC respectively) became the official title of the Mission's commercial enterprise. Originally, trade was not a policy of the Mission. The venture was thrust upon the mission by difficult circumstances. The supply of some essential commodities to the missionaries was difficult because there was no transport, no postal system, no roads, no coinage. Consequently, in 1854 a young missionary was detailed to take control of the missions imports and finances. In addition to taking charge of the Missionary imports which were stored at Christiansborg and later distributed to the missionaries at their various stations, the store-keeper missionary, Hermann Ludwig Rottmann, purchased the coffee grown at Akropong for export. Within five years, the business flourished immensely. This made the Home Board put the business under a special Trading Commission opened to share-holders. The Missionary Society and prominent Basel laymen both held shares. Their aim was to supply European goods to the missionaries, raw materials to the mission workshops and Christian groups, and "to promote the welfare of the people by giving an example of Christian industry in honest commerce".[13] The usefulness of the Factory led to the opening of additional ones at Ada, Akuse and Accra and finally on every main station. The Factories were manned by European employees called "lay brothers". As the business expanded, in 1909, the commercial personnel were separated from the missionaries and the enterprise gradually became secularised. But the fine tradition of industriousness, moral probity and honest trade laid down by the "lay brothers" during the first fifty years of the company's life was maintained after the separation of the personnel from the missionaries.

An Industry Commission was established and it opened workshops at Christiansborg where African artisans were trained in shoemaking, bookbinding, pottery and basketry, in joinery, carpentry, blacksmithing and masonry. Even though this was the only technical training in the Colony after 1858, the Government did not give it any assistance. The apprentices, trained for three years, were paid by the missionaries from one shilling and sixpence to six shillings per week.

Agriculture is an important aspect of industrial development. Consequently, the Basel Mission made persistent efforts to develop agriculture also. The West Indian immigrants brought with them to Akropong crops such as coffee, cocoa, tobacco, cocoyam, the mango, the avocado pear and bread fruit for experimental cultivation. At first coffee alone showed

---

[13] *Ibid.*, p. 59.

real signs of promise and so between 1857 and 1878 the Basel missionary agriculturists established a "farm school" purposely to train the "Africans in the scientific cultivation of the soil and for experimentation with as many crops and fruit trees as possible".[14] Gum arabic, rice, tobacco and cotton also succeeded for a time but eventually by the 1890's all of them including coffee gave way to the cultivation of cocoa.[15]

The profits from the commercial side of the mission work helped the growth of the mission tremendously because part of the income was used to subsidize the building of new mission houses, schools, chapels, the training of artisans, the development of agriculture and the building of roads. These commercial and industrial activities were promoted vigorously until World War I.

From 1870 to 1914, the mission succeeded in extending its missionary work from the Akwapim ridge to Kwahu, Akim and Ashanti, and across the Volta as far as Yendi in the North in 1913.

Difficulties encountered during this period were different from the initial difficulties (invaliding home, sickness, deaths and suspicion of the indigenous people in accepting the Gospel). Now many of the most disturbing problems resulted from the establishment of the cocoa industry, "the expansion of commercial activity, the development of gold mining, the building of roads and railways."[16] All these new changes disturbed the traditional life-style and decreased the earlier zeal with which people had begun to accept the Gospel leading to nominal Christianity. Moreover, new indigenous cults (see Smith p.122) began springing up and the Islamic religion was also being introduced to the Southern section of the country by Moslem immigrants from the North of Ghana.

In spite of all this, by 1914 in the Kwahu district there were twenty one congregations with a total of 2,582 members. Bompata was developed into an industrious Christian village. The Akim area had about 3,400 converts scattered over thirty-two villages and there were about 900 children distributed in about 27 schools. Nsaba, one of the chief stations in the

---

[14] *Ibid.*, p. 60.

[15] *Ibid.*, pp. 60-61. Cocoa, since then, became the economic mainstay of Ghana. It should be noted that it is officially recognized that Tetteh Quarshie was the person who introduced Cocoa to Ghana. But there is documentary evidence which shows that cocoa was first introduced to Akropong by the Basel Missionaries around 1857/58 and in 1868 there was a small missionary cocoa plantation at Akropong. It seems that Tetteh Quarshie has been given precedence over the Basel missionaries in this matter, because it was with his coming with cocoa to Ghana in 1879 that the cocoa seed was widely distributed and the cocoa industry began to flourish as the major economic and social transformer of the country. It is interesting to note also that Tetteh Quarshie was trained at the Basel Mission Technical School at Osu. This gave him employment outside Ghana whence he brought cocoa back to Ghana.

[16] *Ibid.*, p. 109.

Akim area, became the second largest station after Akropong. This phenomenal expansion was possible because the Basel mission trained adequate local personnel to man most of the new stations.

The most frustrating of all the problems during this period was World War I which was declared in 1914. The German missionaries were restricted in their movements by the British in the British Colonies. The restrictions grew more and more severe until, in the second week of 1917, all the German missionaries were rounded up, brought to Accra and deported on 16th December. The work of the Basel Missionary Society was taken over, with the consent of the Basel Mission Home Board, by the United Free Church of Scotland whose ecclesiastical organization was Presbyterian. The Scottish Missionary Society had been working at Calabar in Nigeria, also a British Colony adjacent to Ghana and as we shall see below (chapter XV) it was from the Calabar Presbyterian Church in Nigeria that a missionary was sent to take charge of the Presbyterian work in the Gold Coast after the deportations.

Officially, the Basel Mission was a neutral international Missionary Society. So it was surprising that the British Government took this drastic step against them. From the point of view of Smith, "the closing years of 1917 were a very dark period in the war for Britain, and that there was therefore a natural tendency to feel suspicious of the German".[17] Indeed, a large proportion of the Basel Missionaries who worked in Ghana was German (Smith estimated two-thirds) and naturally they were in sympathy with Germany. Above all, the attitude of the British Governor, of Ghana, Sir Hugh Clifford, impressed upon the British Government that the presence of the non-British in the Colony was harmful to the loyal British subjects of the Colony.[18]

It was a bitter pill for the Basel Mission to swallow after about 90 years' devoted service in this mission field. But they were not dismayed when they considered that:

> In education and in agriculture, in artisan training and in the development of commerce, in medical services and in concern for the social welfare of the people, the name 'Basel', by the time of the expulsion of the Mission from the country, had become a treasured word in the minds of the people.[19]

---

[17] *Ibid.*, p. 152.
[18] Gold Coast, *Legislative Council Debates*, 4th Feb. 1918.
[19] Smith, *op.cit.*, p. 154.

CHAPTER SEVEN

SCOTTISH FREE CHURCH MISSIONARY SOCIETY

The Scottish Missionary Society started their work in Nigeria in 1846 with the initiative from the Jamaican Presbytery. We have noted in the introduction to this volume that the Edinburgh Society was formed in 1796. Later in the early nineteenth century the name of the society was changed to Scottish Missionary Society. It was under this new name that the Presbyterians of Scotland started their Missionary activities in Jamaica in 1824. In 1835, another missionary body in Scotland, the United Session Church of Scotland, also started work in Jamaica. The agents of these two bodies formed the Joint Presbyterian Church in Jamaica.

In 1839 this Joint Presbytery began to consider sending a mission to Africa because the Negroes of the Presbytery became deeply concerned about the spiritual condition of the indigenous peoples of Africa. Their concern was expressed by G. Blyth, as follows:

> Our emancipated people, finding their condition so much improved by freedom, and appreciating their Christian privileges began to commiserate their brethren in Africa .... All our congregations held meetings for consultation and prayer about the subject, and also began to form a separate fund for the benefit of Africa, which in the course of a little more than a year amounted to six hundred pounds. In these efforts they were stimulated by the Baptist congregations, especially that of Mr. Knibb.[1]

Between 1839 and 1840 the Presbytery concerned itself with finding more information about Africa. Then at the Presbytery meeting of 1841 a firm decision was taken to send a mission to Africa and eight of the missionaries offered themselves to proceed to Africa should the need arise.[2]

In Scotland itself, the Home Board was very sceptical of the Jamaican resolution to send a mission to Africa because of the fate of the Niger Expedition in the 1840's. Consequently, the secretary of the Home Board wrote to the Jamaican Presbytery and that letter "was enough to frighten [them], by its long array of previous failures".[3] In spite of this threat the Jamaican Presbytery meeting of 1842 confirmed "that the desire of

---

[1] Groves, *op.cit.*, Vol. II, p. 34 citing C. Blyth, *Reminiscences of Missionary Life* (1851), p. 178.

[2] J. M. Kerrew, *History of the Foreign Missions of the Season and United Presbyterian Church*, (1869), Vol. II, 368-9.

[3] Groves, *loc.cit.*, Vol. II.

members to aid in introducing the gospel into Central Africa (Nigeria) is unabated ... and that they entertain the same sense of their duty in relation to it as at first.''[4]

Eventually, the mission was sent to Calabar on the Cross River, in Nigeria, West Africa. The circumstances leading to the change of the Home Board's attitude was providential. In 1842, two men George Blyth and Peter Anderson, Scottish missionaries in Jamaica were on furlough in England on health grounds. At Liverpool, they met sea captains who had personal knowledge of Old Calabar in Nigeria. They counselled the missionaries that they should look in that direction for their mission field. As a result of this conversation, the two missionaries wrote a letter to the chiefs of Old Calabar expressing their intention to open a mission there. The letter was carried personally by one of the sea men, in question, Captain Turner, who had a personal consultation with the chiefs on the subject and in 1843 he sent the following intelligence to the missionaries:

> The King and the Chiefs say they are desirous of your coming amongst them, and are full of the scheme, hoping to have their children taught in English learning.[5]

These chiefs were motivated by the fact that earlier in 1842 the chiefs of Duke Town and Creek Town had asked for missionaries to instruct their people and introduce them to legitimate trade. Methodists, Anglicans and Baptists had attempted work there but with no permanent results.

Blyth and another colleague, Waddell, warmly accepted the chiefs' invitation. Before they returned to Jamaica Blyth and Waddell corresponded with Captain Beecroft who was the Governor of Fernando Po at the time. He, having much influence with the Calabar chiefs, highly recommended the Scottish missionaries to them. Beecroft, after his interview with the chiefs who re-affirmed their ardent desire to have the missionaries, communicated the same to Blyth and Waddell in Jamaica. Consequently, a special Presbytery meeting was convened in September 1844 and it was resolved that a new missionary society should be formed to carry out their new programme.

In pursuance of this resolution H. M. Waddell was asked to return to Scotland, obtain two years' leave of absence and organize and lead a new mission to West Africa. Other colleagues from Jamaica were to join him in Scotland. Thus in January 1845, the Waddells bade farewell to Jamaica. As a result of Waddell's appeal to the Christian public in Scotland, the United Session Church consented to incorporate the

---

[4] *Loc. cit.*
[5] Groves, *ibid.*, Vol. II, pp. 34-35.

Jamaican proposal into their programme, thus releaving Waddell of the responsibility of organizing the proposed new missionary society. Waddell's appeal for money was also so effective that within a year he raised £4,000 from members of various denominations. The third result of the Waddell's appeal was that Mr. Jamieson, a generous Liverpool merchant placed his vessel of 150 tons, at the disposal of the missionaries and he also offered to give an annual grant of £100 towards running expenses. So on 6th January 1846, the pioneer party of seven persons: Mr. & Mrs. Waddell and their son, Mr. & Mrs. Edgerley, seconded from Jamaica, Andrew Chisolm and Edward Miller, West Indians sailed from Liverpool. After four months, on 10th April, 1846, they anchored in the Calabar River and the Calabar Mission was born.

The Baptists had started work in Calabar in 1845 when a station was opened in Duke Town, but no permanent worker was appointed. Thus when Waddell and his party got to Calabar, Sturgeon, a Baptist missionary in those regions suggested that the Presbyterians might join hands with them to work in union. When the opinion, of the chief of Creek Town, Eyo Honesty II, was sought he permitted the Presbyterians to remain and work on their own. Eyo Honesty II showed great interest in the missionaries' religious activities, and remained their loyal friend he himself acting as their interpreter at Sunday Worship. Due to Eyo's cordial disposition to the missionaries, of the three towns where mission work was started, it was only Creek Town under Eyo's rule, that the enterprise really began to flourish. A school, established by Andrews Chisolm, made good progress and the Sunday congregations were large.

Eyo's character also contributed considerably to the progress of the Church. He was, unlike the other chiefs, a total abstainer from alcohol, his motto being that: "It is not fit for a man who has to settle palavers in the town to spoil his head with rum".[6] He also approved of the education of his people, despised the use of charms and was "prepared to discourage certain customs contrary to the dictates of humanity which were still approved among his neighbours."[7]

After six months' pioneer work, Waddell returned to Jamaica, gave a progress report on the work done and recruited additional workers. The Presbytery reappointed him the leader of the mission and gave him the helpers he wanted from among the European missionaries in Jamaica and the West Indian Churches.

With these new set of workers, including Hugh Goldie, a European who became authority on the Efik language, Waddell returned to the

---

[6] H. M. Waddell, *Twenty-nine Years in the West Indies and Central Africa* (1863), p. 250, cited by Groves, *op.cit.*, Vol. II p. 38.

[7] *Ibid.*, pp. 38-39.

Calabar Mission. This group was joined in 1849 by William Anderson and his wife who had served nine years in Jamaica. Mrs. Anderson gave thirty and Mr. Anderson forty years service to the Calabar mission.

In 1850 Waddell commenced to extend the work higher up the Cross River. This was not an easy task at first because the chiefs feared that if the river was opened up they would lose their lucrative trade as middlemen in the palm oil trade. But thanks to the wisdom of Waddell, the chiefs were courteously reassured and Waddell continued to explore the river and open stations in the course of the exploration.

The presence of European traders along the coast contributed positively and negatively to the work of the missionaries. Positively, they gave material support to the missionaries' efforts at reform. Negatively, however, their moral and religious lives did not encourage the Christian way of life that the missionaries were trying to build.

In 1857, S. Edgerley, who accompanied Waddell in 1846, died and in 1858 Waddell retired from the mission. An appraisal of his twelve years' labours in the Calabar Mission has been recorded by Groves testifying that:

> Waddell had faithfully carried out the commission first entrusted to him in Jamaica more than twelve years before. He left a well-established work, with two regularly constituted Churches in Duke Town and Creek Town respectively, together with various up-river stations.[8]

The Presbytery of Biafra was formed in September 1859 as the local Ecclesiastical authority with William Anderson as the first Moderator. The link with the Jamaican Church was preserved for two generations later. The West Indians continued to serve the mission effectively as teachers but not as settlers. In December 1859 Eyo Honesty II died, thus bringing to an end a prosperous era.

In 1860 Chief Archibong II of Duke Town attempted to expel the missionaries because they established stations up river and destroyed their trade monopoly as middlemen. But Eyo III of Creek Town, defended the work of the missionaries and said at an assembly, that the Duke Town chiefs "might as well try to stop the rain as to prevent God's message from spreading, even if the missionaries went."[9] It was reported that soon after Eyo's address an unexpected tornado gathered and crashed down on them. This dispersed the Duke Town durbar and they never reassembled. The chiefs were greatly astonished and one of them later commented to a Liverpool merchant Irvine: "For true, your God was there that day."[10]

---

[8] *Ibid.*, p. 40.
[9] *Ibid.*, p. 239.
[10] *Loc. cit.*

Creek Town had always been well disposed to Christianity due to the influence of Eyo Honesty II. Thus when in 1874 the Creek Town chieftainship was vacant the choice fell on a Christian who became Eyo Honesty VII. He accepted the post only on condition that:

> The King should govern and the people consent to be governed by the will of God as revealed in the Bible; and that he should be received as King not by a section but by all.[11]

These conditions were accepted by the King and chiefs and ratified in the Church. In conjunction with their expansion work, the missionaries also did a lot of literature work. Three of them developed vernacular books for Church use: William Anderson translated some New Testament portions for printing; Goldie completed the translation of the New Testament in 1862 and compiled a *Dictionary of the Efik Language*; Alexander Robb translated the *Pilgrims Progress* into Efik and William Anderson translated St. John's Gospel, the Romans, 1 Corinthians 8, 9 & 15, the Hebrews and the Proverbs.

The climax of the missionaries' achievements during this period was the ordination into holy orders on 9th April, 1872, of Esien Esien Ukpabio, the first baptized convert and the first African teacher. This date has been kept as the anniversary of the real beginning of the Mission.

The policy of the Scottish mission in Calabar was to use the Cross River as highway and extend its missionary activities from the Coast up the river. Thus after having gained this solid foothold along the coast James Luke led an exploratory expedition in 1884 to Ikotana, about seventy five miles north of Calabar. Luke opened a station here in 1887 and in 1888 he opened another station about 30 miles farther up the river at Unwana. These two achievements spurred Luke on to explore in 1890 an area farther north about 240 miles up the Cross River. He even took a land journey to the east of the river in 1893. These latter explorations did not bear fruit because tribal wars and disease militated against the safety of the missionaries in the area.

In spite of these hinderances the Scottish mission persisted in their aim of opening up the hinterland. It has been estimated that Mary Mitchell Slessor was the one pioneer whose influence penetrated the hinterland more than any other missionary or official.[12]

Mary Slessor arrived at the Calabar Mission in 1876. After twelve years there she was appointed to Okoyong, among a people famous for lawlessness. Mary was satisfied with her new assignment, went and

---

[11] *Loc. cit.*
[12] Groves, *op. cit.*, Vol. II, p. 218.

worked among them. Her love and sympathy for the people and her devotion to service made her eternally famous in Nigerian Mission History. Her influence was officially recognized when she was appointed "as Vice-Counsul in 1892, and her decisions were accepted by Chiefs and people without demur."[13]

In 1903 Mary Slessor went to settle on the west of the Cross River among the Aro Chuku, being the first missionary to do so. She settled at Itu, below the mouth of the Enyong Creek. Here also her success was spectacular as the following report illustrates:

> The head chief of all the Aros, who was the Chief formally in charge of the Long Juju at Aro Chukwu, is one of those most favourable. He has already announced to the other Chiefs his intention to rule in God's ways. He has been the most keen in asking the missionary to come.[14]

Mary Slessor was so loved by most of the indigenous people that until her death on 13th January, 1915, she continued to receive invitations from many people to visit them. It was the result of such invitations which led her to plant the Church at Ikpe, a well-known market and an old slave centre situated up the Enyong Creek.

Further in-land, the Scottish missionary work was carried out by other devoted men. John W. Hitchcock a young medical doctor was commissioned to explore the hinterland of Unwana station, west of the Cross River and north of Calabar. Hitchcock discovered a very populous and a commercially important town called Uburu, about twenty-five miles west of the Cross River. He estimated the population to be 150,000. It was famous as a slave-trading centre and the people held fast to the faith in the "Long Juju". This did not discourage Hitchcock. He established a medical centre there and gradually Uburu gave up "Long Juju" and became an important hinterland Christian outpost.

By 1914, when World War I was declared, the Scottish mission, like the other missions which had preceded it, had made a steady advance into the Igbo interland between the Niger and the Cross River.[15] The war obstructed the easy flow of the missionary staff into the mission field; the influenza (a deadly fever after the war) also took its toll. But the African helpers maintained the work throughout the crises. Thus through many vicissitudes and difficulties, the Church of Scotland mission transformed the life of Calabar and its environs slowly but surely in spite of hindering problems such as seen by McFarlan in these words:

---

[13] *Loc.cit.*
[14] *Loc.cit.*, citing D. M. McFarlan, *Calabar* (1946), p. 117.
[15] Groves, *op.cit.*, Vol. III p. 220.

The growth of the Church in Eastern Nigeria has been slow in comparison with the development in educational and medical work. The Christian insistence on monogamy, without which there can be no true family life, has been a stumbling block in a polygamous society. The Church's high ideal of marriage and purity of the life, set amongst conditions which provoke licence and where common opinion exerts little moral restraint, together with its demand for a renunciation of heathen rites and practices, keep outside its fellowship many who show the Christian religion much good-will so long as they themselves feel no compulsion to obey its standards.[16]

---

[16] D. M. McFarlan, *Calabar*, citing *The Church of Scotland Mission Founded 1846* (Thomas Nelson and Sons Ltd. London), p. 175.

CHAPTER EIGHT

NORTH GERMAN (BREMEN) MISSIONARY SOCIETY

The North German Missionary Society (another Presbyterian organization) was comparatively very late in sending out missionaries to Africa. Among the reasons given for this lateness we may mention the following: First, the German Protestant Churches did not originally have any strong theological support for sending out missionaries to evangelize non-Christian peoples. They were convinced that (a) the church's missionary work should be restricted to the apostate Christian lands; (b) the apostles were the only people called by God to evangelize the world and they had already preached the gospel universally; (c) it was God himself who leads His elect to faith without the continuing help of any human missionary agency; (d) the end of the world was at hand and therefore it was only necessary to develop and extend the already existing churches, and (e) it was the responsibility of civil authorities to evangelize the heathen among whom they worked because church leaders had been called to remain with their congregations.[1]

The second reason for the lateness concerned domestic instability. After the Reformation the Protestant Churches in Germany became involved in the struggle against Roman Catholic secular power. Both the Roman Catholic princes and the Protestants formed defensive leagues in anticipation of possible clashes. Fortunately, however, no war broke out because at the Diet (Church meeting) of Speyer in June 1526 "it was agreed that until the final decision by a national council, each prince could regulate the religious affairs of his domain."[2]

In the eighteenth century, however, the German protestant attitude to the evangelization of non-Christian lands changed for the better. The religious spirit at that time was *Pietism*. Its emphasis was on personal holy living, consequently, it was incumbent on each person, living a holy life, to lead other people into living holy lives. It thus became the responsibility of every Christian to be missionary in the country. Pietism therefore led German Protestantism to form missionary societies. On 11th April, 1836, most of the missionary societies, which had thus been formed in North Germany, came together and constituted the *North German Missionary Society*. Its aim was to send out missionaries to other lands.

---

[1] E. P. Church Ho, "The Formation of the North German Mission Society", Mimeographed, n.d., p. 1.

[2] *Loc. cit.*

The Rev. Johan Hartwig Brauer was chosen the first Inspector of the Society. On 30th October, 1837 he established a school for the training of missionaries in Hamburg with four students. The school made steady progress and by 1842 there were ten missionaries in training most of whom were North German, who by occupation, had been either tradesmen or farmers.

The original targets of the missionary society were New Zealand and India where the pioneer missionaries were sent in 1842 and 1843 respectively. Later, they added a third mission field: Gabon in West Africa. The pioneers who were sent to Gabon were James Graff of Jutland in Denmark, 32 years old; Luer Bultman of Vahr near Bremen, 28 years old; Lorenz Wolf of Bingen on the Rhine, 26 years old and Karl Flato of Horn near Bremen, 25 years old. By profession they were tradesmen: carpenters and leather and shoemakers.

On 17th March, 1847, they left Germany for Gabon in West Africa. When the journey started Lorenz Wolf recorded:

> We set sail. As far as the eye could see, it beheld ships, all in full sail, setting course for the sea. It seems to me as it were war time, as though all were frigates in a hurry to make some conquest, and indeed they are all out for war conquest, the conquest of trade and we are going with them. When we saw the open sea for the first time we sat in the prow of our ship and greeted it with Luther's Hymn: 'A safe strong-hold our God is still'.[3]

They landed at Cape Coast, in the Gold Coast (Ghana), on 5th May, 1847 because there was no boat plying directly between Gabon and Germany. They were well received by the Wesleyan missionary at Cape Coast, the Rev. Thomas Birch Freeman. After 12 days' stay Bultman and Wolf left for Gabon, to examine the possibility of opening a station. Flato and Graff remained in Cape Coast to explore possible avenues for establishing a mission station[4] in the Gold Coast.

The expedition to Gabon was a fiasco. The missionaries were not allowed to remain in the country by the Spaniards who wanted only Spanish Roman Catholic missionaries and by the French Government which ordered Wolf out of the country because it did not want Protestant rivalry with the Roman Catholics. This disappointment was worsened by the fact that soon after their arrival in Gabon Bultman passed away. Worst of all, before Wolf arrived back at Cape Coast, Karl Flato too had been buried. Thus were left Wolf and Graff alone, dismayed but not discouraged. Their next move was to look for a mission field of their own choice.

---

[3] *Ibid.*, p. 2 citing Wolf's diary.
[4] P. Wiegrabe, *Ewe Mission Nutinya 1847-1936* (St. Louis, U.S.A. 1936), p. 1.

About 100 miles east of Cape Coast was Christiansborg, a suburb of Accra, where Basel missionaries had settled since 1828. Graff and Wolf left Cape Coast for Christiansborg in order to consult Basel Missionaries there about possible mission fields to which they could turn. The Basel Missionaries advised them to turn to Eweland. It was a suitable place but could not be occupied earlier by the Basel Mission because Keta had been bombarded as a result of the Anlo opposition to the Danish attempt to halt the slave-trade between the Portuguese and the people of Keta. Although Ada near Accra and Anecho in Togoland were also attractive, the Bremen missionaries could not settle there because the Basel Mission had already included Ada and its environs into its area of operation; the Wesleyan Mission had opened a mission station at Anecho.

Peki in Eweland is 87 miles east of Accra. At that time it had trade links with Accra from where ammunition was sold to the Peki people. While the missionaries were still undecided about their next move, they were approached by Prince Nyangamagu, a son of Kwadzo Dei V, King of Krepi. "The youngman was serving as a hostage at the court of Osu Mantse"[5] and attending the Basel Mission School at Osu. He told the missionaries that his father was very powerful and ruled over hundreds of places[6] and that he would be very pleased to have them. He promised that he would accompany them to his father if only they would agree to go. The missionaries consented to go to Peki. The Prince then sent message to his father about the proposal. Tutu, Togbi Kwadwo Dei V of Peki was so delighted that he sent bearers to help the missionaries in their journey to Peki. The missionaries however did not travel together to Peki. Wolf went alone leaving Graff at Christiansborg. Starting from Christiansborg on 9th November, 1847, Wolf and his party reached Peki on 14th November, 1847. The experiences of the journey and the receptions accorded Wolf at various points have been preserved in a missionary diary and I reproduce them here verbatim:

> Nov.   9: Christiansborg, Labadi, Teshi, Tema, Poni (?) Prampram where we lodged with Mr. Bannerman.
> Nov. 10: Ningo, formerly seat of Danish Governor, breakfast with Mr. Richter, Bator, very hot, passing night in a henhouse at Boku (?) a small place.
> Nov. 11: Headache, fever, high rocky mountains.... Plenty of monkeys marched along with us. On top a big place called Osudoku, where a pagan ceremony is being performed. Kind welcome. Asuchuare in River Volta. Terribly bitten by mosquitoes.

---

[5] G. B. Ansere, "Missionary Work in Peki 1847-1853. From Germany to Gabon and then to Peki", Mimeographed, p. 2

[6] Die Ewe Stammen (Bremen), pp. 25:3; 59:1; 137:1; 139:2.

Nov. 12: Crossing Volta. Akwamu country. Ahanawase (?).

Nov. 13: Abuatia "Now we observed that we had reached Krepi country. We concluded this from the fertility of the land and from the cleanliness and diligence of the natives.

The large village, Asiedu (? Ananse) was so clean and so nicely built that I was very much surprised. I had become the object of curiosity and fear.... My interpreter said my appearance was to them as of a man who had fallen down from the sky. They did not know where I came from. From Abuatia we came to Nkwakubiw where we had to spend the night because a heavy rain poured down. The Chief received us and gave us chicken and plantain". From there I informed the Peki King about my arrival.

Peki for the first time:

Nov. 14: In the morning: Anum. Thousands were assembled in the market place and welcomed me with music and shouts of joy. The chief and his elders wanted to speak with us but as I was in hurry, I asked them to meet me later at Peki.

First day at Peki from Wolf's report:—

Tutu when being informed of my arrival had ordered all people who were free from work to change the path leading from Anum to Peki about half an hour's walk into a broad road so that I might walk in comfort. When I was not far from Peki, the King's son whom I had seen at Accra with some of the confidants of the King met me on the way and said he was sent to lead me home. I shook hands with him and greeted him. My reception and the welcome accorded to me by the people and the King at Peki was too glorious for a poor missionary. The town consisted of three places. When I passed the first one (Dzake) it was the most beautiful African village I had ever seen, clean houses and a line of trees on both sides of the broad street—people shouted with joy and accompanied me by the hundreds. The same happened at the second place (Avetile). The people went with me to the house of the King's son where I was to lodge. I had hardly sat down when two volleys of gun-fire greeted me. It was said Tutu had done this in order to honour me. I knew of course, that he, too, expected something from my side. Gradually the leading men of the town assembled in front of the King's house. I took with me the customary presents:—

Two pieces of cotton cloth and four parcels of tobacco and accompanied by my people, I approached the place where the King sat. There I laid down my presents at his feet. I saluted him.

He is an old man, has a gaunt face and a long black beard. He wore a large cloth and had a silken small cloth on his head. People held over him an umbrella that we (Graff and I) had sent to him from Accra. His linguist sat beside him and behind there were his men, armed with guns. I was given a place opposite the King. A mighty multi-coloured umbrella was held over me. Behind me there were musicians, if one might call them so, and made a horrible music. I waved my hand and when the music stopped I said in English which my interpreter translated in Krepi:—

The King will know already why I am come to Peki because his son did not only see me at Accra but came also into the house of the Missionaries. I have not come here for trade nor for war. I am not going to buy slaves nor do I have in mind to rob people of their land. I came a long way from a country where there are only white people. I wish to show you the source of happpiness: the true God. I wish to proclaim Him from whom come all good gifts and who sent His son into this world of ours. This briefly is the great thing I wish to proclaim amongst the Peki people.

When my interpreter had finished his translation the King said: "Darfe loo!" (Doafe loo) where upon at once music and joyful shouts of the bystanders set in. I was told the king sent messengers to all chiefs to call them together in order to deal with my case. I thanked him and went home. An hour later the King sent me a fine big sheep as a present and a pot of cowries for my carriers. In the evening people came to see me to preach on what I had told them in the morning. I was tired on account of the journey and all the ceremonies, but as it is a Sunday, and people asked me, so I ignored my fatigue and chose Ps.22:23 "I shall praise Thee amongst the people". I showed them in a simple way the plan of our salvation in Christ. It was about seven o'clock. The moon was our light. Nature was quiet. The people listened attentively—

Meeting of chiefs: From Wolf's report again:—

Monday, November 15, 1847. The whole day people from everywhere visited me in great numbers in order to see me. There was no moment that I was not surrounded by some. Towards noon Tutu called on me, and in the afternoon he came once more. I was given yam and plantain in such quantities that I did not know where to store them.

November 17th: Tutu had invited all his chiefs for this day. Then a man asked me in the name of the assembly why I had come and what they could do for me. I said:—

I am glad at, and thank you for, your coming together here. I come to you as your friend and ask you to consider me as such. I told the King already why I came here. I want to preach God and His Son Jesus Christ. I want to instruct your children in all things that make us happy. So have no fear of me! If you can do anything for me, please, build a house for me and give me a place to have a plantation....

There upon a stick was handed over to the King's linguist and he said my word was good one and they were willing to build a house for me, and to give me a piece of land. The King added: He, his people, myself and all white people that might come should be one. I thanked him for his kindness and went home. The sun vexed me very much as I had been in the open air for two hours. The chiefs spoke with Tutu about my case. They said then, they would come together again in three days time and build the house. As it is very unhealthy to live in low rooms, I must praise the Lord that has hitherto kept me in good health although I stay in a room in which I can hardly turn round.—Yes I shall praise Him!— He is faithful indeed![7]

---

[7] Ansre, *op.cit.*, pp. 4-6.

While arrangements were being made to build a Mission House for Wolf, news reached him that Graff had died at Christiansborg. Wolf left Peki on 28th November for Accra to look after their property left by Graff. After a short while Wolf returned to Peki, rekindled the people's enthusiasm and by 14th January, 1848 the Mission House was completed and occupied by the missionary. It was a large house comprising six small rooms and a large one intended for a school and a chapel.

On 8th February, 1848 Wolf opened a school with 14 boys. He taught them Biblical History, Reading, Writing, Arithmetic and Singing using the English Language as the medium of expression. One of the students, King Tutu's son, Dzani, learnt the alphabet and the hymns very fast and out of school hours he would collect the village children of his age and teach them what he had learnt at school.

While organizing the school, Wolf continued to preach, using interpreters who were not always competent and this led sometimes to embarrassment. For example he once wrote the following to his authorities in Germany:

> During my first months I had an interpreter. But his way of life was so immoral that I had to be ashamed of him, besides his interpretation was so bad that it was of very little use.
> He had once to tell, the King: 'In my country, there is no polygamy' but instead he interpreted my words to mean that the King was to give me one of his wives.[8]

But Wolf succeeded considerably in his healing work. He cured the Chief Tim Klu of Wudome of a chronic ulcer. This made him celebrated and as he remarked: "It was now believed that I could perform miracles and that there was magic in my medicine."[9] As a result he won the confidence of the Peki people. For instance, once when two villages were quarrelling and could easily engage in a war, the presence of Wolf reconciled them because, as he recorded, as soon as he appeared on the spot, "every word of war ceased, I know not why, but they listened to my prayers for peace. Many had already been wounded, but the Lord be thanked; in the heat of battle, peace came to reign."[10]

Although the people were co-operative they were not inclined towards giving up their traditional religion. The traditional priests were powerful and were held in high esteem by the people. After a while the priests became so antagonistic to Wolf that they tried to prevent people from attending his little clinic. Even King Tutu was blamed by the priests for ac-

---

[8] Ansre, *op.cit.*, p. 7 and Wiegrabe, *op.cit.*, p. 22.
[9] Ansre, *op.cit.*, p. 6.
[10] *Loc.cit.*

commodating the missionary. Worst of all, when a great drought came, they blamed it on the presence of the white man and his God.

Wolf endured all these difficulties alone at Peki for a year. But on 3rd march 1849 two other missionaries, Groth and Quinius, joined him. Their presence relieved his loneliness but the task remained problematic: there were not many students in the school, the adult enquirers were very few and did not pay attention when the sermons were being preached; the mission house was in ruins; the parents were demanding clothes for their children who went to the school as it was done in Accra; the missionaries were short of money and so could not complete a new mission house for occupation; they could not adjust easily to eating all the local foods; Accra from where European food could be procured was far away; it was very difficult to get correspondence to and from Europe and above all, they were constantly ill.

In spite of it all for 13 months they continued to sow "the seed of the word, mostly by the life lived and no more by word of mouth as usual because there were no good interpreters."[11]

As a result of the ill-health of the staff, shortage of money and the time spent on building a new mission house, the school was closed down in January, 1850. But hope was rekindled on 5th April 1850, when Miss Koroline Deist, the fiancee of the Rev. Wolf arrived at Peki. The school was reopened and all suspended projects were activated. It seemed probable that she came with money from the Home Authorities, though the records are silent about the reasons for the reactivation of the projects. Unfortunately, however, at the time when things seemed to be taking shape Wolf's health failed and he had to be invalided home. Worst for Peki, Groth and Quinius also decided to return home with Wolf. First, they felt that they were unequal to the task at Peki without the pioneering personality of Wolf; second, they wanted to go home to get more information about the financial arrangements for the mission field and finally, the Akwamu were at war with the Peki and the situation was explosive. So, the four missionaries: Wolf, Koroline, Groth and Quinius left Peki and the Gold Coast in January 1851 for Germany. When the ship anchored at Hamburg harbour, Wolf died on 9th April 1851 and was buried in the cemetery of St. George in Hamburg.

So ended the lives of the four pioneer North German missionaries to Africa. They gave their lives on the mission field; but no single convert had been gained. But the Missionary Society did not give up. They were encouraged by these words from the Holy Scriptures:

----

[11] *Loc. cit.*

I am telling you the truth: a grain of wheat remains no more than a single grain unless it is dropped into the ground and dies. If it does die, then it produces many grains. (Jn.12:24)

Accordingly, three other missionaries were despatched from Germany on 12th October 1851. They were Wilhelm Dauble, Johannes Menge and Quinius with his wife. They disembarked at Christiansborg on 23rd December, 1851 and in January 1852 they were at Peki. The missionary fortune at Peki during this second attempt was no better than the first. Quinius lost his first son who was buried at Peki on 6th March 1852. On 22nd April, 1852, Johannes Menge also died and was buried near the grave of the junior Quinius. It seems Johannes Menge was rather careless about his health. He tried to imitate the Basel Mission missionary Simon Suss at Akropong who worked as one of the local labourers at Akropong. But this was too much for Menge's stamina. Thus, although he was outwardly robust, his labours with the Peki workmen in clearing bushes, digging and kneading swish with his feet to provide earth mortar for building their mission house, proved too much for him and so he died suddenly without the sign of any dreadful disease.

Later for health reasons Quinius and his wife had to return to Germany and Dauble was left alone to carry on the work. Unfortunately, however, there were rumours of war again between the Peki and the Akwamu. This made it difficult for the Basel Missionaries in Accra either to send supplies to Dauble or communicate with him at Peki. These problems made him consider transferring the mission station from the interior, Peki, to a coastal town, Keta. He left Peki, came to Accra and from there he petitioned the Home Mission Board to permit him to transfer the work to Keta, an influential harbour town in Eweland. As a result of the petition, Brutschin and Plessing were sent by the Home Board to assist Dauble, but with an order that the work at Peki should not be abandoned because Peki was a strategic missionary point: it was situated between Ashanti and Dahomey. So for the third time the missionaries were at Peki in January 1853. Two months afterwards there were again rumours of war between an alliance of Ashanti and Akwamu and the Peki. Despite great reluctance to leave their work and promises of protection from the King, Peki was abandoned by the missionaries for the third time.

It was not Dauble's intention that Peki should be abandoned completely. But he believed that from the coast Peki and its environs could be won "as the Romans long ago, conquered Carthage from Spain."[12]

---

[12] *Loc.cit.*

The Home Board agreed with Dauble and permitted him to move from Peki to Keta. Thus he and Plessing, leaving Brutschin in Accra because he was sick, went to Keta, landing at Dzelukofe on 2nd September, 1853. They were convinced that Keta was a better starting place than Peki because of its geographical location. It would be easier, on the coast, to obtain the supplies needed by the missionaries from Accra and also to maintain a reliable and regular contact with Germany.

But the big headache was how to recruit the people to be evangelized. Dauble knew that the area beyond the lagoon was thickly populated; Dzelukofe was only a half hour's walk from Keta and was a flourishing market-town, and other quite populous villages were likewise within walking distance. But Keta itself consisted merely of the fort with a garrison of less than 30 men, a factory or ware house belonging to the Commandant of the fort, and a few African huts (as late as 1858 only five in number). "In view of their main objectives the missionaries must often have been plagued with grievous doubts about the wisdom of their choice."[13]

However, there was no going back. Luckily, Commandant Evans received the missionaries well and gladly permitted them to live in the fort until their own house was ready. The missionaries had with them two lads from Peki, Peter Papo and Ababio, a washerman and a cook from Accra, a very competent carpenter, Kwao (Quau), who had been baptized at Cape Coast and their faithful chief African helper John Wright. With the help of these and a few local men hired as labourers, the missionaries started building a very substantial Mission House with walls 18 inches thick. The reason for their planning such a substantial building was that the Commandant had told the missionaries that he was going to develop the village into a very large town.[14]

Endless difficulties were experienced in the building work, of which one of the most serious was the sudden death of Kwao, on 20th October, 1853 as a result of epilepsy. In due course, however, Plessing was able to secure some experienced artisans from Accra. But cruel fate soon struck again when Dauble, who was primarily in charge of the work, suffered from stroke and died on 26th December, 1853. The entire small population of Keta warmly participated in mourning this tragedy. Plessing shouldered all the responsibilities alone, but ill-health was telling heavily on him, as well as everything else. On 6th January, 1854 he was feeling that he had arrived at the end of all his forces when, at 4 p.m., the faithful John Wright ran up to him and exclaimed "Mr. Brutschin is here."[15]

---

[13] E. P. Church Ho, *op.cit.*, p. 10.
[14] Wiegrabe, *op.cit.*, p. 8.
[15] E. P. Church, Ho, *op.cit.*, p. 11.

This meant a new lease of life for exhausted Plessing, and together the two men resumed their work with fresh hope.

Another hurdle was reached when the Paramount Chief of Anlo forbade his subjects to do any work for the missionaries because they had been in the country six months without paying a courtesy call on him to inform him of their presence and purpose. This serious error was frankly admitted, apology duly rendered and the work proceeded again. At the beginning of March, 1854 the two missionaries were able to move into the first of their own new rooms.

In addition to their building projects, the missionaries engaged in evangelistic work in and around Keta. The local people listened to their preaching but very often they requested the missionaries to reward them for coming to listen to them, by asking the preachers to give them gifts of money, alcoholic drinks or tobacco. On one occasion when such a demand was made the missionary responded as follows:

Ne amea ɖe va miagbɔ le zã me, nyɔmi le alõ me hegblɔ na mi be, miaƒe xɔ le dzo bim la, ɖe miabia ga tso esi be, yewoƒe to se efe nyagbea? Menye akpe boŋ miada ne be, exɔ yewoƒe agbe oa? Ke nye amesi le didim be, maɖe miaƒe luwɔ gɔ tso tsieƒe ƒe dzomavɔ me ɖe?[16]

The most serious opposition came from the Yeve cult whose leaders often tried to disrupt the preaching of the Gospel. The priests and priestesses of the other local deities also made the evangelistic work of the missionaries difficult. For example, on one occasion the missionaries invited an indigenous priest to consider accepting Jesus Christ as his saviour. The priest responded:

Kpao! Kpɔɖa, trõwo kata menye naneke o, Yesu hã menye naneke o. Nyigblã ɖeka koe wòle be, woasubɔ. Wo hã va subɔe ekema maganɔ vevie be, nàganɔ hiã kam ɖokuiwò alea gbegbe, anɔ tsatsam le xexẽame katã anɔ yiyimi o. Nyigblã lakpɔ wò nuɖuɖu gbɔ na wò.[17]

The missionaries, however, denied this assertion. In spite of these difficulties the missionary work progressed. In 1855, on 22nd February the first formal school was opened by Schauffler at Keta. The first pupils were all immigrants. The Anlɔ̃ were afraid that if they sent their children to the school, they might become slaves to the missionaries.

---

[16] Ibid., p.10 i.e. Supposing you were awakened in the night and told that your house was on fire, would you ask a reward from the informant because you listened to him? Would you not give him thanks for saving your life? How much more the person who wants to save your souls from hell?

[17] Ibid., pp. 10-11 i.e. Never! Behold, the local gods are nothing, Jesus too is nothing. The only god to be worshipped is Nyigblã. You should also come and worship him and stop worrying yourself so much travelling round the world. Nyigblã will provide you with food.

Schauffler, however, lived only for a short time and died between 9-10 weeks of his arrival. This disappointment was compensated for by another overdue achievement. The first seven converts were baptized in 1855 after the death of Schauffler. Of these seven, only one, John Ababio was an Ewe. Ironically, he was from Peki, the first missionary station of the North German Missionary Society. The missionaries had laboured for seven years, buried seven of their number during the period and now had won seven souls for the Lord. Thus after many years of disappointments the missionaries had the encouragement that their labours had begun to bear concrete fruits.

The period 1855-1893 was one of progress for the mission.

> Using Keta as the base, the missionaries advanced by stages to Peki to resume the work which had been so painfully [suspended]. Progress was rapid. Waya was opened in 1856, Anyako in 1857, Vegbe in 1859 and the first baptism was made at Ho in 1869. By 1881, after 34 years' labour, the missionary work of the Bremen Mission made remarkable progress. Thus by the turn of the century there were three main stations, Ho, Keta and Amedzọfe, with their respective outstations. The total strength of the three stations by 1893 was: outstations, 20; schools, 20; pupils, 591; Church members, 1,247; places of worship, 313, missionaries (1894): men, 18, ladies, 10 including 3 deaconesses; African assistants (unordained), 37.[18]

These achievements could not have been as they were without the help of the African auxiliary workers. The most outstanding of these during the period was John Wright. He was from Teshie in Accra and was baptized by a Basel Missionary. His father was a trader who traded with people in the interior. John used to accompany his father on his commercial journeys. It was during one of these treks that John first came into contact with Lorenz Wolf at Peki and became his interpreter. He was officially employed by the Bremen Mission in January 1852 and had been with the missionaries during their retreat from Peki. He was very helpful to them, both in all their dealings with the other Africans and in the work of evangelism itself. In those days African girls had not yet been Christianized; consequently, John Wright was compelled to marry an unbaptized girl from Teshie. He led her to the Lord and she became a member of the Keta congregation. "Thus John Wright proved to be the first married African Christian worker. Though the marriage remained childless, John remained true to the teaching of the Mission regarding a monogamous family life".[19] He was made a catechist in 1863 and from that time he had regular charge of a congregation. Unfortunately,

---

[18] J. K. Agbeti, "Missionary Enterprise, Education and Nationhood in Ghana Since 1828". Unpublished S.T.M. Thesis, Yale Divinity School, 1967, p. 33.

[19] E. P. Church, Ho, op. cit., p. 16.

however, just after two years' service as a full catechist he died of small-pox. In all, he served the Church for 13 years.

Towards the turn of the century 1894-1912, the work expanded by leaps and bounds. At that time plenty of money flowed into the mission work from Germany. The reason was mainly political. In 1884, Togo became a colony of the German Empire. In Germany many Christians, motivated by nationalist enthusiasm, felt that they owed a divine respon-sibility to the people of the new colony. Consequently, people donated more freely into the Mission coffers than ever before. Thus, one district with a major station, after another, was opened up. It was during this period that the following stations were opened: Agu (1895), Lome (1896), Akpafu (1898), Atakpame (1907), Kpalime (1910) and the districts of the Akposso Plateau and others. Despite the comparative youth of the mis-sion station Lome as the capital of Togo, took precedence over Keta as the Missions' headquarters. The missionary staff rose in numbers to the unprecedented figure of over 50 persons.[20] It was also during this period that the first seven African pastors for the Bremen Mission were or-dained: Rudolf Mallet in 1882, Samuel Newell and Adolf Lawọe in 1901, Andreas Aku and David Besa in 1910, Robert Kwami and Theodor Seḍoḍe in 1911 and Elia Awuma in 1912. Some of these were selected from the twenty young Ewe men who had been trained in Germany for the Church.[21]

The number of outstations also rose to 40, that of catechists to 198, school children to 8,100, Christians to 11,682 members of the missionary church. Surely those who sowed in tears were reaping with shouts of joy, (Ps. 126:5).

This period was also a watershed:

> the old era of peaceful evangelism in a stable political climate had come to an end, and a new, and very different one, was about to commence. World War I, after shaking the missionary church to its very foundations and put-ting its indigenous leadership to severest testing, proved to be the stepping-stone to advance in a new and, in its own way, necessary and desirable direction.[22]

As we shall see later, immediately at the outbreak of the war Togo was captured by the Allies. Some of the German missionaries were taken to Dahomey as prisoners of war. On 21st June, 1916 the missionaries and deaconesses at Keta were removed and interned, and in October 1917 those still left in Togo suffered a similar fate. The only missionary left at

---

[20] *Ibid.*, p. 19.
[21] C.f. J. K. Agbeti, *West African Church History: Christian Missions and Theological Train-ing*, Chapter IV.
[22] E. P. Church, Ho, *loc.cit.*

Lome was Buergi with his wife because they were Swiss and not German. He tried as much as possible to guide the work in both the German and the English speaking zones but he found it difficult because of the political restrictions imposed at the frontiers. Yet he stood firm and pastored the Church during and after the war.

In the English speaking zone the work was passed on to the Scottish Mission while in the old German, now French zone, the Paris Mission assumed responsibility of the schools and congregations. Thus ended the name "Bremen Mission" as the official designation for the church that that mission came to build in Eweland.

During these 72 years, 1847-1919, the Bremen Mission achieved much for the advancement of Eweland. The Gospel was preached, churches were built, schools established, artisans etc were trained.

As a result of the last mentioned achievement

> already, at a quite early stage one missionary writing home delightedly reported that soon they would no longer require basic furniture such as beds, tables, wardrobes, cupboards, or fixtures such as windows, doors, floorings etc. and similar other items.[23]

Above all the mission paid great attention to the training of women and girls. Such a training was begun in 1857 by the wives of the missionaries, Plessing and Brutschin at Keta. Young women were gathered and given training in sewing, knitting, cookery, housecraft and simple hygiene. This informal training was formalized in 1889 by two deaconesses, Hedwig Rohns and Lottchen Rohns. The training they gave the women of their time,

> not only set the pattern and standard for the very high level of Christian womanhood and mother-hood of which our own generation has become the blessed beneficiaries, but also inspired similar efforts at all the other main stations of the mission. Its influence has continued till today , having fructified the present vast and vigorous women's movement within our church, to which we all owe so much.[24]

In their travels, the missionaries made collections of Ewe myths, history, and culture of the land. Also from their writings researchers can find good collections of geographical, historical, religious and cultural material of the greatest interest and value. In order to preserve the Ewe character and individuality the missionaries studied and used the Ewe language as the chief means of communication from Wolf at Peki to Professor Westerman and Paul Wiegrabe of our days. It was by their efforts that the Ewe language was reduced to writing and its literature developed.

---

[23] *Ibid.*, p. 16.
[24] *Loc.cit.*

CHAPTER NINE

ROMAN CATHOLIC MISSIONARY SOCIETIES: SIERRA LEONE, LIBERIA AND NIGERIA

The Roman Catholics returned to resume mission work in West Africa around the mid-nineteenth century. The principal contributory factor for this revival of interest in West Africa was the initiative of Bishop Melchior de Marion Bresillac. On 8th December, 1856 he founded the Roman Catholic Religious Community known as the Societas Missionum ad Afros (SMA) or the Society of African Missions.

Bresillac's intention was to organize a society of young European missionaries, who would devote their lives to the conversion of Africans. They were to spend their whole life among their converts in the mission field, instruct them in the Catholic Faith, administer the Holy Sacraments and work as Parish priests.

About one and a half years after the formation of the society, the Vicariate Apostolic of *SIERRA LEONE* was erected on 13th April 1858 and Bresillac was nominated by Rome as the first Superior. In the following year Bresillac despatched the pioneer SMA missionaries to Sierra Leone. The party, comprising three men, Fathers Baptiste Bresson and Louis Reymond and Brother Eugene Reynaud, arrived in Freetown on 12th January 1859.

The initial problems they noted on their arrival in Sierra Leone were two: the first concerned communication. Sierra Leone was an English-speaking country. It was therefore necessary for these French Roman Catholic pioneers to learn English, otherwise they would not be able to evangelize Sierra Leone and other English-speaking countries along the coast. To solve this problem the Irish Province of the SMA was founded to supply English-speaking missionaries.

The second difficulty was about the low morals of people in the colony. This the missionaries learnt from a remark which the British Governor made on their arrival. He said that "he hoped they would bring some morals to the place."[1]

Fr. de Bresillac, Father Louis Riocreux and Brother Gratian Monnoyeur followed the advance party and arrived in Freetown on 14th May, 1859. This was the year of a devastating yellow fever epidemic. The captain of the ship which took de Bresillac and his party to Freetown

---

[1] John M. Todd, *African Missions, A Historical Study of the Society of African Missions* (London), p. 32.

knowing the havoc that yellow fever could cause advised his crew not to disembark. But de Bresillac would not listen and he disembarked with his party.

The first Mass which he officiated on his first Sunday was disappointing: only two people were present, because "the Europeans were dying like flies".[2] Both the Spanish Consul and the Vice-Consul had died, leaving their residence vacant. On the same day de Bresillac wrote a depressing letter home in which he described the precarious state of existence caused by the yellow fever epidemic; his missionary party was being threatened by the yellow fever and his own health was deteriorating.

In spite of all this the missionaries were happy to be together and make plans for the future exploration into the interior of the country. But all these plans were unexpectedly nipped in the bud: from 2nd June, death began wiping off the missionaries. Before the 18th of the same month, three of them had died. On 25th June the worst happened: the story is told by John M. Todd:

> With his usual kindness Msgr. de Bresillac asked after the health of my children and of Father Reymond. Then he said calmly to me: 'My child, what I have feared is going to take place. The catastrophe is upon us. Do you think Father Reymond is well enough to come to me?' M. Bremond replied that Father Reymond was not well enough; the knowledge of Msgr. de Bresillac's condition might be fatal. de Bresillac's reply was: 'Fait voluntas tua'. But it is very hard to me to die without the Last Sacraments!
>
> M. Bremond then had a qualm of conscience about depriving a 'prince of the church' of the Last Sacraments. He consulted with the doctor and finally decided to inform Father Reymond. On hearing of the situation Father Reymond got up, put on his cassock and a stole, and was led, perhaps carried, to de Bresillac. They were left alone for a moment for confession. Father Reymond then administered extreme unction in the presence of M. Bremond, the brother of the [French] vice-consul and an Irish business man, Quin. At the request of de Bresillac, M. Bremond remained with him till the end which came about two hours later. Towards the end de Bressilac, raised his eyes and said: 'Faith, Hope, Ch....' He was unable to finish the word. Bremond added 'Charity'. Bressilac said 'Thank you'. After a very severe agony of half an hour he died at twenty past one in the middle of the day. He was buried at nine in the morning on the next day in the presence of the Governor, the staff officers, a detachment of soldiers, the consuls of France and America, and all business men and important people of the town without distinction of religion.[3]

There was no Catholic priest able to assist at the burial. The Protestant Bishop had recently died and the junior minister left in-charge said a few words at the graveside.

---

[2] *Ibid.*, p. 34.
[3] *Ibid.*, pp. 37-38.

Three days after the death of de Bresillac, that is on 28th June, Father
Reymond also died and was buried the same day beside his colleague.

Thus the first attempt of the SMA to evangelize Africa suffered a tragic
disaster. From January to June 1859, ''all that was now left of the first
mission of de Bressilac's Society of the African Missions was a series of
graves in which lay the bishop-founder, three priests and a brother''[4] and
yet no converts made.

This tragedy was so frustrating that the SMA did not send any more
missionaries to Sierra Leone. What they had begun was therefore taken
over by the Holy Ghost Fathers in 1864 assisted by the St. Joseph Sisters
of Cluny. They made modest but steady progress. Freetown remained
their only station for a long time. But from 1890 the missionaries began
to reach out and the first outstation was opened on the Sherbro Island.
From there other stations were opened on the mainland. So, slowly but
surely, the Roman Catholic converts increased in numbers and in 1913
there were about 3,250 Roman Catholics in Sierra Leone.[5] Thus after
very distressing disappointments Roman Catholic missionary and educational work in Sierra Leone were being firmly established when World
War I broke out in 1914.

From Sierra Leone the Holy Ghost Fathers were called upon by Rome
to open a mission in *LIBERIA*. It happened that during Father Francis
Borghero's famous 1862 trip to Sierra Leone (see page 96 below) he met
the President of Liberia, Mr. Stephen A. Benson at Cape Palmas. The
President encouraged Borghero to open a mission in Liberia. Nothing
was immediately done in response to the President's request apart from
the brief time which two other missionaries who were on their way to
Dahomey spent in Garraway in Liberia.

As nothing definite was done by Borghero in response to the
President's request, in 1880, the Liberian Government took the initiative
and invited Rome to send missionaries to Monrovia. No response came
from Rome so the invitation was repeated in 1882 again asking Rome to
send Roman Catholic priests to Liberia.

At the time Fr. Blanche, C.S.Sp., was the Prefect Apostolic of Sierra
Leone. He was instructed by the Cardinal Prefect of Propaganda in
Rome to honour the Liberian request. In response, Frs. Blanche and
Lorber went to Monrovia in February 1884. Fr. Lorber remained in
Monrovia and he began the Catholic mission there by dedicating it to the
Nativity of our Lady. Three other colleagues were later sent by Blanche
from Freetown to help in Monrovia. Lorber, assisted by these colleagues,

---

[4] *Ibid.*, p. 38.
[5] K. Latourette, *A History of the Expansion of Christianity*, Vol. V., p. 456.

Fr. Bourzieux and Brothers Langst and Coleman, made satisfactory progress in Monrovia. During the first two years a school was built; Fr. Bourzieux studied the Kru language and translated prayers and hymns into it; finally he also compiled a catechism into the same language.

Bright prospects became suddenly dimmed when illness and death compelled the Holy Ghost Fathers to abandon their work in Monrovia in 1886. No further attempt was made to reopen the station until 1903. On 18th April that year, the Holy See (Rome) erected by a decree the Prefecture Apostolic of Liberia. The Montfort Fathers were placed in charge of the new Prefecture Apostolic. Without much delay the first batch of Montfort missionaries were despatched to Liberia and they arrived in Monrovia on Christmas Eve, 1903.

The fate of the pioneer Montfort Missionaries was not different from that of the Holy Ghost Fathers. Illness and death so disrupted their efforts that towards the end of 1904 the only surviving Monfort missionary in Monrovia closed down the station and went to Europe.

Two years later, in 1906, the Liberian mission was reassigned to the Society of African Missions (SMA) and Father Kyne of Mayo was made the Prefect Apostolic. Under the SMA the Roman Catholic work took root in Liberia. From Monrovia stations were opened at Kekru on Little Cape Mount, along the Kru coast and in the Gola country.

In 1910 Father Kyne had to leave this promising new mission to become Superior of the SMA in Ireland. He was succeeded by Msgr. Jean Oge. Under him also, the work continued to expand. He organized the mission stations at Cesstown, Betu and Cacatown on the Kru coast. Grand Cess was opened as a central station by Fr. Peter Harrington and outstations were opened at Niffu and Nonokya. So by the end of the period under discusion the Roman Catholic work was firmly established in Liberia after many decades of disappointment and setbacks.

It is clear then that the disappointments which the SMA had suffered in Sierra Leone earlier did not make the Society abandon the entire West Coast of Africa. Even long before their advent in Liberia in 1906 the SMA had been very active in *NIGERIA*.

The Nigerian story began in 1860. On 29th August that year, a new SMA Vicariate Apostolic of Dahomey was erected. The pioneer missionaries sent there in January 1861 were headed by an Italian priest Fr. Francesco Borghero in the diocese of Genoa.

On 17th February 1862, Fr. Borghero made an exploratory tour of the Guinea Coast. Among the many places he visited was Lagos where he found the reception given to him most cordial. There as well as at Ouidah, he found a Roman Catholic community made up of "quasi-African Catholics". Most of them were slaves repatriated from Brazil.

They had been converted to the Roman Catholic Faith while they were serving as slaves in that country. There, in exile, they were taught trades such as carpentry, tailoring and masonry. They returned to Nigeria in 1851. They settled in Lagos around Campus Square because the British had ended the slave trade in Lagos in that year by expelling from Lagos the Portuguese and Brazilian slave traders.[6] In their new home the immigrants had occasional pastoral visits from the priests who were serving at San Thome Island. Thus it was that Fr. Borghero found a Roman Catholic community in Nigeria when he arrived.

The Brazilian immigrants had their own catechist, Padre Antonio. When he saw Borghero at first he was suspicious of his true identity as a priest so he tested him by asking him to say the rosary. Borghero said it correctly and Padre Antonio testified to his community that Borghero was a true Roman Catholic priest.

After Borghero's departure from Lagos the Brazilian community continued to expect that he would return to open a permanent mission in Lagos.

This hope was realized in 1868 when a new station was opened in Lagos by Fr. Borghero and put under the charge of Fr. Bouche as the superior. Fr. Bouche did not remain at this station for long. Fr. Borghero was replaced by Fr. Courdioux as the superior of Dahomey in 1870. Courdioux transferred Bouche to Agoue and Fr. Cloud became the new Superior of Lagos.

Father Cloud's aim was to develop an agricultural settlement for a full Christian community. This aspiration was in consonance with the general Roman Catholic educational policy of the period, viz.: to train children to use their minds and hands for

> it would be a sad thing if they were unable to use their hands on leaving school .... Besides, if a love of manual work is fostered, it will prove a thousand times more valuable than mere literary studies alone.[7]

At that time there was a devoted Roman Catholic layman on the coast. He was Sir James Marshall, an English trader and a Supreme Judge for Lagos and Cape Coast. When he learnt of Fr. Cloud's agricultural intentions, he advised the Father to ask the Governor of Lagos for a nine-mile strip of land at Topo, along the coast near Badagry.

Fr. Cloud sent in the application to acquire the land and after careful consideration the land was granted by the Governor on 26th July 1876.

---

[6] Bane, *Catholic Pioneers in West Africa* (1956), p. 147. See also Modupe Oduyoye, *The Planting of Christianity in Yorubaland* (Day Star Press, Ibadan 1969), p. 61 and J. F. Ade Ajayi, "The British Occupation of Lagos, 1851-61", *Nigeria Magazine* 69, August 1961, p. 102.

[7] Todd, *op.cit.*, p. 98.

Fr. Poirer was appointed the first Superior of Topo. With the help of Father Baudin, Brother Elie, four African boys and a cook with his wife, Topo was occupied and the group began to develop the place.

According to Modupe Oduyoye, an added and major reason for establishing Topo was that:

> ...the society's experience in Sierra Leone had taught its missionaries to prefer the untouched native in his paganism to the sophisticated colonial in coastal seaports. They wanted to make converts among the natives; they wanted to effect the social life of the native community with the leaven of Christianity. The method they chose for doing this, however, was to create a separate Christian community where they could teach monogamy and discourage fetish rites, two aspects of the native culture which they judged to be strongest in keeping the native from embracing a Christian style of life.[8]

Thus when Topo was occupied local Nigerian families were offered residence. Those who consented to live there were to farm. In appreciation for the land granted to them, the families were to pay rent in kind and help to clear further areas for development. The progress made during the first decade was fantastic:

> hundreds of acres had been cleared, ten thousand or more coconuts had been planted, there was a herd of sixty cattle and great plantations of cassava; fifty-four traditional religious worshipper families worked on the land and eighteen children, orphans or redeemed from slavery, were in the care of the priests.[9]

Later in 1892 a convent was established there for girls.

The Topo experiment was a practical demonstration of the Roman Catholic evangelizing policy for Nigeria. The mission was determined ''not to give a literary education that would produce clerks who would be unable to earn their livelihood except they sought employment from the Government or from commercial firms.''[10]

Unfortunately, however, most of the farm children did not appreciate the dignity of agricultural labour. When they grew up they went to either Lagos or Porto Novo to enjoy city life. In spite of this apparent failure John Todd has recorded that:

> Topo created an atmosphere of happiness and industry which had its effect throughout the neighbourhood. The influence was of the same kind as that exercised by the Benedictine monasteries of the Middle Ages throughout Europe which often did not have any direct religious effect, but suffused the

---

[8] Oduyoye, *op.cit.*, p. 63.

[9] *Loc.cit.*

[10] *Ibid.*, pp. 63-64, citing J. F. A. Ajayi, *The Journal of the Historical Society of Nigeria* 2, 4th Dec. 1963, pp. 520-521.

whole of society with a tangible visible ideal of industry and prayer, so that gradually without any striking conversions society was changed.[11]

From 1877, when the SMA recorded their first confirmation in Lagos, the work of the mission began to develop: the construction of the Holy Cross Cathedral was began in 1878 and was completed in 1881; ten years later in 1891, Msgr. Chausse was consecrated Bishop of Lagos in Lyons, becoming the first Bishop of West Africa since the death of Bresillac in Sierra Leone; in 1889 the mission work was extended to Abeokuta under Fr. Hooley and to Ibadan in 1895 where the society's first seminary in Africa SS Peter and Paul was opened in 1905.

In their missionary activities, the Fathers were assisted by a contingent of nuns. The first four nuns to work for the society in Nigeria arrived in Lagos in 1872 from the congregation of the Franciscan Sisters of the Propagation of the Faith in Lyons. The number was increased by two in 1874 and the six sisters served in educational and medical work. Sister Colette who died in 1916 gave a firm foundation to the Roman Catholic educational work which was expanded by her successors.

After 1876 the supply of sisters to the mission field became steadier because, in that year, Augustin Planque opened the first House of the Sisters of Our Lady of the Apostles at Lyons.

These early missionaries and sisters were faced with language problems in Nigeria. Dahomey was French-speaking but Nigeria was English-speaking. The Missionaries of the SMA were for a very long time, invariably, French-speaking. A few, however, like Borghero were Italian. In order that the society might be able to supply English-speaking missionaries to Yorubaland where English was the dominant European language an apostolic school was opened in Ireland in 1878 to produce the badly needed English-speaking missionaries. Thus responsibility of the greater part of Roman Catholic Missions in Yorubaland was transferred to the Irish Province. So on 4th June 1883 due to the same language problem the Dahomey Mission was divided into two by Rome. The English-speaking section was designated the Vicariate Apostolic of the Bight of Benin stretching from Oueme in the East to the Niger and Fr. John Baptiste Chausse became the Provicar of the Holy See.[12]

Soon after this, in 1884, Chausse visited Oyo where the chiefs granted him a large site for a mission, and in 1886 Fr. Bel started work there whilst Chausse opened a convent at Abeokuta. On 12th May, 1891, Chausse was nominated the Vicar Apostolic of the Bight of Benin, a

[11] Todd, op.cit., p. 201.
[12] Bane, op.cit., p. 151.

bishopric he held only for three years when he died in France on 17th January, 1894.

Bishop Paul Pellet succeeded Chausse and under his jurisdiction the work continued to expand. It was during this period that the first Roman Catholic Mission was opened in Ibadan (Oke Are) in 1895.

Pellet's work came to an end in Nigeria when he was recalled in 1901 and made Vicar General of the Society of African Missions. His successor Bishop Joseph Lang assumed office in 1902 when he was consecrated Bishop in the Lagos Cathedral.

Lang's extension work was so spectacular that his period became known as the "era of outstations". He concentrated his efforts on the Ijebu area and opened missions at Ibonwon and Eshure and from these centres in 1911, he opened many outstations in the vicinity including the central station at Ijebu-Ode the capital of the Ijebu country.

In the East, Bishop Lang was helped by his colleagues. From 1906 they began to open stations at Issele-Uku, Igbuzo, Ogwashi-Uku, and Onitsha-Olona in Igbo country reaching Shendam north-east of Benue in 1911. Later during that year Bishop Lang was invalided home where he died on 2nd January, 1912. Shendam mission field was later erected the Prefecture Apostolic of Eastern Nigeria and separated from the Prefecture Apostolic of Western Nigeria. It was from Shendam that Msgr. Waller and his colleagues extended the work to the North-eastern Provinces of Nigeria.

The work in Northern Nigeria made slow initial progress due to religious and political factors. The Muslim rulers restricted the Christian missionary activities. They were not allowed to proselytize the Muslim population.

The indigenous people had been conquered by the Hausa and later by the Fulani. But these colonialists could not assimilate the indigenous tribes because the indigenous tribes regarded them as invaders and hated them. It was because of this that the conquered did not embrace the Islamic religion. For similar reasons, the indigenous peoples were suspicious of the Christian missionaries whom they looked upon as foreign intruders.

Lang's successor, Bishop Ferdinand Terrien, continued the extension work of the Mission. By 1914 stations in Oshogbo and Benin City were opened and Northern Nigeria was politically added to Southern Nigeria forming a unitary country.

The British administration which developed throughout the new Nigeria, took literate workers from the South to the North. Most of these literates were Christians and they formed the nucleus of Christian communities in many centres in the North.

Kano mission was opened in 1919 by Msgr. Waller and the first six adults were baptized on the Palm-Sunday of that year. A few neophytes were also confirmed and two marriages enacted. By the end of 1919 many parts of the North were being occupied by the missionaries and so from difficult beginnings the work continued to expand in Nigeria.

CHAPTER TEN

ROMAN CATHOLIC MISSIONARY SOCIETIES: GHANA AND THE GAMBIA

West of Nigeria was the *GOLD COAST* (GHANA). The Roman Catholics were comparatively late in establishing themselves there. Their pioneer missionaries Frs. Auguste Moreau and Eugene Murat arrived on Pentecost Tuesday, 18th May, 1880. A Roman Catholic historian, Helena Pfann stated that the Roman Catholics found it difficult to send missionaries to the Gold Coast because of the ravages malaria was causing among the Europeans on the coast. She claimed that the Gold Coast then was "a country where no European would escape catching a tropical disease and dying".[1] This is not a convincing reason in the light of the Roman Catholic missionary activities along the West African Coast during the period under discussion. Roman Catholics were in Sierra Leone in 1859 despite the fact that Sierra Leone was famous as the "White man's grave"; they were also in Liberia, Dahomey and Nigeria in the 1860's. In Ghana itself other European missionaries had worked since 1828, remained on the field and made converts in spite of the fact that many of the missionaries died. A stronger reason than Pfann's will be required to explain the Roman Catholic inactivity in the Gold Coast earlier than the 1880's. It seems to me that the Roman Catholics did not want any unhealthy competition with the Protestants. By the 1850's there were two very strong Protestant missions already in the Gold Coast, the Wesleyan Methodists monopolising the Western section of the country while the Presbyterians were predominantly active in the Eastern sector.

Ironically, it was this presence of the Protestants in the country which led the Roman Catholics to change their attitude in 1879 in response to the lamentation of Sir James Marshall, one of the English men on the coast who was also a Roman Catholic. Originally, Marshall was baptized an Anglican and was trained an Anglican priest. Later, he changed his denomination and became a Roman Catholic. After studying Law, he was appointed a judge for the Gold Coast and Lagos. For some time he resided at Cape Coast in Ghana. Through his travels along the West Coast he discovered that "although there were (Roman Catholic) Missions in Liberia and Nigeria, nobody had thought of bringing the Catholic Faith to the inhabitants of the Gold Coast."[2] Consequently, he wrote from Cape Coast to some newspapers in England stating that:

---

[1] Helena Pfann, *A Short History of the Catholic Church in Ghana* (1965) p. 11.
[2] *Ibid.*, p. 10.

There is no country in the world, where a Catholic Mission could be established more easily. Contrary to what we see in many other countries in Africa, there is nothing to fear from the native population .... Yet on the whole of the Gold Coast there is not a single Catholic priest.[3]

As a follow up Marshall appealed to the Roman Catholic Fathers working in Nigeria to write to their superiors in Europe and request them to send Missionaries to the Gold Coast (Ghana). One of the Fathers travelled to Rome and discussed the request with the Sacred Congregation of the Propagation of the Faith composed of Cardinals who directed missionary work all over the world on behalf of the Pope. After careful consideration the Cardinals erected the Apostolic Prefecture of the Gold Coast in 1879 and entrusted it to the SMA. These were the circumstances which led the Roman Catholics back to Elmina in 1880.

When the pioneer missionaries, mentioned above, Fr. Auguste Moreau 33 years old and Fr. Eugene Murat 31 years old, arrived at Elmina, in the Gold Coast, they were met by a Frenchman Mr. Bonnat who was living at Elmina. He took them to lodge a small European hotel in the town. It comprised two rooms and a verandah where they celebrated their first mass on an improvised altar. As soon as they settled down they began their pastoral visit from house to house, paying respect to the chief, Nana Andoh, the elders, councillors, sub-chiefs and the people. Initially, Mr. Bonnat served as their interpreter because he had studied Fante, the local language. Wherever they visited, the general request from the local people was: "When will you open your school".[4] Before the first week was over, the Governor Herbert Taylor Ussher from Accra paid the missionaries a visit and spurred them on to open the grammar and agricultural schools they hoped to found.

It will be recalled that the Portuguese had settled at Elmina in the fifteenth and sixteenth centuries. So also did a group of Augustinian monks but their work suddenly came to an end when the five monks died. Although the Portuguese and the other Roman Catholics had left Elmina 250 years earlier, in 1880 when the missionaries arrived traces of Roman Catholic influence were still extant among the Elminians.

For example, they noticed that there was a fellowship called Santa Mariafo;[5] they observed also a local birth ceremony which was reminiscent of a Christian rite: on the seventh day after the birth of a baby, a crucifix and a lighted candle were presented to the baby on whom water was sprinkled three times. Wiltgen thinks that these were Portuguese

---

[3] *Ibid.*, p. 11.

[4] R. M. Wiltgen. *Gold Coast Mission History 1471-1880* (Illinois: Techny, Divine Word Publications 1956), p. 142.

[5] *Loc. cit.*

Roman Catholic ceremonial rites. "For about 250 years, 1637-1880, the people had passed down from generation to generation as much as they could remember of the ceremonial and doctrine taught them by their Portuguese priests."[6] Thirdly, they discovered a shrine called *Nana Ntona* in the town. It was a hut which contained the crumbled pieces of an old statue probably that of St. Anthony, left at Elmina by the Portuguese. The worshippers at the shrine called themselves Santonafo. The cultic ceremonies celebrated in connection with the shrine were very reminiscent of certain Roman Catholic rites. For example, the week beginning on Good Friday was set aside for *Nana Ntona* celebrations every year. "During that week nobody was allowed to work. Like their forefathers, the *Santonafo* knelt down to pray not only for themselves but also for their brethren in the town."[7]

The significance of all this was that when Moreau and his colleague noticed these practices, they had bright hopes that it would not be difficult to evangelize the people. Indeed, the Roman Catholic work there assumed form and progress more easily than elsewhere in West Africa.[8]

But the progress did not come without the familiar handicaps. Within ten days Fr. Moreau fell sick and was advised by his doctor to have a sea voyage. In response he and Murat travelled to Lagos. There they met an educated Gold Coast youth, *James M. Gordon*. This boy was redeemed from slavery by Sir James Marshall, in 1873, during the battle between the Fante and the Ashanti at Abakrampa. The English Commander, Captain James Gordon took charge of the boy for some time and later transferred him to his original master, James Marshall. When Sir Marshall was transferred from Cape Coast to Lagos, he took the redeemed boy, John Ashanti, along and sent him to a Roman Catholic school there. He became converted at the school and was baptized James Marshall Gordon in appreciation of what these two Europeans had done for him. After his meeting with the missionaries in Lagos he became their very good friend, taught them the Fanti language, served as interpreter after Bonnat, became a teacher, helped at the celebration of the Mass and was among the very first Roman Catholic catechists at Elmina.

Soon after the missionaries returned from Lagos to Elmina, Fr. Moreau was compelled to write to Fr. Plangue, the Superior General of the SMA: "Yesterday evening at five o'clock, I performed the first public

---

6 *Ibid.*, p. 146.

7 Pfann, *op.cit.*, p. 16.

8 It is not quite clear whether this easy success was due to earlier Portuguese influence. But it might be due to the fact that by the 1880's, the local people were beginning to realize that through Christianity and mission education people were improving their social and economic status.

function of my ministry —alas! it was the burial of good Fr. Murat...''.[9]
In the same letter he requested that reinforcement be sent. Without any
delay Murat was replaced by Fr. Michon and some financial help was
also sent. Now that some money had been sent Moreau and his new colleague moved out of the hotel and secured lodging in an abandoned boarding school which had been run by a certain George Amile Amissang. It
was called Louis House and was situated at the foot of Java Hill.
Although the new abode was not in perfect condition it was more suitable
than the hotel. It was so spacious that some of the rooms were converted
into classrooms. After the renovation an Elementary School was opened.

The school served as the backbone for evangelism. It is true that the
pupils studied secular subjects such as English, Reading, Writing and
Arithmetic. But through the Religious Instruction given, the pupils
learnt to serve at Mass and sing hymns. Every Sunday, the parents
followed their children to the little improvised chapel in the new Mission
House to hear their children sing. As the roll of the school increased so
also did the adults at Elmina begin to demand instruction for themselves
in the religion of their children. On Christmas Day, that year, five of the
pupils were baptized following the example of George Auguste Salmon
who was the first to be baptized in 1880 after the Christmas Midnight
Mass. From 1881, annually, more and more of the pupils of the school
were baptized. Some of them became catechists—the first lay apostles
through whom the Roman Faith was spread from Elmina:

> Wherever they afterwards happened to settle, it was due to their fervour and
> zeal that little Roman Catholic communities were founded and the way
> prepared for the establishment of Missions.[10]

Fr. Moreau felt that though more and more of the school boys were being baptized "no lasting results would be obtained until the girls were
also instructed in the new Faith."[11] Consequently, he made arrangements with the Lyon Superiors to send nuns to open a girls' school
at Elmina. The pioneer Sisters of Our Lady of the Apostles (OLA),
Sisters Ignatious (Irish) and Sister Potamienne (Swiss) arrived at Elmina
on 26th December 1883. They were housed in a large building near the
bridge overlooking the lagoon. They occupied the second floor and on
31st March 1884 the school for girls was opened on the first floor with 26
pupils.

In addition to his emphasis on educational work, Fr. Moreau travelled
extensively. He visited Denkyira in 1880 and the King asked him to open

---

[9] Wiltgen, *op.cit.*, p. 152.
[10] Pfann, *op.cit.*, p.18-19.
[11] *Ibid.*, p. 23.

a Roman Catholic Mission at Jukwa his home town. In 1882 Fr. Moreau was in Kumasi and a day after his arrival, on Sunday 23rd April, the first Roman Catholic Mass was said in the Ashanti capital. This was followed by a visit to Accra.

As the prospects of the mission were bright Fr. Moreau encouraged the congregation at Elmina to help him in building a new Mission House. All the people rallied round him and secured a site and building materials in readiness to start the building. Unfortunately, however, before the work could be commenced Fr. Moreau's health failed and he was invalided home on 18th March, 1886. Three days after his departure from Elmina he died on 21st March aboard a ship off Axim and the corpse was silently slipped into the boisterous waves.

Moreau's successor continued the Mission House building project but he died of black water fever six months after his arrival. Under the next missionary, Fr. Pellat, the Mission House was completed and occupied by the missionaries on 27th June, 1887. After this the OLA Convent near the Mission House and a new more spacious chapel were built. The chapel was dedicated to St. Joseph on 29th December, 1890.[12]

It was also during the time of Pellat that the Roman Catholic attempts to open stations outside Elmina met with success.

The Cape Coast station was opened on 1st September, 1889. On that day Chief Daniel of Amanful was enrolled as a catechumen and on the following day a school was opened there with Mr. Francis William Haizel Cobbina, an ex-pupil of Moreau, as the teacher. At the end of the year there were 227 pupils in the school.[13]

In the following year, 1890, the OLA Sisters opened a Girls' school at Cape Coast where the girls were taught Religious Instruction, Reading, Writing, Sewing and Housecraft. A little dispensary was also opened. The services the Sisters rendered to the sick so endeared the Catholic Church to the people of Cape Coast that the work progressed satisfactorily and steadily. A new Mission House was erected in 1896 and in the same year the Headquarters were transferred from Elmina to Cape Coast for administrative convenience, Cape Coast being the capital of the Central Province (now Central Region) with all the Government offices there. Mail and cargo-boats stopped there and roads were better from Cape Coast into the interior of the country than from Elmina. Although

---

[12] A member of the Church, Mr. J. B. Nelson, a storekeeper, provided bank drafts and persuaded other traders who were members to supply goods on credit for work on the chapel. It was this help given by Mr. Nelson that helped Fr. Pellat to complete the building so rapidly.

[13] Pfann, *Ibid.*, p. 29 See also footnote 8 in this chapter.

it was difficult for Elmina to give in, the reasons for the transfer were so obvious that the transfer was inevitable.

Upon a request made by Nana Graham, the chief of Low Town Saltpond, for Roman Catholic missionaries, Fr. Pellat sent Frs. Ulrich and Groebli to open the Saltpond station in 1890. Good progress was initially made: the adult fisher folk were enthusiastic in attending the catechumen class because Chief Graham persuaded them to do so and a school was opened at Upper Town and entrusted to the care of Mr. R. B. Quaison from Saltpond. Unfortunately, the usual problems: sickness and death robbed the station of its missionaries and Fr. Pellat had to close down the Saltpond station only a year and a half after its establishment. During the interim, Master Quaison supervised the Saltpond Roman Catholic work and kept the school and chapel alive until the missionaries returned in 1894 and from 1897 consolidated the work there.

Keta in the Volta Region came under the supervision of the SMA in Ghana in 1890. Originally the Keta Mission was an outstation of the Roman Catholic Mission in Dahomey. From Agoue (pronounced Aguwe) the missionaries founded a small community at Keta. During a war between the French and Dahomeans, Dahomey detained the French missionaries in the territory. Consequently, Keta was left without any pastoral visitations. When Fr. Pellat heard of the sorry plight of the Roman Catholics at Keta he despatched two of his colleagues Fr. Wade and Fr. Thuet to visit the community. They arrived at Keta on 28th May 1890.

With the help of Chief Akolatse a permanent site was acquired from Chief Tamakloe and Mr. Jacobson. They settled down and despite initial financial difficulties the missionaries revived the Roman Catholic work in the Volta Region. Schools were opened at Dzelukoḟe and the OLA Sisters travelled from Cape Coast and opened a girls' school at Keta. By 1914 Roman Catholic stations had been opened at Denu, Kpando and Gbi-Bla or Hohoe (Xǫxǫe).

From Elmina a station was opened in Axim in the West. The first attempt made to establish a permanent station there in 1882 failed because, in the first place, the pioneer resident priest Fr. Michon could neither speak English nor the Vernacular. Secondly, a gold mine had been opened in those regions and this made it practically impossible for the inhabitants to pay sufficient attention to the missionary and his message. Thirdly, the missionary was invalided home and the station remained vacant until 1902.

But the station was kept alive during the interim by African initiative. Mr. C. A. Rhule, born and baptized a Roman Catholic at Elmina went to reside at Axim. He rallied round the immigrant Roman Catholics there and they built a bamboo chapel and continued to worship according to the Roman Catholic rite on Sundays. There were about 50 members in the church and about twenty young men were on the catechumen roll being instructed by Mr. Rhule.

This was the position when Bishop Albert revisited Axim in 1902. He was pleased with the little flock and promised them a resident priest. Mr. Rhule offered a coconut plantation whose proceeds should be used in maintaining the missionaries and also offered part of his residence to the missionaries until a Mission house was built.

When the new missionaries arrived at Axim they built a school because the people were very anxious to have one. From that time Axim remained a permanent and a central station whence the Wassaw districts were evangelized.

The first attempt made by Moreau to open a station in Kumasi in 1882 failed because of internal political problems. The Asantehene Mensah Bonsu did not allow his subjects to fight the Gyaman and the Banda and sent to ask advice from the Governor. This displeased his war party. Furthermore there was no internal peace because his people disliked his immoral life. Thus, although the Asantehene promised that he would recall Moreau later, the promise was not fulfilled before he was destooled in 1883.

In 1893, however, the Roman Catholics had the privilege of appointing a chaplain to accompany the British Army to fight in Kumasi because there were many Roman Catholics in the British Army. The missionaries had hoped that this might offer them a new opportunity to open a station in Kumasi. Unfortunately this venture did not bear the anticipated fruit either, because the English Governor who had promised to give a site for the establishment of the mission did not fulfil his promise.

Unknown to the missionaries, Roman Catholic immigrants out of their own initiative had been building the Roman Catholic Church wherever they went. Thus when Bishop Klaus went to Kumasi in 1905 he was welcomed by a Roman Catholic congregation of about eighty members. The congregation had been assembled in 1903 by Mr. James Cobbina, an Ashanti, who had been baptized at Cape Coast. Although this discovery was encouraging to Bishop Klaus, he could not grant the request of the Kumasi congregation for a resident Parish Priest immediately because of financial difficulties. In one of the reports he sent home then he lamented:

> The expense of keeping open the existing stations exceeds our income by £800 a year. It means that we have to beg for that amount and if kind people do not help us, I shall see with tears in my eyes our Christian communities

discouraged and losing interest. Dear Father, be the instrument of Providence, come and help me. When I think of it, I must pray but I can no longer write.[14]

In 1908 Klaus's successor, Bishop Ignatious Hummel visited Kumasi and succeeded in acquiring a piece of land on Zongo Hill for the Roman Catholic mission. On 20th July, 1908, the Kumasi Roman Catholic Mission was inaugurated when the deed was signed for the lease of the mission land. Fr. Muller was immediately appointed the first resident priest. Muller began erecting a mission house in 1910. The House was ready in 1913 to house permently, the missionaries, a school and chapel on Zongo Hill.

The Roman Catholic activities in Accra were not exciting from the beginning. In 1893 the British Governor and some European Roman Catholics in Accra invited Fr. Pellat to open a mission there, in the capital town of the Gold Coast. Two missionaries were despatched, but due to the lack of money, little could be done. The yellow fever epidemic which broke out in 1895 worsened the situation. Many of the missionaries died and it was difficult to keep the new stations opened. Consequently, the missionaries sent to Accra were recalled to Cape Coast and Accra was abandoned until after World War I.

Northern Ghana, formerly known as the Northern Territories, was not evangelized by the Roman Catholics who worked in the Southern section of the country, but by the **WHITE FATHERS** from Ouagadougou. The White Fathers community was founded in 1868, in Algeria by a Frenchman, Cardinal Lavigerie, who was then the Archbishop of Algiers. The Cardinal, it is believed, loved Africa so much that he wanted its inhabitants to become Christian without losing their own African personality. So he ruled that before attempting to convert them, his missionaries should try to copy as much as possible the Africans in dressing, eating and other habits of life. Lavigerie believed that this method of evangelism would help the Africans to accept the Christian faith without any fear that they would lose their identity.

The White Fathers started work in North Africa, always travelling in caravans like the Arabs and moved southwards across the Sahara desert to the Sudan as far east as Uganda. It was from the Sudan that some of them entered Waga-Dugu, the capital of Upper Volta.

At the turn of the nineteenth century Roman Catholics were persecuted in France and anti-clerical laws were passed as a result of the Dreyfus Affair. The White Fathers in Upper Volta fearing that they might be expelled from this French territory, applied, in 1905, to Colonel

---

[14] *Ibid.*, p. 53.

Watherston, the Chief Commisioner of the Northern Territories "for permission to open a mission station somewhere between the 10th and 11th parallels of the north latitude."[15] At first the permission was not granted because

> the Northern Territories was not yet sufficiently settled to render the establishment of missions advisable. The colonial administration was also unwilling to make itself responsible for the protection of the lives and property of missionaries especially those of a foreign power.[16]

In 1906, however, the White Fathers were given permission to open a mission station at Navrongo under these conditions:

> The mission station was to be near an administrative post; only the English Language would be taught in the mission's future schools. The mission was to open a school as early as possible and was to conform to such regulations as may be passed from time to time for the administration and management of schools in the Northern Territories.[17]

The missionaries accepted these conditions and on 23rd April, 1906 Fr. Morin, Fr. Cholett and a Brother arrived in Navrongo with some redeemed slave boys. They were well received by the English Commissioner who allotted to them a piece of land for the mission. With the co-operation of the local Chief a few of the inhabitants helped the missionaries to erect six little huts, one of which was used as the chapel where the missionaries said Mass for the missionary party.

Due to Muslim influence in Navrongo and also to the people's ignorance of white men, the local people at first stood aloof from the missionaries. But after the missionaries had opened their school in 1908, the local people became interested in the missionaries and in the chapel they had built. Any time the people visited the chapel the Fathers talked to them about Jesus Christ. Consequently, on Christmas eve 1910, at the midnight Mass, five catechumen out of the 150 being instructed were baptized.

Following that, with the help of local devoted men and women such as Pascal Fela, Peter Sayere, Madam Teresa Abatey and others the missionaries opened outstations around Navrongo. And so the work continued to expand until the outbreak of World War I.

The Holy Ghost Fathers entered the *GAMBIA* in 1849 and opened their first station in Bathurst now Banjul. As they did not reach out from Banjul until the 1930's their main missionary activity falls outside the scope of the present study.

---

[15] Benedict Der, "Church-State Relations in Northern Ghana, 1906-1940". *Transactions of the Historical Society of Ghana*, Vol.XV (i) 1977, p. 41.

[16] *Loc.cit.*

[17] *Loc.cit.*

PART TWO

MISSIONS FROM THE UNITED STATES OF AMERICA

CHAPTER ELEVEN

INITIATIVE FROM THE AMERICAN COLONIZATION SOCIETY

Towards the end of the eighteenth century, some of the clergymen in America became concerned about the presence of the Negroes in the States. They thought that the deplorable condition of the Negroes in America would be made better if they could be repatriated to new colonies in Africa. Consequently, in 1770, the Rev. Samuel Hopkins then serving in Newport, made plans to send the Gospel to Africa through Negroes. His plan was to train two Negro men in his congregation: Messrs Quamine (a freed man) and Yamma, a servant.

Another minister, the Rev. Ezra Stiles also had a similar plan: his was to recruit thirty to forty well trained and convinced Christian Negroes and send them out to Africa as colonists.

The two ministers came together in August 1774 and decided to solicit support for the project among the churches of Massachusetts and Connecticut.[1] The appeal was well received and in November the same year, Messrs. John Quamine and Bristol Yamma sailed from New York and then to Princeton, where they received training in preparation towards coming to Africa. Neither, however, set foot on Africa because Quamine was killed during the revolutionary war and Yamma died in North Carolina in 1794. Hopkins had envisaged in 1770:

> A colonial scheme whereby free Christian Negroes would voluntarily emigrate until all of the blacks in New England and even the middle and southern states had gradually been drawn off. Thus slavery would come to an end. The colony in Africa would proclaim Christ by precept and example and tend to stop the slave trade at its source.[2]

In 1773, an Education Society was formed to translate this scheme into reality. But nothing actually emerged. This, however, did not discourage other individuals from their efforts to make plans to repatriate the freed Afro-Americans to Africa. But during the revolutionary wars, circumstances changed and people became more concerned with internal stability than colonial expansion. Consequently, during the wars the individual efforts being made to repatriate the freed Afro-Americans to Africa declined, though the colonization spirit was kept alive.

---

[1] Walter Cason, "The Growth of Christianity in the Liberian Environment" (Unpublished Ph. D. Thesis, Columbia University, 1962), p. 11.

[2] *Ibid.*, p. 12.

Thus after the revolutionary wars, lay individuals such as Paul Cuffe (probably Paul Kofi) a Massachusetts merchant and ship owner single handedly, in 1815, took thirty-eight colonists to Sierra Leone. Cuffe's efforts were of special significance because he was a Negro and the first individual who actually landed colonists in Africa many years before the American Colonization Society began to do so.

Before the death of Cuffe in 1817, other individuals who were moved by similar colonization sympathies met in the State of Washington and organized themselves into the American Colonization Society in December 1816. In the following month, January 1817, the Society was formally constituted under the designation: "The American Society for Colonizing the Free People of Color of the United States."[3] Its first President was Bushrod Washington, the nephew of George Washington. This Society was truly national because unlike other State Colonization Societies, it admitted adherents from all the other States. It also became the parent of the first colony in Liberia.

It seems that the principal aim of the Colonization Societies was the eradication "from American life, a particular 'evil', i.e. the free Negro."[4] Thus, the idea of the planting of Christianity in Africa seemed to be secondary. This may explain why the pioneer colonists sent to Liberia by the Colonization Societies pursued secular interests such as politics, trade, agriculture and were "not all flaming Evangelists."[5]

Despite the fact that the aspirations of the Colonization Society were secular, the church lent its support to it. In the first place, individual ministers such as Hopkins, Stiles, Mills, Finley and others gave addresses, wrote explanation pamphlets in support of the colonizing spirit and joined "with influential members of the Washington Society to give the movement an air of religious respectability."[6] Secondly, the church synods and conferences also endorsed the aspirations of the Colonization Society.[7] The church's endorsement was not just theoretical: arrangements were made by the congregations for collections to be taken at worship services towards the colonization project, and ministers were seconded to the Colonization Movements for employment.

The position was not the same in all the Churches. The Bethel Church of Philadelphia for example, had a protest meeting during which the Philadelphia Negroes raised objections to the motivation of the Colonization Movements and resolved:

[3] Groves, *op.cit.*, Vol. I, p. 250.
[4] Cason, *op.cit.*, p. 25.
[5] *Ibid.*, p. 29.
[6] *Ibid.*, p. 34.
[7] Philip John Staudenraus, *The African Colonization Movement, 1816-1865* (New York: Columbia University Press 1961), p. 48.

That we view with deep abhorrence the unmerited stigma attempted to be cast upon the reputation of the free people of color, by the promoters of this measure.... That we never will separate ourselves voluntarily from the slave population of this country; they are our brethren by the ties of consanguinity, or suffering, and of wrong and we feel that there is more virtue in suffering privations with them, than fancied advantages for a season .... That without arts, without science, without a proper knowledge of government, to cast into the savage wilds of Africa the free people of color, seems to us the circuitous route through which they must return to perpetual bondage.[8]

The fears expressed by the Philadelphia brethren were shared by others and in 1831 similar protest meetings were held by Negroes in New York, Baltimore, Washington, Hartford, Pittsburgh and other places. In the same year, 1831, five of the protesting States met as "the first Annual Convention of the People of Colour". They deplored the activities of the American Colonization Society and when they met again in 1832 "they called upon the society to cease their unhallowed persecutions of a people already sufficiently oppressed."[9] The meeting later suggested that if the worst happened the exiled Negroes should be sent to Canada rather than to Africa.

There is the third group of liberal Negroes who did not reject all the principles of the Colonization Society. They favoured the idea of only partial emigration of the free Negroes. That is, those free Negroes who would like to migrate to Africa could do so but they should be left free to return to America if they chose to do so. It was from among this group that Negro leaders were selected later to lead those emigrants who went out from America as colonists to Africa. Some of them "were men of training, integrity and ambition who were to participate in founding a new nation."[10]

Finally, the Abolition Movement severely questioned the intentions of the Colonization Society. The reason was that while the Colonization Society was supposedly concerned with improving the lot of the Negroes, some of its members actually continued to promote slavery. Groves states that 12 managers of the Society were slave owners.[11] This weakness was brought out most forcefully by the abolitionist, Mr. Garrison. The effect was that the popularity of the Colonization Society diminished especially when the abolitionists maintained that the society was actually preserving slavery through those of its supporters who promoted the trade.

---

[8] Cason, *op.cit.*; p. 36 citing Lloyd Garrison, *Thoughts on African Colonization* (Boston: Garrison and Knapp, 1832) part II, p. 9.

[9] Cason, *op.cit.*, p. 38.

[10] *Ibid.*, p. 39.

[11] Groves, *op.cit.*, Vol.I, p. 290.

The Churches were forced, by these conflicting circumstances, to take a stand either in support of the abolitionists or the Colonization Society. Naturally, as many of the White Christian churches had lent support to the Colonization Society from its inception they stood by it. Not only that. From the beginning, most of the white Christian leaders had anticipated that the new colony would serve as a fertile ground for American Missionary work in Africa. So, though the Negro Convention and the abolitionists opposed the Colonization Society, the dominant white churches and some liberal Negro church leaders supported the movement unreservedly.

The Negro supporters had good reasons for doing so. First, the one area in which the Negroes in America enjoyed freedom was in the church. In line with the policy of segregation from the whites, the Negroes produced their own places of worship. From the late eighteenth century, it was mainly within these churches that Negro leadership developed and the black people freely expressed themselves. By the time that the founding of Liberia was completed in 1847 Negro freedom in the black people's churches had been clearly developed.[12] The liberal Negroes anticipated that when they moved away from America to the new colony in Africa they would have the fullest advantage to develop their freedom and leadership to the utmost.

The other reason why some of the Negroes supported the Colonization Society was their concern for the Africans at home. Their aspiration was that they might extend the freedom they had attained in the church to other places. This is why most of their sermons were about how Moses freed the Hebrews from Egyptian slavery.

With this support of the church, the Colonization Society in 1818, sent Messrs Samuel J. Mills[13] and Ebenezer Burgess to the West Coast to prospect for a suitable location for the proposed freed Negro colony. First of all, they went to Sierra Leone where some Negroes, under the auspices of the British Philanthropists, had been settled.[14] There, they met one Mr. John Kizell, one of the earliest immigrants. He was believed to have hailed originally from that part of West Africa. Under Kizell's guidance the

---

[12] Benjamin Elijah Mays and Joseph William Nicholson, *The Negro's Church* (New York: Institute of Social and Religious Research 1933). Also Carter G. Woodson. *The African Background Outlined* (Washington D.C. The Association for the Study of Negro Life and History. Inc. 1936). In some cases, however, white denominations such as Baptists and Methodists attracted some black Americans because such congregations were less formal and allowed more freedom in their worship.

[13] Groves, *op.cit.*, Vol. I, p. 291. Footnote 1 states that this Mills "was one of the four signatories to the Andover students' letter that prompted the founding of the American Board in 1810—First Ten Reports of A.B.C.F.M.,[10]"

[14] c.f Chapter II above.

colonizing party visited Sherbro Island, some thirty miles south of the Sierra Leone Peninsula, where Kizell had established a settlement and was acting as its Christian leader. He advised the commission to consider Sherbro Island as a possible location for the establishment of the new colony. They were satisfied with the proposal and took it back home. Mills, however, died on the return journey and Burgess was left alone to give the report to the Society.

As a result of the favourable report received, the Colonization Society sent pioneers to Sherbro Island in 1820. The party comprised eighty-eight freed Negroes under the leadership of three white Americans: Samuel Bacon, a minister, John P. Blankson and Dr. Crozer. They did not succeed in founding a colony because many of the group died of fever. Those who survived, left Sherbro Island and went to settle in Sierra Leone.

The second party was despatched from America in 1821. After some period spent prospecting for a new site, Cape Mesurado was selected and early in 1822 a third party arrived again from America and joined those of the second party who were still alive. It was this third party, under the leadership of Elijah Johnson, a colonist (a freed Negro emigrant), which decided to occupy the high ground of Cape Mesurado because that part was healthier than the lower elevation. It was at this new site that Monrovia is now located. Soon after this the fourth party of fifty-three colonists arrived from the States. They were led by a white leader Jehudi Ashmun. "For a critical six years he guided the fortunes of the little settlement of freed Negroes and left it well established";[15] thus he proved himself the real founder of the colony, Liberia.

Apart from the problem of illness and death the indigenous people were very hostile to the colonists. The Cuban slave traders in the neighbourhood also resented the coming of the colonists because their presence was a threat to their trade. Accordingly, they supplied arms to the indigenous people who invaded the settlement. The settlement was able to repel the attack and through the diplomacy of a British traveller, Major Laing, an understanding was secured between the colonists and the local people.

In 1824 a further 105 colonists arrived. Among this group was Robert Gurley, who was charged to draft a constitution for the settlement. The names Liberia for the country and Monrovia for the capital town were proposed by General Harper. Gurley worked fast and in the same year the names and the provisional constitution were ratified by the Government of the United States. Ashmun then had the opportunity to develop

---

[15] Groves, *op.cit.*, Vol. I, p. 292.

the colony in an atmosphere of stability. He extended the boundaries of the settlement by treaties with the chiefs. Unfortunately, however, he was invalided home in 1828, and there he died in New Haven, Connecticut, in the same year.

Other groups also began to show interest. In 1831, the Maryland Colonization Society sent thirty-one colonists led by Dr. Hall, a white American. This group eventually settled at Cape Palmas in 1833 because the earlier settlers in Monrovia did not co-operate with them. Probably the temperance tenet of the Maryland group, which led them to prohibit liquor, was not conducive to the Monrovia group. Other groups came in from Edinburgh, Pennsylvania, and from Mississippi and by 1838 the total of American emigrants in Liberia was 2,281.[16] At this stage, a new constitution was prepared to cover all the various settlements except Maryland in Africa (Cape Palmas).

One important feature of these settlements was that the colonists did not mix freely with the indigenous people. The initial hostility which the local people had expressed was not completely wiped out by Major Laing's intervention. Thus when the work of evangelizing the people actually began in Liberia the missionaries had two distinct groups to deal with:

> The American newcomers already aware of civilized standards and demands, and the African tribes with a primary interest in trade, the slave-trade for preference, but trade with liquor in it.[17]

The newcomers had been Christianized in America. Therefore most of the pioneer colonists carried their Christian faith with them to Liberia. In addition, as most of the Churches in the States had lent much support to the Colonization Movement from its inception, they also saw to it that the teachers who accompanied the colonists were men who had strong Christian convictions. For example, Ashmun had decided to become a missionary at a time when the Colonization Society was looking for a suitable man to direct the colonists. When Ashmun offered his services the Colonization Society appointed him to the post because of his missionary zeal. It was with such convinced Christian men that the American Missionary Societies began their work in Liberia.

Good examples are Lott Carey and Collin Teague, two of the colonists in Ashmun's party in 1822, whom the Baptist Board of Foreign Missions for the United States used as their missionaries in the new colony. Similarly, the American Roman Catholic Church, the Methodist Episcopal Church of the States, the American Board and others com-

---

[16] *Ibid.*, p. 294.
[17] *Loc. cit.*

menced their evangelical work in Liberia between 1820 and 1838 with convinced Christian colonists.

From these small beginnings emerged the various American denominations which we find in Liberia today. But it must be noted that American Missionary Societies did not work in Liberia alone. They also laboured in some of the British colonies in West Africa such as Sierra Leone, Ghana and Nigeria. We cannot, however, study all these American Missions now because of lack of space and funds. We shall therefore tell the story of a representative selection from among them. The criterion for the choice is based mainly upon the availability of local materials during the period of these researches.

CHAPTER TWELVE

SOUTHERN BAPTIST CONVENTION MISSION

American Baptist missionary work in West Africa was initiated by the General Missionary Convention of the Baptist Denomination in the United States commonly referred to as the Triennial Convention. Missionaries were sent by the Convention to accompany and spiritually care for the colonists of the American Colonization Society who migrated to *Liberia.* Lott Carey and Collin Teague mentioned in Chapter XI were the pioneer Southern missionaries sent by the Triennial Convention.

The unity of the Baptist denomination in the United States of America did not endure for long. There occurred a cleavage between the Northern and Southern sections in 1845. The immediate cause concerned the divergence of policy relating to the question of employing slave-holders as missionaries or agents of the Triennial Convention. While the Northern members of the Convention did not think it wise to include slave-holders as missionaries, the Southerners insisted that it was expedient to include them provided their conduct and motives were satisfactory. As all efforts to come to a compromise failed, the Southerners withdrew from the Triennial Convention at a meeting held at Augusta in 1845 and gave birth to the Southern Baptist Convention. From that point the Northern section was reorganized and known as the American Baptist Missionary Union.

It was not the intention of the new Convention in the South to depart from the general scriptural principles upon which the Triennial Convention was founded. This they made explicit in their resolution:

> That for peace and harmony, and in order to accomplish the greatest amount of good, and for the maintainance (sic) of those scriptural principles in which the General Missionary Convention of the Baptist denomination of the United States was originally formed, it is proper that this Convention at once proceed to organise a Society for the propagation of the Gospel.[1]

Accordingly, the Board of Foreign Mission was formed at a meeting held on 20th February, 1846. It chose West Africa as its mission field, particularly Liberia on the advice of a committee chaired by Mr. Crane. Liberia was peculiarly attractive because most of the colonists who had gone to that country were from the Southern States of America and most

---

[1] George W. Sadler, *A Century in Nigeria* (Bredman Press: Nashville, Tennessee, 1950), p. 31.

of them were Baptists.[2] Another reason was that it was believed that the cost of living in Liberia was less than in the other West African countries. Finally, it was thought that Afro-American missionaries who would be sent there might have easier access to the local Africans whose colour and background were similar to theirs.

Due to this last consideration the Convention agreed that only Afro-American missionaries should be sent. But Mr. William Crane maintained that it was "peculiarly important, that at least two well educated, well qualified missionaries, fitted for the work, should be employed there as leaders."[3] Mr. Crane clearly meant white missionaries when he referred to "well educated, and well qualified missionaries" because soon after his suggestion the Convention set out to search for white missionaries to go to Liberia as leaders. However, after searching for a whole year Crane had found no white man prepared to offer himself. Reasons for this lack of interest have not been documented. It may be conjectured, however, that they were frightened by the reputation of the Guinea Coast as the "white man's grave". Indeed, at the time of the search, 109 missionaries of other missionary societies had died in Sierra Leone.[4] The white Presbyterian missionary who went to Liberia in 1832 died and so the Presbyterian missionary society decided after the death of six of their white missionaries there, to send only Afro-American missionaries. All these might have caused the reluctance of the White Baptist ministers of the South.

Thus the only avenue left for the Board from which to recruit missionaries was to appoint Afro-Americans. But here too it was difficult to recruit the required personnel because of the poor education of the Afro-American pastors.

In the interim, while the search for missionary personnel was going on in the States, the Board appointed some of the resident colonists in Liberia as missionaries. The first to be thus appointed in 1846 were Brother John Day and Brother A. L. Jones. The latter passed away soon after his appointment. Thus Brother John Day remained as the first missionary of the Southern Baptist Convention in West Africa.

John Day was born at Hicksford Virginia on 18th February 1797 and was baptized in 1820. In the following year he was licensed to preach. He was among the colonists who arrived in Liberia in 1830 and worked part-time as missionary of the Triennial Convention. After the disruption of the Convention he relinguished his services with the American Baptist

---

[2] *Ibid.*, p. 32.
[3] *Ibid.*, p. 33.
[4] *Loc. cit.*

Missionary Union and accepted the invitation of the Southern Baptist Board. He sold his business, resigned his post as a judge and worked full time for the Southern Board.

John Day was instructed to occupy Grand Bassam and work among the indigenous people in that region. He had a keen interest in education and with the consent and approval of the Board, he established an industrial School at Bexley in 1849.

Meanwhile, at home, in America, people were responding to the call to offer themselves for work in Liberia. From among those who applied in 1847 only one of them, Rev. B. J. Drayton, was qualified because he had good education. He was followed by J. N. Harden, who, despite inadequate education, proved to be a most valuable worker.[5]

With the reinforcements which trickled in from America, Brother Day and his colleagues toiled fervently in Liberia. In 1854 Day became the pastor of the Baptist Church in Monrovia. Here he founded and presided over a High School where he had hoped to train the pupils in elementary, classical and theological disciplines.

As the Superintendent of the Liberian mission field Rev. Day travelled extensively preaching in the villages, visiting and establishing Sunday schools. It has been estimated that by the time he died in 1859 he had preached to about ten thousand heathens.[6]

In 1861 the fruits of the labours of Rev. Day and his colleagues were enumerated and it was found that in that year there were in Liberia and Sierra Leone 24 stations, 18 pastors, 1,258 members, 26 teachers and 665 pupils and 68 baptized.[7]

Unfortunately, however, the mission in Liberia was suspended after the American Civil War in 1861. This was due to the fact that during the five years immediately following the War no financial support was sent from America because of the reconstructions taking place in the States then. But the work was maintained to some extent through local initiative.

In 1871, A. D. Phillips was sent by the Board to survey the West African missions. During his visit to Liberia and Sierra Leone he engaged eight mission workers in Liberia and gave limited financial assistance.

Soon after these developments, in 1873, Phillips resigned his post as the superintendent of the West African work and the Board suspended all

---

[5] *Ibid.*, p. 34.

[6] H. A. Tupper, *A Decade of Foreign Missions, 1880-1890* (Richmond: Foreign Mission Board, Southern Baptist Convention, 1891), p. 22.

[7] Baker J. Cauthen and others, *Advance: A History of Southern Baptist Foreign Missions* (Broadman Press. Nashville, Tennessee, 1970), p. 141.

the missionaries working in Liberia excepting B. P. Yates and J. J. Cheeseman who were the supervisors of the mission and a gratuity of $500.00 was distributed among the dismissed missionaries.

The reason is obvious. The civil war made the South destitute and the poverty was worsened by the reconstruction. But the work had been begun along the West African Coast. It was true that the war had had adverse effects on the missionary efforts: the work in Nigeria was tottering towards extinction. But the Board was determined to continue the enterprise despite the difficulties and in 1874 the Revs. W. J. David and W. W. Colley (an Afro-American) were appointed for work in West Africa. They were charged by the Board "to determine whether it would be possible to renew the work in Yoruba country and, if not, to attempt a new mission among a tribal group in Liberia whose King had shown a friendly interest."[8] So in January 1875 they left the States for West Africa.

They visited Liberia first where Colley was left to encourage the churches. When David reached Nigeria he was given a warm welcome by the languishing little congregations in Lagos, Abeokuta and Ogbomosho. On his return to Liberia he found that the projects there were not as hopeful as those in Nigeria. Accordingly, David settled all debts and closed down the Liberia Mission in 1875 and returned to Lagos together with Brother Colley.

When Colley returned to America in 1879 he resigned as a missionary of the Foreign Mission Board and organized the Afro-American Baptists to form their own national missionary Board. He became their first secretary and from 1880 the Liberian work was sustained by these Afro-American groups. They sent workers to Liberia as pastors and teachers entirely supported from Afro-American church funds and prayers.

These soldiers of Christ worked mainly along the coast and established churches and schools among the immigrants. But they did not completely neglect the indigenous people in certain areas reaching into parts of the interior with the Gospel.

Although these Baptists had been in Liberia before other denominations arrived there they lagged behind the other denominations. The explanation simply was that as they did not have sufficient money, the Baptists could not maintain adequate schools and support properly trained pastors. Hence their work remained weak until the Southern Baptist Foreign Mission Board returned to resume its abandoned work eighty-five years later, in 1960.

---

[8] *Ibid.*, p. 143.

I have mentioned earlier that in 1861 the statistics of the Baptist mission was taken for Liberia and Sierra Leone together. The *SIERRA LEONE* Baptist work had been started in 1792 by the Afro-American immigrant David George, an evangelist from Canada. He worked in Freetown and founded a small Baptist congregation there. Three years later, in 1795, the British Baptists also attempted to establish themselves there but failed because they did not find the place suitable.

The Baptist congregation established by independent Afro-Americans remained and continued to spread Baptist influence in Freetown. In 1849, during the first visit of Bowen, Goodale and Hill, Goodale acquired some land for the Southern Baptist Mission at Sama and opened a school there. In 1853 when Bowen, Dennard and Lacy were on their way to Nigeria they stopped in Freetown and ordained two ministers, J. J. Brown and George R. Thomson at the request of the Baptists there. In that year there were 13 stations and 11 day schools with 400 pupils under Afro-American ministers and teachers.

In the following year, 1854, the Rev. John Day of Liberia was authorised by the Foreign Board to visit Sierra Leone. He was to advise whether or not the Southern Baptists should revive the Baptist churches there and, among other things, to find men to join the brethren of the Yoruba Mission at Lagos, the Board meeting the expenses of the agency.[9]

As a result of John Day's report the Foreign Mission Board, in 1855, assumed the support of the ministers of the Freetown Baptist Society.

Four years later there were two churches one in Freetown with 72 members and one called Waterloo church with 34 members and a school was opened in Freetown.[10] From that time Liberia and Sierra Leone were administered together.

The work in Sierra Leone was mainly among Afro-Americans who had been christianized in Western countries prior to their immigration to Sierra Leone. During the period of this study apparently no effective evangelization of the indigenous people took place.

It has been mentioned earlier in this chapter that Thomas J. Bowen, Harvey Goodale and Robert F. Hill visited Liberia where Goodale died in Sama country. These men had been commissioned and sent as missionaries to Central Africa (Northern Nigeria), on 22nd February 1849. So Liberia was not their destination. They just stopped over there in order to acclimatize before moving on to their destination.

The particular location where their work was to begin was Igboho, a large city northwest of Yorubaland, in *NIGERIA*.

---

[9] Sadler, *op.cit.*, p. 39.
[10] Cauthen et al., *op.cit.*, p. 141.

After the death of Goodale, Bowen left Monrovia leaving Hill behind and sailed for Badagry in 1850. On 5th August that very year Bowen landed at Badagry and from there travelled to Abeokuta. He was warmly welcomed by Anglican and Wesleyan missionaries who had been working there. He could not immediately proceed to Igboho because he was refused permission due to inter-tribal strife between Akitoye and Kosoko.[11] This delay gave Bowen the opportunity to start learning the Yoruba language and to visit Eruwa, where he was well received by the Chief and his people and he opened an outstation there.

Fortunately, in 1852 he was invited by Kumi, the Chief of Ijaye. He accepted the invitation and when he arrived at Ijaye, north of Abeokuta in the direction of Igboho, chief Kumi asked him to select any site of his choice for a mission. After selecting a suitable site he encountered some difficulties: he had no money with which to build a house and he was in poor health. Under these circumstances he went on furlough in February 1853 to report the progress he had made.

The six-months furlough was fruitful: Bowen got married, found reinforcement for the staff and financial assistance. With these advantages he left the United States on 6th July, 1853 and landed at Lagos on 28th August the same year.

The party comprised Thomas Bowen, Mrs. Bowen, J. S. Dennard, Mrs. Fannie Dennard, J. H. Lacy and Mrs. Olivia Lacy. After some delay at Lagos, due to the rebellion of Kosoko against the British the party moved on to Abeokuta. Immediately after arriving members of the group fell victims to Malaria. Mr. Lacy was so seriously sick that he and his wife were repatriated home. When the rest regained their health, Mr. Dennard returned to Lagos, to plant a station and also to serve as a forwarding agent of goods to colleagues living in the interior of the country. Six months later Mrs. Dennard died in Lagos and Mr. Dennard had to return to Abeokuta where he too died a while later. So within a brief period after the arrival of the party in Lagos only Bowen and his wife were left to proceed to Ijaye.

They were received well by chief Kumi and they rented quarters in a local house. Arrangements were quickly made to erect a Mission house and by February, 1854, the Bowens moved into the new house which was nearing completion. When the Mission House was completed, a chapel was built the same year and the first convert, a man named Tella, was baptized on 23rd July, 1854. The first Holy Communion was administered on the same day.

---

[11] See Chapter IV of this book.

Two months later Bowen received reinforcement in the person of W. H. Clarke of Lumpkin, Georgia. After his arrival more converts were baptized. The Bowens remained and worked for a year, together with Clarke at Ijaye and then transferred to Ogbomosho. There they opened a new station on 23rd September, 1855 leaving Clarke to take charge of the Ijaye station.

After the arrival of Clarke on the coast many other missionaries folowed between 1856 and 1858 but most of them were obliged to return to the States because of ill health after spending only a short time on the field.[12]

Early in 1856 the Rev. & Mrs. Bowen had to return home. His Home Board was anxious to arrange for the publication of the Yoruba grammar and dictionary which Bowen had compiled.[13] Unfortunately, the Bowens did not have the opportunity to return to Africa. After three years' service at home Bowen went to Rio de Janeiro where he was to work among Yoruba slaves.[14] The experiment did not succeed and Bowen returned to America disappointed and with failing health.

There were nine male and seven female white missionaries left in the field at the time of Bowen's departure. The years 1856 to 1866 were very difficult for both missionaries and the Home Board. Financially the missionaries did not receive in time the money voted for them; there was tribal war in Nigeria and in 1860,

> the annual meeting of Yoruba Mission could not be held on account of the war there prevailing, and requested that supplies should be forwarded for the interior without waiting for estimates on the salary drafts of the missionaries.[15]

In addition there was some confusion among the missionaries. For example, R. P. Priest refused in 1859, to place himself under the authority of the Yoruba Mission, and would not have anything to do with its meetings.[16] Stone was captured by Ibadan warriors because he was considered to be a spy and the Ijaye were on the verge of collapse as a result of the Ibadan-Ijaye war.

At home in America, the Board had serious internal problems: some of the Baptist members were agitating for the dissolution of the Foreign Mission Board. They favoured "the primitive and Gospel plan." According to this scheme individual congregations supported their itinerant ministers. So the dissenting group wished to withdraw from the Board

---

12 Sadler, *op.cit.*, p. 60.
13 *Ibid.*, p. 61.
14 Cauthen and others, *op.cit.*, p. 140.
15 Sadler, *op.cit.*, p. 63.
16 *Ibid.*, p. 64.

and assume direct responsibility of their pastors serving the Mission Board overseas. Consequently, the Rehoboth Association of Virginia withdrew from the Board and planned to take over the support of Reid in Nigeria. The Association planned, however, to continue to transmit their funds to Africa through the Board to ease transfer transactions.

Above all the clouds of the American civil war were on the horizon. In April 1861 the war broke out and the Foreign Mission Board ''resolved that no additional appropriation be made to the Yoruba Mission for 1861.''[17] The missionaries were thus left to fend for themselves material-ly. Naturally they turned to material pursuits spending little time on their regular missionary work. The Board was compelled by the serious war conditions at home to condone this shift of emphasis as change was clear-ly articulated by the Board in its resolution on 5th March 1863:

> That in the present difficulty of transmitting funds, the Board approve of any suitable arrangements which our missionaries may adopt for the pur-pose of sustaining themselves in whole or in part by secular pursuit.[18]

It was a difficult time. It seems other alternatives which the Board sought to use to reduce the problems of the mission field failed.[19] In any case four of the missionaries: T. A. Reid, A. D. Phillips, R. H. Stone and Mrs. Stone, endured the hardships until conditions improved. In ap-preciation of their endurance the Board, on 12 March, 1866 resolved to send financial help and more missionaries to the field. This could not be done immediately because the war had rendered the South ''prostrate; reconstruction left it maddened.''[20] So in 1868 T. A. Reid was advised not to return to Africa when he went on furlough.

Those left in Nigeria had further complications. The war between the Egba and Ikorodu near Lagos hit Abeokuta mercilessly and as a result Abeokuta expelled all the missionaries because the British Government lent a helping hand to Ikorodu.[21] The missionaries sought refuge in Lagos for a period until boats were available to convey them home. The last of them, Rev. Stone was invalided home in 1869.

Thus the first phase of the Southern Baptist work in ''Central Africa'' (Nigeria) was almost abortive. Most of the missionaries died, others were invalided home and civil wars forced the rest out of Nigeria. The first sta-tion, Ijaye, and the work at Abeokuta were destroyed by the civil wars. But there was left a flickering light which was kept aflame during the absence of the missionaries by devoted African converts such as J. C.

---

[17] *Ibid.*, p. 66.
[18] *Loc. cit.*
[19] *Ibid.*, pp. 66-67.
[20] *Ibid.*, p. 68, quoting Adams, *The Epic of America*, p. 286.
[21] Cf. Chapter IV above.

Vaughn,[22] a carpenter from Liberia, some young people and "a godly African widow," who was the wife of J. M. Harden (an American-Liberian).

Thus the Nigerian work was abandoned without funds and supervision from the Home Board until 1874.[23] In that year W. J. David and W. W. Colley, an Afro-American were appointed as Missionaries and charged-by the Home Board "to determine whether it would be possible to renew the work in Yoruba country."[24] They sailed for Africa in 1875 landing first in Monrovia as mentioned earlier in this chapter (p. 123). Leaving Colley in Monrovia, David travelled to Nigeria. From the satisfactory report he gave after his visit to Lagos, Abeokuta and Ogbomosho the Board decided to resuscitate its collapsing work in Nigeria.

Accordingly, David and Colley left Monrovia and went to settle in Lagos where they arrived on 14th October 1875. The efforts of the missionaries at this time were so successful that on 1st January 1876 they organized a church, comprising 52 members in Lagos. While Colley was left in charge of the congregation in Lagos, David moved to Abeokuta and Ogbomosho and organized the scattered flocks in these places into churches.

After their first furlough, W. W. Colley did not return to Nigeria but remained in America and organized the Afro-Americans for work in Liberia.[25] David returned with a wife and another Afro-American whom he left in charge of the Abeokuta work. After 1880 more new recruits were sent to the Nigeria mission field. The work progressed so steadily and with so little difficulty that in 1887 a "stately" church was built with materials imported from America for the Lagos congregation— the first Baptist Church sanctuary which is still being used.[26]

The educational aspect of the work also progressed satisfactorily. Primary schools were built in almost all the mission stations. With the growth of primary schools came the need for higher education. This led David to establish the Lagos Baptist Academy in Lagos, in 1886. The son of the J. M. Harden mentioned earlier was made the first principal and David Brown Vincent (afterwards known as Mojola Agbebi) the headmaster of the elementary department.

---

[22] It seems from the records that Vaughn adopted the name Moses L. Stone in appreciation of his missionary benefactor, R. H. Stone, cf. Cauthen and others, op.cit., pp. 142-143 and Sadler, op.cit., p. 71.

[23] Cauthen and others, op.cit., p. 143.

[24] Loc.cit.

[25] See above under Liberia, p. 123.

[26] This is the building in which Gen. Obasanjo and President Carter worshipped in April, 1978.

A year after the chapel was completed in Lagos, that was in 1888, there was schism in the Lagos church and the separatists constituted themselves into the "Native Baptist Church" currently known as "Ebenezer Baptist Church." It all happened because Moses Stone, one of the teachers in the Lagos Academy, was not satisfied with his salary. This led to a dispute between him and the missionary David whom he assisted as pastor of the Lagos congregation. As no satisfactory compromise was reached, Stone withdrew from the First Baptist Church. In sympathy with him about two hundred members of the church also withdrew, leaving only about twenty-four of them in the Lagos church.[27]

The new group made Stone their pastor and organized the Ebenezer Baptist Church which for some time became stronger than the mother church.[28]

The effect of the schism spread through all the Baptist churches in the country. This brought the administration to question the strained relations between the African members of the church and the missionaries. Consequently, W. J. David had to leave Nigeria in 1889 for America never to return to the land where he was an originator and pastor of the first American Baptist Church, Lagos, 1875 to 1888.[29]

David was succeeded immediately after his departure by C. C. Newton who arrived in Nigeria in 1889. In order to help in bringing reconciliation Moses Stone in 1892 returned to the ministry of the American Baptist Mission currently known as the First Baptist Church in Lagos. Although he did not succeed in reconciling the two factions, he was able to guide the Lagos First Baptist Church to purchase its independece by leading the congregation to raise funds with which they purchased the church building from the Mission and became self-supporting in 1900.

Meanwhile Mojola Agbebi took charge of the Ebenezer Baptist Church. He preached widely, visiting neighbouring West African countries. Because he was sound in doctrine he was able to preserve the dissenting group from drifting into syncretism.

Between 1901 and 1910 the work continued to expand in spite of the schism. A few new missionaries were sent, a new station was opened at Shaki and the staffing position of the pastors' Training College started in 1898 by C. E. Smith at Ogbomosho, was strengthened. The Baptist medical work was begun by George and Lydia Green and a girls' school, "Idi Aba", was established by Mrs. Carrie G. L. Lumbley at Abeokuta,

---

[27] *Ibid.*, p. 146.
[28] *Loc.cit.*
[29] Sadler, *op.cit.*, p. 91.

in 1910. This eventually became a secondary school which later developed into a teacher-training college.

Between 1912 and 1914 arrangements were made towards the formation of the Yoruba Baptist Association. In 1912 Duval invited representatives of the independent Baptist churches to attend the annual conference of mission "native workers". They found the fellowship so rewarding that steps were taken to create a regular meeting with officers. Consequently, from 11th - 12th March, 1914, at a gathering at Ibadan, the Yoruba Baptist Association (Synod) was constituted. Its first president was Mojola Agbebi, who was called the "dynamic leader of the independent movement."[30]

The foundation members of the new Association consisted of 31 churches comprising 2,880 members of which 14 churches with 1,646 members were independent and 17 churches with 1,254 members were mission. This brought together once more the two factions in the Baptist Churches in Nigeria. Thus the schism which dated from 1888 was healed to a large extent. The result was that a strong indigenous Baptist organization was later developed and the name of the Association was changed to the "Nigeria Baptist Convention." Thus at the beginning of World War I the Nigerian Baptists reorganized themselves and embarked upon a united venture for the spread of the gospel and the development of Baptist institutions and churches.

The most important development during the war was the formation of the Baptist Women's Missionary Union which came into being at Ogbomosho in April 1919 with Mrs. Agbebi as its first president.

So the seed which had been sown in tears by the Southern Baptist Missionaries did not die but germinated and took firm roots which withstood the storms of the 1914-1918 war.

---

[30] Cauthen and others, *op.cit.*, p. 148.

CHAPTER THIRTEEN

UNITED BRETHREN METHODIST MISSION

The United Methodist Church of Sierra Lenone of today was established by the United Brethren Church (UBC) Mission. This Missionary Society was formed, in the United States of America, on 7th January, 1853. Its aim was:

> to aid the Annual Conference in extending their missionary labours throughout America, and to Foreign lands by preaching the gospel of Jesus to all men in all countries in its unmixed and original purity.[1]

As Africa was among the primary targets, Sierra Leone was selected as their pioneer mission field in Africa.[2] The first missionaries Messrs Flickinger, Shiney and D. C. Kumler, M. D. sailed from New York on 23rd January 1855, and after thirty-four days' journey arrived in Freetown on 26th February the same year. They were welcomed by the missionaries of the congregational American Missionary Society which had preceded them.

From Freetown the pioneers travelled extensively, preached through interpreters and reached as far as Mokolleh, about sixty miles east of Mattru Jong. After their first furlough, Flickinger was able to return to the mission field in 1857 with two new colleagues Mr. W. B. Witt and Rev. J. K. Billheimer. During this second tour, the missionaries were offered a one hundred acre piece of land at Shenge by Chief Caulker.

The first permanent Station was established there and the missionaries were so satisfied with this location that they sent the following intelligence home:

> There is no spot on the African continent of greater interest to the United Brethren in Christ than Shenge, the place where our Church began permanent Missionary work in Africa. It is beautifully situated, sixty miles southeast of Freetown, being on a peninsula with the waters so nearly surrounding it that it is almost an island. Extending out into the sea as it does, it is likely the most healthful resort in the Protectorate of Sierra Leone. Adjacent to it on a little Island, called Plantain Island, are remnants of the old slave pen of John Newton. Shenge is the home of the Caulker Family, one of the most intelligent families in all that country.[3]

---

[1] H. J. Williams, "An Outline of the Early Beginnings of the United Brethren Church Now United Methodist Church in Sierra Leone, West Africa" (Mimeographed, Freetown, 1972), p. 2.

[2] See Chapter III above p. 19 for the reason.

[3] Williams, *ibid.*, p. 3.

With this satisfaction, the Rev. J. K. Billheimer commenced his evangelization, by holding worship services and Sunday School every Sunday at Chief Caulker's court house which was situated in the centre of the village. The first three converts came from the Chief's family: they were Madam Lucy Caulker, Tom Caulker and Chief Caulker himself whose conversion and interest in the Church inspired others to accept the teachings of the gospel. Thus Shenge grew quickly to become the head-quarters of the Shenge Mission. A Mission House, a Training School, a Chapel, a Boy's Home, Parsonage and minor buildings were put up there.

During the pioneer period, the main aim of the Missionaries was evangelism. Flickinger having studied the people and environment, observed that

> the introduction of the gospel among them is the only remedy for their physical sufferings, as well as for their spiritual maladies; and we have the means in abundance to give them a preached as well as a written gospel.[4]

Thus, during the first six years, no schools were opened; the attention was focused on preaching the gospel. As a result, stations were opened outside Shenge within the Kagboro Chiefdom at Rembee, Mofus, Mocobo and Mambo.

In 1861, however, the missionary activities were expanded beyond evangelism alone. On 9th May, that year, the Board of Missions met in Johnsville, Marrow County, Ohio, and received a report that the first Day School was opened at Shenge. Part of the report stated that:

> A Day School was also in progress part of the year; the Shenge people showed increased interest in the success of the Mission, and the adjacent towns are anxious to receive religious instruction. A Sabbath School of twenty-five members is progressing.[5]

From its inauguration in May 1861, formal eduction became an additional method of evangelism. Thus the school and the preaching of the gospel became the most powerful tools which the missionaries used in evangelizing the people.

Another change took place in 1870. Owing to the constant deaths and sickness of the white missionaries the Home Board was compelled to revise its policy regarding the appointment of the missionaries. It was decided that Negro missionaries should be sent to the African mission field instead of the white ones. Thus the Gomer family was sent in December, 1870 to assist their white predecessors still active in the field.

---

[4] *Ibid.*, p. 4.
[5] *Loc.cit.*

Mr. Gomer was an African in the Third United Brethren Church in Dayton. When they arrived in Sierra Leone, the Gomers were received with enthusiasm by the local people among whom they worked tirelessly. True to the anticipation of the Home Board the Gomers were completely immune to the hazards of the climate. As a result, unlike the white missionaries, the Gomer family stayed on the coast from five to seven years before they went on their first furlough. During their first tour Gomer and his wife taught the people cleanliness, Godliness and industry. Their most important achievement then was that the Palli Church in the Bompeh Chiefdom was built and dedicated.

By 1877, the work of the mission in Sierra Leone began to bear more concrete fruits of success. On 3rd January, 1877, the Rev. J. K. Billheimer wrote a letter home from Sierra Leone and observed among other things that:

> Twenty years ago this part of the Sherbro country was without the gospel. Very few had ever heard of a saviour. The grounds upon which the station is built were in the bush. Today flowers and fruits are growing on the borders of the walk in the shade of the cotton tree. Twenty years ago Shenge was the abode of many illiterate people. Today pen, ink and paper, newspapers and books are in the requisition.[6]

This is not only a good commentary on the evangelistic work of the missionaries, but it is also an eloquent witness of the effective formal educational training given to the local people.

It has been mentioned earlier in this chapter, that this mission introduced formal education in 1861 when the first day school was opened at Shenge. In 1877, Night Schools were opened at Shenge, Bompetoke and Rotifunk in addition to the day schools and Sunday Schools.

The significance of the Religious and Educational activities of the United Methodist Church in Sierra Leone lies in the fact that unlike the Missionary Societies which had preceded them, they did not concentrate their endeavours in the colony; rather they penetrated the hinterland. From 1855 to 1904, "they laboured single handed to bring benefits to the Sherbro, Mende, Temne and Kono who were the indigenous people and the majority in need."[7]

The achievements in the field of education did not come without difficulties. In 1868, that is, seven years after the establishment of the first day school, the roll increased only to twenty scholars. Most of these were from King Caulker's family. Many who had enrolled did not persevere; most of them absconded from the school. In spite of poor enrolment the

---

[6] *Ibid.*, p. 5.
[7] *Ibid.*, p. 6.

work was effectively maintained by the Rev. Gomer, the Superintendent with his assistants, the Rev. and Mrs. Warner, Rev. J. A. Evans and Mrs. M. B. Hadley.

The second day school was opened at Bompetoke in May 1875. In that year the greatest difficulty was no longer that of lack of pupils but of teachers. Thus when the Gomers went on furlough to the United States in 1876, they launched an appeal for teachers and this resulted in the recruitment of two new missionaries. With this addition, the Executive Committee of the Board of Foreign Mission instructed that an Industrial School should be opened at Shenge with agricultural and mechanical departments connected with the work. A sum of $1,800.00 was raised by the Annual Conference of which part was to be used for the purchase of tools for the industrial section.

It seems that the project was a great success, for Williams commenting on the achievements of the school said:

> The proceeds from this Industrial section were amazing in money and service. With knowledge acquired in farming the boys extracted oil, and sold kernels which they cracked. They planted cassava and arrow-root which they sold. Their sample of cotton was sent to England. The children lived happily on their farm products.[8]

As the Industrial school experiment was successful, the missionaries became convinced that they had reached a stage in their missionary work in Africa, where they must enlarge their plans and cultivate with more diligence the land they had acquired. Their aim was that:

> The boys must be taught to cultivate the land, to build and operate mills and factories, to construct dwellings, to make highways, to build rail-roads, to open up mines, to utilise their forests, to carry on commerce, in a word, to live and grow, and flourish as a civilized, Christian Nation.
>
> The girls must be taught how to dress themselves decently, how to make their clothing, how to cook, how to keep a house, in a word, how to become and continue as Christian mothers, and how to teach and do, and live after the manner of Christian women in Christian countries, and to do this, something more than schools to teach them letters, is required.[9]

It was also in 1876 that the first post-primary school was established. Two years later, on 17th December, 1878, Mr. & Mrs. D. F. Wilberforce served as pastor and teacher in the Training School. Nine years later, in 1887, the second post-primary school, for sacred learning, the Rufus Clarke and Wife Training School, was opened under the Principalship of the Rev. D. F. Wilberforce.

---

[8] *Ibid.*, p. 8.
[9] *Ibid.*, p. 7.

The foundation stone of this Academy of Sacred Learning was laid by the Rev. D. K. Flickinger on 31st January, 1887 and on 2nd February, 1887, the first five theological students were enrolled. This number quickly increased to twelve at the end of the second year and by 1890 there were 18 students in the school.

Rev. D. F. Wilberforce did not restrict himself to the activities of the Theological Institute alone. He was very concerned about building secular schools. Thus after a short period he was able to open schools at Mano, Mambo, Thumba, Bompekote and Rotifunk.

It was not in education only that the work was extended beyond Shenge. Congregations were also founded in the outstations. Work at some of the important outposts will now be described.

The *Mission at Rotifunk* was founded by the Rev. Gomer in 1876. It happened that on 21st October, 1875 a Missionary Convention was held in Dayton, Ohio, U.S.A. by the United Brethren Church. Among the decisions taken at the convention was one concerning Africa. It was overwhelmingly decided that volunteers and money should be released for the establishment of a new school, in Sierra Leone, up the Bompeh River, a thickly populated area. The Rev. Gomer was authorised to visit the area and select a suitable site. With his recommendation the Mission was located at Rotifunk, on the Bompeh River, about 55 miles from Freetown.

Rotifunk, was a strategic location. It was linked with Freetown by railway and with Shenge by river. It was a good point for provincial missionary operations and a supply station for places north-east of the Rokel River.

Before the advent of Christianity, Rotifunk was a slave trading centre so the importance of a Christian presence there cannot be overemphasised.

The prospects for the work looked so propitious that, soon after the opening of the mission, a chapel was erected and Miss Beeken was appointed as a representative in 1877 and charged to train the local girls. At first, she did not have adequate local support; but gradually, the Headman of the village, Pa Souri, became interested, gave up drinking and smoking and built a *barri*. The Women's Association in America also erected a mission house on an elevated spot near the town. During her nineteen months' stay at the station Miss Beeken established two schools and conducted public worship in the surrounding towns.

After nineteen months she was succeeded by Mrs. M. M. Mair from Glasgow, Scotland. She had previously served in other parts of West Africa for twenty-six years. She landed in Freetown on 19th October, 1877 and went to Rotifunk in November, the same year.

The work these two lady missionaries did among the Temne girls was considerable. They established the first Girls' home for the Mission. The pupils were taught sewing, washing, ironing and house-work of various sorts.

> They were trained in the Christian way as capable wives of Native workers and together established Christian homes. Some took the Bible home on holiday from which they read and interpreted passages for the benefit of their friends and relations. This gesture was most satisfactory to the Missionaries who felt that their seeds had been successfully sown in the hearts of the girls they trained.[10]

Although from the beginning the parents did not encourage their daughters to go to school[11] the Missionaries were not dismayed. In remembrance of the work of Miss Beeken and Mrs. Mair the Mary Sower's Memorial Girls' Home was built and dedicated on 13th December, 1888. The dedication service was held in the Chapel at 10.00 a.m. in the presence of the Revs. West, Wilberforce, Gomer, and Evans who officiated. Later the Architect's wife Mrs. Sage, who was also present wrote the following about the dedication.

> We feel that this home is as really consecrated to the use and service of God as any church building, and we pray that the daughters of the King may here, through the Holy Spirit, be made all glorious within, and may go forth from this house as corner-stones polished after the similitude of a palace to be living stones in the spiritual temple of our God as well as a blessing to their own home which they shall rear for themselves in the future.[12]

The progress made at this Home was a fulfilment of the hopes expressed by Mrs. Sage. In a short time, the news of the school, which now enrolled boys with the girls, spread into the hinterland. The Paramount Chief of the region, Chief Bai Marro was so impressed about the progress made by the school that he sent his son Manka and a daughter, later baptized Laura Monga, to the school. The institution continued to make such good impact on the people that, by 1898, there were forty pupils on the roll including Josiah, Eric and Santigie, the sons of Sorie Kessebeh, the Chief of Rotifunk.

Unfortunately, in the midst of progress, the school met with a tragedy in 1898. About the beginning of that year, the Missionaries were told that some nationalists were planning to invade them. At first the Missionaries

---

[10] *Ibid.*, p. 15.

[11] Williams' reason for this unwillingness of parents to send their daughters to school is that at that time eduction for women was of no importance, and the girls were regarded as goods and chattels.

[12] *Loc. cit.* Although the emphasis at Rotifunk was the training of girls, boys were also admitted.

did not take the rumour seriously until the information was repeated by Pa Lemon, an ex-frontier soldier of Daru Barracks. This now alarmed the Missionaries and, realising the gravity of the situation, they attempted to evacuate the Mission station, but they were too late.

On 2nd May, 1898, in the morning, a great local warrior, Pa Gberi, sent the traditional two pieces of tobacco leaf to the Missionaries, to announce the war had been declared by him against all the educated people of the community.

The line of action which the warriors took has been recorded thus:

1. All persons wearing English sewn materials were suspects and should either be killed or captured. Boys and girls were requested to use locally woven cloth in form of a gown. Beneath it was a *vomi* (locally known as knickers).
2. On the night of May 2, 1898, a crier named Koro Tamba, announced war with his horn and warned them to go into hiding. The result was an empty town with only the Missionaries and other educated people left.
3. To further entrap the educated element within the township an expression in the form of an exclamatory statement was introduced as follows: '*Aa Kiye*' meaning a surprise in Mende. Again when asked 'Gberi', the answer should be 'Gbonge' or in short '*Gberi-Gbonge*'. Only a successful answer exonerated the individual from difficulty.[13]

On 3rd May, 1898, as the custom was, the school assembled and had the morning devotion and sang the hymn, "A shelter in the time of storms." Soon after they had dispersed, the Rev. Cain and Dr. Archer went to the dispensary. Some warriors followed, arrested and shot them. Other warriors set the Mission house on fire and when Mrs. Cain, saw the house aflame she, in a frantic mood, ran into the fire and perished. Dr. Hatfield, who had been confined to bed, managed to get up, went to a nearby street and knelt down to pray. Her assailants waited until she finished praying and then beheaded her.

The revolution was not limited to Rotifunk only. Missionaries in other localities such as Taisma were ruthlessly massacred. Missionaries other than those of the UBC, such as the Methodists and other denominations were similarly treated at Bompeh, Tikonko and Gbangbala.[14] The only UBC Missionary in Rotifunk who escaped death was the Rev. Ward who was then in Freetown getting ready for his wedding.

The Government took retributive steps when news about these atrocious massacres reached the official quarters. A regiment was despatched to Rotifunk to put the rebellion under control. The regiment was resisted at Rotawa; but with difficulty it succeeded in passing through to

---

[13] *Ibid.*, p. 19.
[14] Groves, *op. cit.*, Vol. III, pp. 247-248.

Rotifunk. There, the Colonel-in-Charge ordered the burial of the corpses lying around. After things had returned to normal at Rotifunk, the Governor of Sierra Leone sent the following instructions to the Acting Colonial Secretary on 28th July, 1898.

> Please inform the District Commissioner Kwalu, that owing to the atrocious murder of the Missionaries, Mr. and Mrs. McGrew, at Taiama, I consider that (sic) place ought never to be allowed to be re-inhabited, that the buildings should be razed to the ground and the site of the town blotted out. The District Commissioner will be so good as to take the necessary action when opportunity offers to effect this.
> Rotifunk, which was the scene of so many murders of Missionaries ought to be treated in the same way but for the fact that the Missionary Society of which the victims were members possesses considerable property in lands there and wishes to resume work there as soon as the disturbances are quelled—but I think a zone round the Mission Station should be cleared of all native buildings and shall be glad if the District Commissioner will carry this out when practicable.[15]

Shortly after the raids, when peace had returned to Rotifunk, the Mission was rebuilt by Dr. J. King. The school which was a *barri* was rebuilt by a sub-chief, Pa Manso. The rehabilitation of the buildings brought new Missionaries and great changes in the missionary activities there. For example, the girls were transferred to Moyamba in 1900 to begin a new school named the Moyamba Girls' School, the Martyrs' Memorial Church was built in 1902, the Hatfield Archer Dispensary in 1904 and a new Primary School Foundation Stone was laid by the Rev. W. R. Funk, D. D. on 27th January, 1908. These changes took place during the period when the Rev. E. E. Todd, 1899-1904 was in charge of the station. In his farewell message to the Mende people on 4th December, 1904 he said among other things, that "we have given them another chance to hear."[16] This was an important challenge to the local Church and the people of Rotifunk. It is a joy to observe that the Church at Rotifunk has continued to grow.

The next outstation of importance is the *Moyamba Church*. In 1899 five persons from Moyamba became converted and were baptized. Thus there was a small nucleus of a Christian community at Moyamba when the Mary Sower's girls school was transferred there in 1900. The aim of this school was to expose the girls to effective Christian life so that through them model Christian homes might be developed. In order to give effective backing to this aim, a chapel was built and dedicated on 22nd June, 1902, with the Rev. J. E. King as the Missionary-in-Charge.

---

[15] Williams, *op.cit.*, p. 2 citing local official correspondence from the Governor of Sierra Leone, to the Acting Colonial Secretary, *Local Confidential*, No. 73, 28 July, 1898.
[16] Williams, *op.cit.*, p. 20

King then built a parsonage and planted an orchard of pawpaw, pineapple, banana, mango, orange and lime with cassava and plantain on the compound.

After the chapel and the parsonage had been completed, a school and a home for missionaries and girls were built in 1905 and 1907 respectively. From this main centre other outstations such as Kuelu, Lunge, Yoyema and Makouri were opened in the district.

Kuelu is of special interest. The evangelist there was Mrs. Juliana Thompson. As a result of her work, the first baptism was performed on 8th November, 1903 by the Rev. J. E. King. Among the three men and a woman baptized was one Abraham. On the day of the baptism, Abraham gave a testimony of his conversion and renounced the devil "by shaking his gown as if to shake the devil off and said, 'But my prayer is, if the Lord will let me speak a little English before I die, I shall be glad'".[17]

Another incident of interest at Kuelu concerned the conversion of two Moslems. "Murray-man" and his wife were Moslems. They had two sons. One of them was called Bockari. This son was often advised by his father not to join the heathens who called themselves Christians. But as the influence of the Church began to spread, Bockari and his brother often attended the Christian services. Eventually, Bockari became converted. He tried to lead his mother also to accept Christianity. But as she was hesitating, Bockari told her: *"Mammy, anybody who follows God no go shame. I don join you go join, too. If we all in this house die, we all go die one place."*[18]

Bockari and his mother became Christians. The mother, Sister Lydia, worked among the women while Bockari rose to become the President of the Young People's Christian Union of Kwelu (Kuelu).

The next outstation of relevance to this history is the *TAIAMA Mission.* It has been mentioned above, in the Governor's despatch to the Acting Colonial Secretary in 1898. There it was that the Rev. & Mrs. McGrew were cruelly beheaded. The Mission was first established in 1896, when the chief granted 120 acres of land to the Missionaries for their work. In addition to the gift of land he also built a *barri* for church and school purposes.

The pioneer Missionaries were the Rev. &Mrs. McGrew. Just after two years' missionary activity in the area, the 1898 rebellion against the foreigners disrupted the progress of the work. It was during that upheaval that the Rev. & Mrs. McGrew were beheaded.

---

[17] *Ibid.*, p. 24
[18] *Loc.cit.*

After the hostilities were brought under control, an indigenous pastor, was sent there in 1901 to reopen the station. As a result of his hard work, a permanent Mission House was built in 1904, a chapel built and a congregation organized in 1906.

From Taiama the work was extended to Senehum, Njama, Monghere, Dambia, Makori, Mano, Hangha and Pendembu.

Among the indigenous pillars of the Taiama church were brother Inskip and his wife Charlotte of whom the following testimony has been recorded:

> Brother Emmanuel Inskip and his good wife Charlotte led a Christian life in the community. Brother Inskip lived in a thatched house with boys he taught. He travelled on a donkey and recruited a large number of boys from illiterate parents for school and religious training.
>
> He was an itinerant (sic) while his wife taught. Mr. Riebel lived with them until the Mission house was constructed, but left after the death of his wife and preferred to remain at Rotifunk with the other Missionaries.[19]

The progress of the work at Taiama was considerable between 1900 and 1915. On 11th February, the Rev. J. E. King travelled to Taiama from Kwelu (Kuelu), administered the first Lord's Supper and baptism. It was during this visit that children of Brother and Sister Inskip were baptized and Brother Inskip himself was chosen a Class Leader. Bishop Howard also visited the station on 24th December, 1906 and baptized seven people in the River Taia.

The Taiama Elementary School for manual training made good progress. On 1st December, 1906, the handiworks of the pupils were exhibited at the Wilberforce memorial Hall in Freetown. The audience highly appreciated their effort and the judges awarded the Taiama School six prizes in Boys' Industrial Handicraft, Kindergarten Work, and Plain and Fancy Sewing.

In 1913 a new larger Taiama School block was built in place of the old mud structures because the roll continued to increase as the parents became satisfied with the training given to the pupils. The satisfaction which the parents derived from the missionary training received by their children encouraged them to join the church.

The growth of the *Mende Mission* makes interesting reading. In 1839, Don Pedro Martinez carried Mende slaves from the West Coast of Africa to Cuba, in spite of the fact that in 1820 the British Government had paid £400,000 as indemnity to the Spanish Government for lost slaves. By that agreement Spain consented to end the slave trade. Spain honoured the

---

[19] *Ibid.*, p. 30

treaty and banned the importation of slaves into Spanish territories. But in Cuba the Spanish slave dealers disregarded the ban.

From Havana the Mende slaves were resold and transferred in the ship the Amistead for Puer and then to Principe. They were so badly treated that the slaves mutinied, seized the ship and compelled the crew to return them to Africa. The ship was captured by the American Navy. The American Government immediately intervened and in 1841 provided an American Judge. He so ably defended the Mende in the U.S. District Court of Connecticut that they were set free.

During the period of the trial the Africans were exposed to Christian instruction at the First Church of Farmington. After a while plans were made by an Amistead Committee to repatriate the slaves to Sierra Leone. Under the supervision of Congregational Missionaries, one white, Raymond and two Negro American families, the Rev. & Mrs. James Steele and Mr. & Mrs. Henry Wilson, the party left America on 25th November, 1841 and arrived in Freetown about the middle of January, 1842. This Mende Mission did not make much progress because the emigrants did not co-operate with the Missionaries when they landed in Africa. Consequently, the Missionaries joined some of the other Missions from the U.S.A. to form the American Missionary Association in Sierra Leone.

This Association continued to work in Sierra Leone until 1882 when it decided to transfer the whole of its work to the United Brethren Church. Lands, buildings and boats were turned over to the UBC. In addition, the American Missionary Board paid to the UBC five thousand dollars annually for a period of six years to enable them rehabilitate the new Mission Stations such as Good Hope at Bonthe, Kwa-Mende on the Jong River and Mo-Tappan on the Big Boom River.

After the handing over of the Mission the UBC work gradually increased in Mendeland under the leadership of the Rev. R. E. Cookson-Taylor who became the Minister-in-Charge in 1898.

A testimony to the able leadership of Mr. Cookson-Taylor during the period was the fact that a strong Mission church was built at Bonthe on the east end of the Sherbro Island. About 200 people worshipped there regularly: there was a good Sunday School, and Junior and Senior Christian Endeavour Societies with 60 and 59 members in them respectively. Cookson-Taylor gave loyal and devoted service to Bonthe until his death in 1906.

As a memorial to the efforts made by the Amistead immigrants the UBC built the Amistead Memorial School at Bonthe in 1914.

These accounts of the growth of the UBC Mission, starting from Shenge are only samples of how the work of the Mission was expanded in Sierra Leone.

After the 1898 revolution the Mission consolidated itself. From 1900 to 1915 the Mission's growth was unprecedented in evangelization. It was during this period that Moyamba became the district Headquarters of outstations, such as Kwelu (Kuelu), Lunge, Yoyoma and Makouri. The Mission field was organized into five major districts, Taiama, Kono, Rotifunk, Shenge and Moyamba which administered the government of the Mission. By 1915, there were twenty-seven organized Churches, thirty-two Bible Schools with 2,086 pupils in attendance, thirty day-schools with an enrolment of 1,212 pupils belonging to the UBC in Sierra Leone.

With these results to serve as the foundation for re-assessment after World War I, the Superintendent Minister, the Rev. E. M. Hurah, in 1915 spelt out the future aspirations of the Mission as follows:

> The greatest heritage of these sixty years in Sierra Leone is a new attitude toward the gospel, a changing social consciousness in African leadership, progressive ideals, and ever-enlarging field, waiting, suffering for the Kingdom of God. Our heritage becomes a new challenge. To conserve the past, to develop a strong African Church, to fully occupy and evangelize our whole field, to maintain and enlarge our present medical service, and save a people from physical as well as spiritual degeneracy; to educate and train more leaders through our schools; to maintain and conserve, on a large scale, the natural resources through our industrial work and plantations; and finally, to stem the tide of Mohammedan movements which is the challenge that claims a response in men and money.[20]

These are hopeful words and a stimulating challenge for postwar ecclesiastical reconstruction and development.

---

[20] *Ibid.*, pp. 43-44.

CHAPTER FOURTEEN

AFRICAN METHODIST EPISCOPAL ZION MISSION

The African Methodist Episcopal (AME) Zion Church grew in 1820, out of the American Methodist Episcopal Zion Church.

It all began in 1796. In that year the "coloured" people in a Methodist Episcopal Church in New York separated from the white members of that congregation. Their purpose was to hold "meetings in which they might have an opportunity to exercise their spiritual gifts among themselves, and therefore be more useful to one another".[1] Similar separations took place in other mixed congregations and in 1820 all the "coloured" separatist groups organized themselves into one unit known as the "African Methodist Episcopal Zion Church" which was most strongly based in North Carolina.

The Christianization of Africa was one of the aims of the AME Zion Church.[2] Consequently, when the mission had the first opportunity a station was opened in *LIBERIA*, West Africa. The story makes an interesting reading. Toward the end of the 1870's, it was felt by the members of the African Methodist Episcopal Zion Church that they should "drive into the vast continent and develop [their] Father-land for Christ Jesus."[3] In pursuit of this aspiration one of them the Rev. Andrew Cartwright offered himself as a missionary for Africa. He had had a rich experience of building churches in Plymouth, North Carolina, where it was estimated that in ten years he established twelve churches.[4]

On 7th January 1876 he sailed for Liberia. On his arrival he settled at Brewerville and organized an A.M.E. Zion Church there on 7th February 1878. Soon afterwards, in November the same year, he established a second church at Clay Ashland and a third in 1880 at Antherton. The members were so enthusiastic that in May 1880 the three churches sent a formal report to the General Conference assembled in Montgomery, Alabama.

In the report they commended the splendid beginnings of Cartwright's work and requested that he be given power to call a local conference and

---

[1] Hans W. Debrunner, *A History of Christianity in Ghana* (Accra, 1967) p.234 citing W. E. W. Du Bois, *Negro Church* (1903), p. 45

[2] William J. Walls, *The African Methodist Episcopal Zion Church Reality of the Black Church.* (Charlotte NC 1974) p. 229.

[3] *Loc.cit.*

[4] *Loc.cit.*

also to recruit more preachers. Three years later, Cartwright went on furlough to America. He attended the meeting of Bishops on 28th March, 1883 at Petersburg, Virginia. There he was granted authority to hold local Annual Conferences and appoint suitable preachers and teachers on the mission field.

On his return to Liberia, due to lack of funds, Cartwright could not expand the work fast enough to justify the inauguration of the Conference in Liberia. In 1886, for example, a new station was opened at Cape Palmas with 40 members and 50 Sunday School scholars. But the work collapsed because funds were not available to sustain it.

The work at Brewerville was, however, maintained through the sacrifice of the Rev. and Mrs. Cartwright. During the period when no missionaries were sent from America because of financial difficulties Mrs. Cartwright was employed as a teacher to start a school for an annual salary of $300.00. This was the position at Brewerville until 1892 when the General Conference felt that its financial position had improved and so firmly resolved to rekindle its interest in the African work. In appreciation of the Cartwrights' devotion to duty, the Rev. Andrew Cartwright was made the Presiding Elder over his own work. He held this post until the first Bishop, John Bryan Small (see below) was appointed to oversee the African Mission Field.

In 1887 Bishop Small had his first pontifical visit to West Africa. He arrived in Liberia on 7th August and visited the Cartwrights at Brewerville. He noticed that the mission was in difficulty: there was lack of finance; the local members wanted a resident Bishop as the other denominations but the Home base was undecided about providing a resident bishop. In spite of all this, before Bishop Small left Liberia for Cape Coast in Ghana (then Gold Coast) he founded a Church at Johnsonville.

Bishop Small was convinced that the General Conference should provide spiritual and financial stimulation for the work in Liberia. Consequently, on his second visit to the coast in 1902 he ordained Brother Lewis B. Dudley as a deacon at the request of the local members of the Brewerville Church. Unfortunately, however, Cartwright did not live to enjoy the fellowship of Dudley for long. On 14th January, 1903 he died leaving Dudley in loneliness.

The Rev. H. T. Wright succeeded Cartwright in 1903. After seven years' labours in Brewerville Wright was succeeded by the Rev. Drybauld Taylor—an African pastor who became the Presiding Elder. The next Missionary from America was the Rev. J. J. Pearce. He was appointed by Bishop Walters the successor of Bishop Small who died on 5th January, 1905. It was during the time of Taylor and Pearce that the Liberian Annual Conference was inaugurated on 3rd March, 1910.

From that time the Liberian work began to bear fruits of steady growth. Bishop Walters ordained pastors wherever he visited to carry on the work. As a result of the increase in the ministerial strength, new stations were opened in Monrovia, Po River, Roysville, Pleasant Hill, Suahn and River Cess.

During World War I Pearce returned to America in 1915 and because of travel difficulties during the war he was not replaced and the Liberian work was left without supervision from America until August 1919 when the Rev. Thomas E. Davis was appointed.

The most extensive evangelistic work in West Africa was done by the AME Zion Church in the *GOLD COAST (Ghana)* during the period under discussion.

It happened that towards the end of the nineteenth century the Ashanti rose up in arms against the British. As a result the British Government brought the West Indian Regiment into Ghana to maintain peace. The Regiment was stationed at Cape Coast between 1873 and 1896. Among the soldiers was a clerical sergeant called John Bryan Small from Barbados in the West Indies. He had been trained for the Christian ministry by the Episcopalian Church in Barbados prior to his enlistment into the army.

He remained in Cape Coast for three years and three months. It was during this period that he decided that if he lived to return to the West Indies, he would retire from the army, seek ordination into Holy Orders and return to West Africa as a missionary. After his return home he retired from the army and visited the United States on his way to England. In the States he came into contact with the Rev. R. H. G. Dyson and Bishop J. J. Clinton who persuaded him to join the African Episcopal Zion Church. In 1896 he was consecrated the Bishop of Mobile in Alabama.

Soon after his consecration Bishop Small visited West Africa. When he was in Ghana at this time he visited his old friends such as Albert Barnes (an eminent engineer), Christian Selby, and the Rev. Kobina Fynn Egyir-Asaam of the Wesleyan Church.

At that time, in 1898, the Rev. Kobina Fynn Egyir-Asaam was the Head Teacher of the Collegiate School, Cape Coast. When Bishop Small returned home he wrote to Rev. Asaam and asked him to recruit:

> suitable young Africans of piety and promise for training in the highest institution of learning of the African Methodist Episcopal Zion Church in America, and to be prepared as ministers for preaching the gospel and evangelizing the people of the Gold Coast (Ghana)[5]

---

[5] F. N. Manuel, "A Brief History of the A.M.E. Zion Church, West Africa" (private manuscript, Cape Coast), p. 3.

The selected institution was to be Livingstone College, Salisbury, North Carolina, U.S.A.

Later, although the Rev. Egyir-Asaam was a Wesleyan Methodist, Bishop Small appointed him Elder and representative of the A.M.E. Zion Church in the Gold Coast. This was possible because Rev. Egyir-Asaam had resigned from the Wesleyan Methodist Church.

It all happened as a consequence of certain political issues taking place during that period. At that time the Rev. Samuel Richard Brew Attoh Ahuma formerly called Samuel Solomon Attoh Ahuma, a Wesleyan Methodist minister, was the editor of a local newspaper, *The Gold Coast Methodist Times*. When the Colonial Government introduced the controversial Lands Bill[6] which sought to vest all "waste land" in the Crown, the chiefs and the intelligentsia opposed it because they felt that the bill was an encroachment on their rights of ownership. The colonial Government was motivated to introduce the Bill because the mining industry was beginning to show signs of prosperity and people were scrambling to acquire concessions. The Bill was intended to check this rush. But since the whole intention was seen as a threat to the rights of owenership, the *Gold Coast Methodist Times* became a vanguard of opposition. The European missionaries of the Methodist Church in Ghana became worried because they were of the opinion that the paper was becoming more political than religious. The editor, Attoh Ahuma, disagreed with his missionary colleagues and declared in 1897:

> We have been indoctrinated as to how a religious paper should be conducted ... we do not intend to wrap up our religion for Sunday use only: we shall continue to go on, so long as we are permitted to be organically connected with this periodical. Our silence on matters political, so far as they traverse the fundamental principles of the Christian faith, will only synchronise with our absence from the editorial chair which position, of course, we occupy on sufferance.[7]

The Methodist Synod was not prepared to compromise their attitude on this matter. They maintained that a Church newspaper should concern itself with religious matters only.

During the same period the Methodist Church in Ghana, through the European missionaries, brought into question the moral integrity of the Rev. Egyir-Asaam. These two events, the uncompromising attitude of the Methodist Synod in the matter of the functions of *The Gold Coast Methodist Times* and the European missionaries' suspicion of the moral

---

[6] See W. E. F. Ward, *A History of Ghana* (London, 1967), passim.

[7] D. Kimble, *A Political History of Ghana*, p. 348 citing. *The Gold Coast Methodist Times*, 15th Nov., 1897. See also Debrunner, *op.cit.*, pp. 233-234.

character of Rev. Egyir-Asaam made Rev. Attoh Ahuma and Egyir-Asaam resign from the Methodist ministry. Rev. Asaam had informed Bishop Small about the friction.

Another Methodist promoter of the A.M.E. Zion Church aspirations in Ghana was Thomas Birch Freeman, the son of the veteran missionary of the Methodist Church in Ghana. He had also resigned from the Methodist Church because he was accused of making a certain woman pregnant.[8]

In 1898 Freeman was authorized by Bishop Small to organize an A.M.E. Zion Church on the Gold Coast. Freeman responded to the invitation and organized the first African Methodist Episcopal Church in Ghana at Keta, Volta Region and later the same year at Cape Coast.

The nationalistic motivation of the AME Zion Church cannot be disputed. Egyir-Asaam confirmed this opinion when a few months after the inaugurations he reported that:

> It is indeed, an entirely Negro Church; organized by Negroes for Negroes, manned, governed, controlled and supported by Negro energy, intellect, liberality and contributions. In fact, it is the sentiment of the Church, that however great may be the friendship, intellect or interest of any white man, in the well-being, Christianization and enlightenment of the Negro race be he European, American or Asiatic, he cannot successfully reach the emotional feelings of the masses of our people.[9]

Soon after the inaugurations, Egyir-Asaam implemented Bishop Small's request that suitable African boys might be recruited for training in the States. The first person to be sent was Emmanuel Kwegyir-Aggrey who at the time was a tutor at the Cape Coast Collegiate School.

Aggrey was born on 18th October, 1875 son of Kodwo Kwegyir and Abena Andowa. He was educated in Anomabu and Cape Coast in Wesleyan Methodist Schools. After his studies he became a teacher and taught at Abura Dunkwa and Cape Coast Wesleyan Schools prior to his appointment to the Collegiate school.

Although he was at first sceptical about Bishop Small's intentions he was persuaded by friends to accept the offer, to go to America. So on 10th July, 1898, Aggrey sailed on the S.S. Accra for England whence he continued his voyage to America.

His education in the States was sponsored by the A.M.E. Zion Church in America. After graduating from Livingstone College, Aggrey decided to remain in America to acquire more knowledge and experience thus

---

[8] Ghana Methodist Archives (Accra): *Gold Coast Synod Minutes, 1885 and 1887.*

[9] Debrunner, *op.cit.*, p. 235, citing Kimble, *op.cit.*, quoting *The Gold Coast Aboriginees*, 26th November, 1898.

defeating the original purpose of the scheme which was to prepare local boys in America as ministers for preaching the gospel to and evangelizing their own people.

In November, 1902 he was ordained as a minister in the African Methodist Episcopal Zion Church in the United States of America. His pastoral work was done mostly in America. Ghana was not to have the privilege of having Aggrey as pastor, as he returned from America only in 1920, in the company of the Phelps-Stokes Commission.

The second pious boy selected by Rev. Asaam to go to America after Aggrey's failure to return home was Frank Arthur who, later on, became known as Frank Ata Osam-Pinanko. He was born on 18th June, 1875 at Dominasi-Abeadzi near Mankesim in the Central Region, son of Egya Ata Otsiwa and Maame Esi Nsedua. He was educated in Wesleyan Methodist schools at Saltpond and Winneba. After finishing his elementary education in 1890 he was appointed a teacher for a year after which he gained admission into the Collegiate School at Cape Coast where he studied for three years, 1891-1893. From the Collegiate school he served as headmaster of the Winneba and Dixcove Wesleyan Schools respectively from 1894 to 1897. In the following year, 1898, he served as a tutor at the Collegiate School under the Rev. Egyir-Asaam.

It was at this time that Bishop Small made a request for the second pious boy to go for training in the United States of America. Rev. Asaam selected Frank Arthur "purely on merit"[10] and despatched him to America in 1899. He studied for four years at Livingstone College graduating with honours, as a Bachelor of Arts in May, 1903. Before the end of his under-graduate studies, he had been ordained a deacon in 1900 and an elder in 1903.

At the end of his studies, unlike Aggrey, he consented to return to his home country and organize the African Methodist Episcopal Zion Church at Cape Coast where he arrived in 1903.

The A.M.E. Zion Church at Cape Coast started to flourish from the time that the Rev. Osam Pinanko arrived back from America.

Soon after his arrival at Cape Coast, the Rev. Pinanko now known as Rev. Frank Arthur organized the African Methodist Episcopal Zion Church (West Gold Coast Conference). The ceremony took place on 25th October, 1903 at de-Graft Hall on Cheetham Street, in Cape Coast. Unfortunately, no record seems to have been preserved relating to the names of the foundation members present at the meeting. But it has been conjectured by Mr. Manuel, the local church historian for the A.M.E. Zion (West Ghana Conference), that people such as Elizabeth Hagan

---

[10] Manuel, *op.cit.*, p. 8.

(Araba Eku) of Jackson Street, David Sam (Rev. Frank Arthur's ward) and chief Amissah (Rev. Arthur's uncle) might have been present.

On Monday, 26th October, 1903, the day following the organization of the Conference, a school was opened at Cape Coast with six boys and a girl as foundation members.

Three months later the church and the school were transferred from de Graft Hall to Hockman's Hotel on Ashanti Road because the former house was found to be inadequate for expansion. The first floor of the Hockman's Hotel was used as the Mission House and the school, designated "Varick Memorial Institute" or "Ata's School", occupied the rest of the Hotel.

Six months after the organization of the church it became necessary to employ a second teacher to help the Rev. Frank Arthur who had been the first and only teacher of the school. The reason was that the number of the pupils on the role increased so much that the Rev. Frank Arthur could not cope with the school and his pastoral work. Consequently, on 9th April, 1904, Mr. Isaac Sackey was employed as a teacher.

The circumstances which led to the employment of Mr. Sackey were providential. It happened that Mr. Sackey gave his pair of shoes to a cobbler, Charles Ata, for repair. Mr. Sackey waited for a very long time without getting his pair of shoes back. Afterwards he learnt that the cobbler had moved to a new station at Cape Coast. Mr. Sackey pursued him to Cape Coast and picked a quarrel with him. During the course of the argument the cobbler, who was a brother to the Rev. Frank Arthur Osam Pinanko, cooled down Mr. Sackey by telling him that his brother, Rev. Arthur had returned from America, had opened a school and needed teachers urgently. Mr. Sackey showed interest and became calm. He requested to be introduced to the Reverend gentleman and the cobbler obliged taking Mr. Sackey to the Rev. Arthur by whom he was immediately employed.

After the employment of Mr. Sackey the enrolment continued to grow and this led to the employment of other teachers. They were Mr. Dziewu Frans, Mr. Isaac Edward Daniel Hayfron and Mr. W. W. Whyte a West Indian. Most of these men were later ordained into Holy Orders.

Meanwhile, the Rev. Frank Arthur Osam Pinanko was free to concentrate his attention on evangelical work. He was a zealous evangelist and through open air preaching on Sunday afternoon and moonlit night open air services during the week days, he won many members, some of whom defected from sister churches in Cape Coast. The most significant of his achievements at the initial stage was the conversion of some of the members of a Cape Coast traditional singing band known as "Baanan". The group used to compose music whose words were designed to expose evils perpetrated secretly by some of the influential members of the community. Through Rev. Pinanko's teaching and preaching four of the group's leaders, Kodzo Apa, S. Tom Otoo, Robert Mensah and David Kofi Brown became converted, joined the church "and used their melodious voices and talents in the laudable service of our Lord Jesus Christ".[11] Later, in 1910, Brown was ordained priest.

Having laid the foundation firmly at Cape Coast the Rev. Frank Arthur Osam Pinanko reached out. The first call came from Twifo in 1906. In response the Rev. Moses Dziewu Frans was sent there to organize the church.

The second call came from Winneba in 1908. The opening ceremony of the Winneba church was conducted by the Rev. Frank Arthur Osam Pinanko accompanied by lay delegates from Cape Coast. Through the evangelical zeal of Sackey, stationed at Winneba, other stations were opened at Akim Akroso, Akim Manso, Agona Asafo, Tekyiman and Osenasi in the Akim Abuakwa district.

Attention has been drawn above to the beginning of the A.M.E. Zion educational work. The small educational beginning in Cape Coast in 1903 developed to become an important feature of the AME Zion evangelical work. Wherever a church was opened a school was attached. Thus during a brief period there were many AME Zion primary schools in the country.

A few secondary schools were also established, the most important of which, during the time of writing this book, was the Aggrey Memorial Secondary School, a co-educational institution at Cape Coast, the Headquarters of the A.M.E. Zion Church, Ghana (the Western Conference).

The first A.M.E. Zion Annual Conference in Ghana was convened at Cape Coast in February, 1908 under the chairmanship of the Rev. Frank Arthur Osam Pinanko. The second one was convened in March 1910 under the chairmanship of Bishop Alexander Walters who was on a visit from the United States of America. It took place at Prospect Hill in Cape Coast. At this conference Bishop Walters ordained into the Christian ministry David Kofi Brown, Isaac Sackey, Isaac Samuel Cole, Moses Dziewu Frans and Samuel Banson.

With this band of ordained ministers many more stations were added to the first three: Cape Coast, Twifo and Winneba. As most of the missionaries were nationals the Zion Church did not feel the impact of the 1914 war on the progress of their work. Many stations from Sekondi in the West, to Koforidua in the east, were opened during the war. Many of the achievements of the A.M.E. Zion church (Western Ghana Con-

---

[11] *Ibid.*, p. 44.

ference) during the period under discussion were made possible because of the zeal and devotion of the pioneer missionary, the Rev. Frank Arthur Osam Pinanko.

Meanwhile, in the Eastern Section of the country, the A.M.E. Zion Church, organized in 1898 by Thomas B. Freeman Junior at Keta was making progress. At first Freeman could not reach out because of lack of money. For example, although he was an energetic pioneer and tried to open stations at Accra, Lagos and a few other places his efforts outside Keta did not succeed. He was able to survive the strains of poverty at Keta because Bishop Small and others sent him donations. For instance Bishop Small sent him $50.00 and also persuaded the General Conference in 1900 to remit Freeman $100.00. Another benefactor was the Rev. Dr. Owen L. W. Smith, Resident Minister and Consul General to Liberia at the time. He also donated $50.00 to assist Freeman establish firmly the A.M.E. Zion Church in the Eastern Section of the Gold Coast. Gradually the financial position improved and by 1902 Keta was a flourishing A.M.E. Zion mission station with a school. The leading Missionary was the Rev. Joseph D. Taylor assisted by William Hockman, S. F. Abbam and C. L. Acolatse.

On March 31, 1910 Bishop Walters organized and held the first session of the East Gold Coast Conference at Keta. There were five ministers and nine lay delegates present and Brothers Harold Nkwaun and G. A. Tay were ordained deacons. Three teachers were also admitted to the Conference. The strength of the Keta congregation then was 300 members and 270 day school scholars.

During World War I Mrs. Henrietta Peters and Miss Lillian Tshabalala were sent to Keta and by 1919 Rev. R. E. Peters was in charge of the East Gold Coast Conference. Full expansion of the A.M.E. Zion Church in the East Gold Coast Conference took place after the end of the period being discussed in this book.

PART THREE

CONCLUSIONS

CHAPTER FIFTEEN

CHRISTIAN MISSIONS IN CATASTROPHE 1914-1919

The period 1914-1919 was catastrophic for the world. World War I broke out in August 1914 between Germany and the allied nations: Britain and France. The disabilities the war imposed on the world had a far reaching impact on the church all over the world.

In West Africa, Togo was one of the theatres of conflict because she was the main German territory and was flanked by two territories belonging to the allied nations: British Gold Coast and French Dahomey.

Togo capitulated to the allied forces early in the war and came under the control of Britain during the rest of the war. At first, Britain did not disturb the German missionaries working in Togo and the Gold Coast. The Gold Coast Government appreciated so much the good work the Basel missionaries were doing that at the onset of hostilities it directed that they should not be molested. In fact the Government called for penalties on any "who seek to molest those who have for many years been amongst us as our good friends and guests."[1]

The Basel mission had Swiss foundation but most of its missionaries working in the Gold Coast at the time were German. In spite of that and in response to the Government's generosity the missionaries declared their neutrality claiming that they were not German but Swiss.[2]

As Togo came under the British sphere of influence the fate of the missionaries there was also determined by the policy of the Gold Coast Government. Consequently, they too were also protected from molestation.

In practice this generous policy did not last long. Before the end of 1914, in November, the Basel Mission missionaries in the Gold Coast were removed from their stations to Accra. After a few days they were released to return to their various stations. They had to report to the police regularly and some restrictions were also imposed on their movements. For example, with the exception of leave to visit the schools, they had to request permission before they travelled beyond a few miles from their stations. Later they were permitted to visit their village congregations but official permission was to be sought from the Gold Coast Government before other head stations were visited.

---

[1] Groves, *op.cit.*, Vol. IV p. 18 citing *International Review of Missions*. IV (1915), 41, n.2.
[2] *The Gold Coast Leader* (Cape Coast), 5th Sept. 1914.

In 1915, the Government's attitude to the missionaries hardened. On 19th August of that year the Acting Colonial Secretary wrote to the General Superintendent forbidding the Basel missionaries on the Gold Coast to hold any meeting while the war continued and warned that:

> any proved case of an attempt by a missionary to use his influence disloyally to the British administration will be dealt with very severely and that any individual misdemeanour may be punished by the immediate internment of the German missionaries.[3]

In the following year the British Government requested the Basel Mission to send, in future, only native-born Swiss missionaries to the Gold Coast. The Mission Board in Basel refused to accede to the request on the grounds that such an action would defeat the international character of the Basel Missionary Society.[4] The British Foreign Office reacted angrily to the Basel Mission Board's view point and gave notice that the Basel Mission would no longer be permitted to operate in a British dependency because the Mission was German in sympathy.

A year later, on 10th December, 1917, the Colonial Secretary wrote to G. Zurcher, the General Superintendent of the Basel Mission in the Gold Coast saying that

> I am directed by the Governor to inform you that His Excellency has received instructions from the Secretary of State for the Colonies that all Basel missionaries of German nationality are to be deported with the least possible delay and that action is being taken accordingly.[5]

It seems that this reversal of the previous sympathetic attitude of the British Colonial Government towards the Basel Mission was precipitated by the Press in the Gold Coast. There appears to have been some trouble in Kumasi and *the Gold Coast Leader* published an article reporting that:

> The rising has been caused through certain Basel missionaries trekking up and down the country and persuading the poor ignorant people into the belief that the Hun is sure to come out victorious in the present world struggle and that he would have no favour for them if they did not kick against the veritable pricks—the allies.[6]

Altough the Rev. Zurcher wrote a letter on 23rd May, 1917, to the Colonial Secretary, refuting the allegation nothing could revert the

---

[3] Smith, *The Presbyterian Church of Ghana, op.cit.*, p. 147 citing *Scottish Mission records*, "Colonial Secretary to General Superintendent", 19th August, 1915.

[4] *Ibid.*, pp. 19-21. "The ecumenical and international character of the Mission is illustrated by the sphere of labour entered into by men trained at the seminary [in Basel].

[5] *Ibid.*, p. 150, citing *Scottish Correspondence*, "Colonial Secretary to General Superintendent," 10th December, 1917.

[6] *The Gold Coast Leader* (Cape Coast), No.769, 5th May, 1917, p. 2.

Government's decision. So in December 1917 the missionaries were arrested.

The occasion at Akropong Seminary was a pathetic spectacle. On 7th December, 1917, the usual teachers' end of year examination was in progress. The Rev. Stricker, a native Swiss and head of the Teacher Training Department was invigilating late in the afternoon. The other members of staff were conversing together outside when a District Commissioner accompanied by an escort policeman arrived in the school and enquired for Mr. Stricker. Mrs. Stricker met the D. C. and the news was divulged: Stricker was made to convey to his German colleagues that the Government had decided to deport them, and that they were to be taken down to Accra that very evening.[7]

They were allowed only one hour to pack their baggage. After that the Principal of the Seminary, Jehle, together with Nothwang, Morninger- and Grau were placed in a lorry without roof and conveyed to Accra. Stricker and Mrs. Grau alone remained at Akropong: Stricker because he was a native Swiss and Mrs. Grau because she was in the family way. On account of this Grau was allowed to return to Akropong the following day. Thus Grau alone had the chance to dispose of his personal effects before he and his wife left for Accra.

The people of Akropong did not desert the missionaries at the time of misfortune. They crowded round them and everybody felt it was not easy to say good-bye without tears.[8] So by 16th December, 1917 the interned missionaries were deported.

The eight non-German missionaries were left behind. Six were native Swiss: H. Stricker in charge of the Akropong College, G. Zurcher at Aburi and H. Henking at Abetifi; one was American, N. Rohde also stationed at Abetifi and the other an Australian, F. Jost, at Kumasi.

To the utter surprise of these missionaries, it became illegal as from 12th January, 1918, for any European alien to remain on the Akwapim ridge. Zurcher tried to negotiate with the Government for permission to remove the seminary from Akropong to Odumase or Anum; but the request was not granted and on 2nd February, 1918, the remaining missionaries were ordered to leave the country by the next boat. Zurcher protested against the expulsion order but his protest was rejected by the Colonial Secretary and the order was implemented. "Thus", says Smith, "after close on ninety years of dedicated endeavour, during which

---

[7] G. G. Gunn, *A Hundred Years, 1848-1948: The Story of the Presbyterian Training College, Akropong,* cyclostyled ed. (Akropong, 1966), p. 8.

[8] *Loc. cit.*

the mission initiated far reaching religious and social changes ... it was thrust out of the country.''[9]

The fate of the German missionaries in Eweland was similar to that of the Basel missionaries described above. Those who were working in the English speaking territory of Eweland such as Keta were arrested in June 1916 and by 10th January, 1918 all the Bremen missionaries with the exception of the Rev. Ernst Burgi and his family were deported. Burgi was permitted to remain behind in Eweland because he was native Swiss. He supervised all aspects of the Bremen mission work alone during the crisis.

The most far-reaching impact of the crisis on the Bremen mission in Eweland was that it became divided into two: the Ewe Presbyterian Church of Togoland and the Ewe Presbyterian Church in the Gold Coast. The division came about as a result of the war. At the end of the war, Togoland (formerly German) was partitioned between the French and the British—the allies—whose combined forces defeated German Togo. By the terms of the Paris Conference in 1919, Lome and the whole of the coast line of the former German jurisdiction in Togo together with part of the interior were assigned to France as mandated territory; whilst Britain was given mandatory powers over Kete Krachi, Yendi and Ho districts. So ended the history of one Bremen Mission in Eweland.

After the hostilities the British Colonial Government invited the Scottish Presbyterians who were working in Nigeria, another English-speaking territory, under the auspices of the United Church of Scotland, to continue the Presbyterian work in the Gold Coast. Accordingly, the Rev. A. W. Wilkie, Secretary of the Calabar Mission Council of the United Free Church of Scotland was permitted in 1918 by his Home Committee to move to the Gold Coast and take charge of the Presbyterian work. Thus with the arrival of the Rev. Wilkie in the Gold Coast in 1918 "one important orphaned mission was allotted its foster parents.''[10]

It was not only in the German territories that the war had a negative impact on the missionaries' activities. In the English-speaking areas also the missionaries endured many hardships which hampered their activities. During the war it was difficult to send new missionaries to the field and this led to the reduction of missionary man power. Secondly, the belligerent conditions restricted vital supplies to the missionaries because mail boats were irregular due to the fear of submarine warfare. In spite of this problem, however, the allied control of the seas maintained a trickle of supplies throughout the war years. Thirdly, inadequate

---

[9] Smith, *op.cit.*, p. 152.
[10] Groves, *op.cit.*, Vol. IV, p. 20

supplies naturally increased the cost of commodities. Finally, these problems taken together curtailed the recruitment of new staff to the mission field despite the fact that Harris's[11] evangelism between 1913 and 1915 had brought into the Christian community in West Africa, especially Ghana, a motley collection of new converts who needed post-conversion training and Christian education.

In spite of all these problems the church endured the storm because the African ministers and lay workers rallied round the few missionaries left behind and together kept alive the church throughout the frustrating experiences of World War I.

And through it all the Christian Missions in English-speaking West Africa emerged successfully standing on the threshold of new opportunities, opportunities destined to lead the Churches in West Africa after 1919 from Missionary control to that of autonomous African Churches.

---

[11] William Wade Harris was a Kru man of the Grebo tribe in Liberia. He had a vision and became an itinerant preacher along the West Coast of Africa during World War I.

CHAPTER SIXTEEN

APPRAISAL

The common feature running through the preceding pages is the stubborn persistence with which Western missionaries flocked to West Africa, during the period discussed, despite heart-rending disasters. The obvious question to ask is "why did they take such dangerous risks to come and evangelize the African?"

The answer to be deduced from the records is that they were motivated by the poor image they had had about the African. For example, Mary Kingsley observed that most of the early missionaries regarded

> the African minds as many jugs, which had only to be emptied of the stuff which is in them and refilled with particular form of doctrine they, the missionaries, were engaged in teaching....[1]

Again a Baptist missionary from America described Africans as "the dark race... constitutionally inferior to the white [but] are capable of being elevated by the same forces that elevate others."[2]

Another example, for our purpose, is taken from the Church Missionary Society. In the Society's publication *Nigeria, the Unknown* (London), p.8 Nigeria was described as:

> A land formless, mysterious, terrible, ruled by witchcraft and the terrorism of secret; where the skull was worshipped and blood-sacrifices were offered to *jujus*; where guilt was decided by ordeal of prison and burning oil; where scores of people were murdered when a chief died, and his wives decked themselves in finery and were strangled to keep him company in spirit land; where men and women were satiated with feeding on human flesh; where twins were done to death and the mother banished to the bush; where semi-nakedness was compulsory; and girls were sent to the farms to be fattened for marriage.[3]

Apart from these particular illustrations, it is true in general terms, that most of the early missionaries thought and believed that the African had no religion of his own, he had no system of traditional education and he had no culture of his own. Consequently, they, the missionaries felt

---

[1] Max Warren, *Social History and Christian Mission* (London, 1967), p. 75 citing Mary Kingsley, "The Development of Dodos", *The National Review*, Vol. XXVII (March to August 1896)— March, 1896.

[2] Sadler, *op.cit.*, p. 43.

[3] *Ibid.*, p. 56.

themselves divinely called to take their Western religion and civilization to Africa.

This Western derogatory attitude has been clearly articulated in this German hymn, specially composed, for mission fields in India, Africa and non-Western countries.

Nu nyui geɖewo sɔ gbɔ
Le nuto mawo me.
Anyigba ya nyo ŋutɔ
Gake ameawo gble.
Mawu ƒe dɔmenyonyo
Gba go ɖe wo dzi dzro
Ati kple kpe wosubɔ,
Womenya Mawu o.[4]

From this so-called depraved nature the Western missionaries, regarding themselves as a superior people, felt themselves called to deliver the Africans. This is why they composed and sang:

Can we, whose souls are lighted
With wisdom from on high,
Can we to men benighted
The lamp of life deny.
Salvation! O salvation!
The joyful sound proclaim,
Till each remotest nation
Has learned Messiah's name.[5]

Thus, from the foregoing, it may safely be concluded that the Western missionaries risked their lives to come to Africa because of the derogatory and poor image they had about Africans. They felt that they were divinely commissioned to save the perishing people from "errors chains." But this is not the whole truth. It was also the case that some of them believed that they would be rewarded in a special way in the life hereafter if they laboured successfully in the mission field. It appears that this was one of the reasons why, during the period covered in this book, the criterion used by the missionaries in evaluating the success of their efforts was mainly numerical and geographical expansion. The extent of the expansion determined the nature of the ultimate reward.

Although their intention may seem humanitarian and attractive to the missionaries many Africans levelled numerous criticisms against their

---

[4] E.P. Church Hymn Book No.166 in Ewe. This verse may be paraphrased in English thus: In those regions (Africa and India) the land is fertile, but the inhabitants are corrupt; may they have a share in God's grace; they worship wood and stone, they do not know God (they have no religion).

[5] Methodist Hymn Book No.801.

work. The gist of the criticisms has been summed up in these words by Ayandele:

> ...missionary activity was a disruptive force, rocking traditional society to its very foundations, denouncing ordered polygamy in favour of disordered monogamy, producing disrespectful, presumptuous and detribalized children through the mission schools, destroying the high moral principles and orderliness of indigenous society through denunciation of traditional religion, without an adequate substitute, and transforming the mental outlook of [West Africans] in a way that made them imitate European values slavishly, whilst holding in irrational contempt valuable features of traditional culture.[6]

This is why probably some of the African critics maintain that the main aim of the missionary was exploitation and not evangelism.

The reason why the critics had this negative attitude to Christianity in Africa is that they maintain that the introduction of Christianity into Africa brought conflict between the indigenous values and the Western ones.[7] For example, the missionaries opposed some of the traditional social and religious practices which were the foundations upon which African societies were built. Ancestor worship, a vital aspect of West African Traditional Religion, for instance, was banned in the Church. Other taboos imposed by the missionaries include the prohibition of polygamy, a socially accepted African system of marriage; forbidding of slavery, a viable economic arrangement among the Yoruba. Above all Christianity displaced the authority of the traditional elders; the very nature of the faith of the new converts made them flout the authority of unconverted chiefs, parents and the extended family.

It is true that missionaries were trouble shooters in the mission field as illustrated by the stories narrated in the preceding chapters of this book; indeed the missionary was a revolutionary because the Christian message does turn the world upside down. This is why Ayandele observed that "no society could be Christianized without its being upset to a considerable extent."[8] It is because of this revolutionary nature of Christianity that we may agree with the critics that the missionaries in actuality brought with them some process of disintegration in West African societies. They incited slaves against their masters in Nigeria; they broke tribal solidarity by building Salems (Christian quarters) for the new converts; they requested polygamist converts to divorce all their wives but

---

[6] Ayandele, *The Missionary Impact on Modern Nigeria, op.cit.*, p. 329. For an examination of specific criticisms, see Harris Mobley, *The Ghanaian's Image of the Missionary* (Leiden, E. J. Brill, 1970) and Ram Desai ed., *Christianity in Africa as Seen by Africans* (Denver, Alan Swallow 1962).

[7] *Ibid.*, p. 18.

[8] Ayandele, *op.cit.*, p. 330.

one; they introduced the concept that what was important for a person was his relationship with God and therefore he, not the family or the group, must make the decision;[9] but in Africa, a person exists because he belongs to a group; even death does not disintegrate his group solidarity. In later years Ghanaian Christians in Ashanti rebelled against traditional taboo's such as the Asaase Yaa taboo. Certainly Christianity was to some extent revolutionary, disruptive and divisive in West African societies.

In spite of this conclusion the study of both secular and ecclesiastical histories of West Africa shows evidence that most of the critics have not been sufficiently objective in their approach; they were extremely biased against the missions. Consequently, they over-estimated their prejudices at the expense of all the facts.

In order to put this right a clear distinction must be drawn between the Westerners who were missionaries and those who were administrators. The truth about Christianity is that although it is revolutionary and possesses "subversive" potentialities, the missionaries did not have any compulsory tool for compelling people to accept their revolutionary teaching apart from suspending culprits from membership for a time or denying them the sacrament of the Lord's supper. In Ashanti, the Christians could not change the Asaase Yaa taboo as they had wished. Many chiefs did not approve of some of the vital changes, which the missionaries would have liked to make. In such circumstances the missionaries did compromise. For instance, Ayandale observed that in the interior of Yorubaland the missionaries compromised "their culture and Christian principles by joining *Ogboni*, by giving polygamists positions of responsibility in the church and by allowing their wards to take 'pagan' titles."[10]

As regards slavery, marriage, ancestor-worship and other cultural prohibitions by the missionaries, it is clear that the African Christians did not accept the ban introduced by the missionaries. Slavery continued among the Yoruba Christians of Nigeria because "inheritance was attached to it (slavery), and as inheritance was a family issue, 'pagan' and Muslim relatives had an interest in the preservation of the institution."[11] The social and economic value of slaves in Nigeria coupled with the Yoruba custom where relatives but not children inherited a man's property, made it difficult for the Yoruba Christians to accept the Western teaching on slavery. The best way out of the problem for the missionaries was a kind of compromise. Slave owning Christians were not excom-

---

[9] *Loc.cit.*
[10] *Ibid.*, p. 331.
[11] *Ibid.*, p. 333.

municated. Rather some of the mission bodies, such as the CMS in
Nigeria and the Bremen mission in Eweland of Ghana redeemed some of
the slaves according to the traditional practice of redemption and gave
them freedom and Christian training.

The absolute destruction of slavery was hastened by the Colonial
political administrators but not by the missionaries. The administrators
instructed their soldiers to set slaves free arbitrarily, that is without the
payment of redemption fee to their owners. This method promoted more
dissatisfaction and disruption in West African slave owning societies than
the missionary approach described above.

The church has always outlawed polygamy. Yet the denominations all
over West Africa tolerate polygamists in the churches and accept their
material gifts with appreciation and blessing. It is outside the scope of this
work to examine the vital reasons why polygamy has persisted in the
church in spite of the missionary ban of it.[12] But the point being made is
that in introducing Christian marriage in the West African Church, the
missionaries did not disrupt the society as much as the critics would have
us believe. It was again the Western administrator who actually did. For
when the divorce laws were introduced by the Colonial administrators into the "Native Courts" in West Africa an individual could, without the
traditional arbitration by the families of the couple, pay a minimum sum
prescribed by the 'Native Courts' and obtain divorce even on trivial
grounds. Traditionally, the marriage of two people was a matter for two
families. Both families had it as their responsibility to try as much as
possible to prevent divorce by wise arbitration. So some scholars maintain that in traditional West Africa:

> divorce was very rare and it needed the commitment of the gravest crimes
> by the husband—not poverty or misfortune—before the consent of all
> members of the wife's extented family... could be obtained for such a
> disgraceful decision.[13]

There are other ways in which the Colonial administration disturbed
West African societies more than the missionaries. For example, some of
the Colonial commissioners did not accord respect to the local chiefs and
therefore undermined their authority and prestige. This led to the in-
subordination and disobedience of some of the inhabitants majority of
whom were not yet converted because the chiefs could no longer inflict
traditional punishments such as death, flogging etc. But both the missionaries and administrators were equally disruptive of society in matters

---

[12] Those who are interested in this aspect of polygamy may turn to Ayandele, *ibid.*, pp.
334 ff.

[13] *Ibid.*, p. 337.

of industrial and technical training. In the case of the missionaries the industrial and technical (practical) education they offered made some of the scholars desert the villages for the towns to earn more money. A few, like Tetteh Quarshie, left their countries and went to neighbouring states in search of more lucrative jobs. As for the administrators they were interested in developing their administration in the towns. Consequently, they recruited into the towns some of the men academically trained by the church for work in the villages. They were employed for white-collar jobs, comparatively, an easier way of earning money than manual labour. As a result some of the converts trained in the agricultural institutions by the missionaries left agriculture and drifted to the towns for white-collar job employment. Probably, this need for clerks explains why the missions, except the Presbyterians lay more emphasis on learning English rather than on the vernaculars. Surely the exodus from village life into "city" life is a strong force of disruption of the traditional society. But by and large the methods used by the missionaries (the temporary suspensions and the denial of certain privileges) to make their converts acquiesce to their new teachings were not generally as decisive as the political and military methods used by the colonial administrators in subduing the Africans.

From the foregoing it may now be agreed that those critics, who consider missionary work as being the *only* agent of disruption and being productive of only negative results in West Africa, have not examined carefully all the relevant facts.

This conclusion is supported by other more objective critics who agree that the Christian missions introduced some revolutionary and disruptive elements into the West African society. In some instances, Christianity *did* undermine some of the cherished cultural and integrative values of traditional African Society. But they also agree that Christianity has produced some concrete and positive results in West Africa. For this class of critics let Dr. E. Amu speak:

> There is no denying the fact that of all Europeans in Africa the missionary is the African's best friend. But there are those who, whilst realizing the many human failings with which Christianity has unfortunately come to be identified as well as serious mistakes made in the past as regards the method of approach to Christianity, are nevertheless filled with thanks to God for what He had done in Africa through the missionaries and are themselves helping in every way to carry into effect the new Africa for which so many missionaries gave and are still giving their lives.[14]

---

[14] Harris W. Mobley, *The Ghanaian's Image of the Missionary* (Leiden, E. J. Brill, 1970), p. 144.

In concluding this book it can be asserted that Christian missions during the period surveyed succeeded in founding the Christian Church in West Africa. In the process of their work they used methods some of which commenced the process of social change and disintegration in West African Societies. This latter point made some West African critics look upon the work of the missions without any favour.

Yet in spite of the mistakes which the missionaries made their work did bear some useful fruits: the schools they built did not only serve as fertile grounds for evangelism; they also produced nationalists whose patriotism and Christian concept of freedom originated educated opposition to Colonial rule. Agricultural and technical training were introduced by the missionaries as a vital aspect of evangelism but the colonial administrators did not encourage this aspect of the missionary training.

The factors which contributed to the success of the work of the missionaries during the period include: the pre-nineteenth century unsuccessful attempts made by the Castle chaplains and individual Christians, the spiritual conviction of the missionaries that they were divinely charged to preach the Gospel to Africans; the quality of the sermons they preached; the divine grace which made the hearers respond to the gospel message; the continual assessment of their strategies and efforts; the material benefits the educated derived from attending the schools; the medical work introduced in the stations; other social welfare activities carried out among the converts; the help given by the Colonial administrators in subduing strong nationalist African opposition to the missionaries and the work and sacrifice of the African agents, itinerant traders, farmers and government officials. From all this it is more true to say that the main aim of the missionary was evangelism rather than exploitation.

But the West African Churches established by the missionaries at the end of this survey had a very serious weakness; most of the African members of the churches were hypocrites; they lived a life of double standard. This was unconsciously encouraged by the missionaries themselves. It had been pointed out already that the missionaries denied the validity of most of the traditional beliefs and taught the converts to deny them too.

For example, in the Gold Coast (Ghana) the Christian Council asserted "that witchcraft was not a reality but only a psychological delusion."[15] I was told that at one of the meetings of some of the officials of the same Christian Council a person who claimed to be a wizard was in-

---

[15] Desai, *op.cit.*, p. 130.

vited to talk to the Council officials about his experiences. At the end of
his address, he offered to demonstrate the reality of witchcraft to the officials. They were excited and asked him to go ahead. He requested that
any of them might offer one of their children upon whom he would exercise his witchcraft. But the officials, who had published in a pamphlet on
witchcraft that witchcraft was a psychological delusion, refused to offer
their children and asked the gentleman to exercise his witchcraft on a
ripened pawpaw fruit.

The point of this story is the fact "that no amount of denial on the part
of the Church will expel belief in supernatural powers from the minds of
the African people."[16] From the reaction of the Christian Council officials referred to above it is clear that some African Christians denounce
certain beliefs and practices only superficially. This kind of attitude does
lead to hypocrisy. This was what precisely happened to the West African
Christian during the period discussed.

The missionaries did not believe in the existence of other supernatural
beings apart from their God and the Holy Spirit. So they taught the
African converts that their belief in witchcraft and other divinities was a
superstition i.e. "belief in something which does not exist." Superficially
the converts accepted the teaching but deep-down the heart, they did not.
This is so because we Africans live:

> in a world of mysterious forces, natural and supernatural, and [our] ideas of
> these are very different from those of [western] culture.[17]

We have already referred to the church's negative attitude to the other
social and religous heritage of the African. All these produced a
disintegrated African Christian. He did not completely absorb Christianity and did not entirely sever himself from vital traditional beliefs and
practices. Consequently, he behaved as a "Christian" in the
missionary's presence; but behind him in the real crisis of life he went
secretly to the traditional medicine man or spiritualist.

This, in my opinion, was a very disheartening weakness of the missionary church in West Africa. Whether or not Christianity in West
Africa would take firm root depended upon how the missionaries and
African Christians dealt with this weakness after the period of this
survey. The church had to reappraise itself. Missionaries had to
recognize that their idea that African supernatural beliefs were supersti-
tions is not Biblical but an expression of Western scientific approach to
life. African Christians had to recognize that one of the attitudes Jesus

---

[16] *Ibid.*, p. 131.
[17] D. W. T. Shropshire, *The Church and Primitive Peoples* (London, S.P.C.K. 1938) cited
by Desai *op.cit.*, p. 131.

found most grievous and condemned was hypocrisy and it was incumbent on the church to cure its members of double living. If the church were to succeed in this task it has to sift authentic Christianity from Western cultural accretions and adopt a new approach to African social, spiritual and religious heritage. This is the challenge for the future.

BIBLIOGRAPHY

Agbebi, Mojola, *Inaugural Sormon Delivered at the Celebrations of the First Anniversary of the African Church* (Lagos, 1902).

Agbeti, J. K. "Missionary Enterprise, Education and Nationhood in Ghana since 1828." Unpublished S.T.M. Thesis, Yale Divinity School, U.S.A. 1967.

—— *Christian Missions and Theological Training.*(ms)

Agyemang, Fred. *We Presbyterians* (Accra-North, 1978).

Ajayi, J. F. A. *Christian Missions in Nigeria 1841-1891. The Making of a New Elite* (Longman, 1965).

—— and Epsie, Ian eds. *A Thousand Years in West AfricanHistory* (Ibadan, 1965).

Ansre, G. B. "Missionary Work in Peki 1847-1853. From Germany to Gabon and then to Peki." (Mimeographed, n.d).

Ayandele, E. A. *The Missionary Impact on Modern Nigeria 1842-1914. A Political and Social Analysis* (Longman, 1966).

Bane, M. J. *Catholic Pioneers in West Africa* (Dublin, 1956).

Bartels, F. L. "Jacobus Elisha Capitein 1712-1747." *Transactions of the Historical Society of Ghana.* Vol. IV Part I.

—— "Philip Quaque." *Transactions of the Gold Coast and Togoland Historical Society.* Vol.I Part V.

—— *The Roots of Ghana Methodism.* (Cambridge, 1965).

Beecham, John. *Ashantee and the Gold Coast* (London, 1841).

Biggs, Wilfred W. *An Introduction to the History of the Christian Church* (London, Edward and Arnold, 1965).

Birtwhistle, A. W. *Thomas Birch Freeman* (London. 1946).

Burns, A. *History of Nigeria.* (London. 1969).

Blyth, G. *Reminiscences of Missionary Life* (1851).

Cason, Walter, "The Growth of Christianity in the Liberian Environment." Unpublished Ph. D. Thesis. Columbia University, 1962.

Cauthen, Baker J., et al. *Advance: A History of Southern Baptist Foreign Missions* (Broadman Press. Nashville, Tennessee, 1970).

Cooke, J. E. *Frederic Bancoft. Historian and three hitherto Unpublished Essays on the Colonization of American Negroes from 1801-1865* (Oklahoma, 1957).

Crowther, D. C. *The Establishment of the Niger Delta Pastorate 1864-92* (Liverpool, 1907).

Debrunner, H. W. *A History of Christianity in Ghana* (Accra, 1967).

—— "Notable Danish Chaplains of the Gold Coast." *Transactions of the Gold Coast and Togoland Historical Society."* Vol. II, 1956.

—— *The Church in Togo. A Church between Colonial Powers* (London 1965).

Der, Benedict, "Church State Relations in Northern Ghana, 1906-1940." *Transactions of the Historical Society of Ghana.* Vol.XV(I), 1977.

Desai, Ram. *Christianity in Africa as Seen by Africans* (Denver, Alan Swallow 1962).

Die Ewe Stammen (Bremen).

Duval, L. M. *Baptist Missions in Nigeria* (Richmond, Virginia, USA, 1928).

Ellis, A. B. *History of the Gold Coast of Africa* (London).

E. P. Church Ho. "The Formation of the North German Missionary Society." Mimeographed n.d.).

—— *Hymn Book*

Epelle, E. M. T. *The Church in the Niger Delta* (Port Harcourt, 1955).

Findlay, G, and Holdsworth, W., *History of Wesleyan Missionary Society*, 4 Vols. (London 1921-24).

Fox, W. *History of Wesleyan Missions in West Africa* (Lon., 1850).

Forster, R. S. *The Sierra Leone Church. A Contemporary Study* (London SPCK., 1961).

Freeman, T. B. *Journal of Various Visits to the Kingdom of Ashanti, Aku and Dahomey* (London, 1844).

Garrett, T. S. and Jeffery, R. M. C. *Unity in Nigeria* (London 1965).

Garrison, Lloyd. *Thoughts on African Colonization* (Boston: Garrison and Knapp, 1832).

Glover, Lady. *Life of Sir John Hawley Glover.* (1897).

Gold Coast, *Legislative Council Debates 4th Feb. 1918.*

Goldie, Hugh. *Calabar and Its Mission* (Edinburgh, 1890).

Gray, J. M. *History of the Gambia* (Frank Cass &Co.).

Grimley, John B. and Robinson Gordon E. *Church Growth in Central and Southern Nigeria* (1966).

Groves, C. P. *The Planting of Christianity in Africa*, 4 Vols. (London, 1948-58).

Gunn, G. G. *A Hundred Years, 1848-1948. The Story of the Prosbyterian Training College, Akropong.* Cyclosted (*Akropong, 1966*).

Halligey, J. T. F. *Methodism in West Africa* (*London, 1907*).

Hatton, D. J. *Missiology in Africa Today* (Dublin, M. H. Gill & Sons Ltd., 1961).

Hayford, C. M. *West Africa and Christianity* (London, 1901).

Herskovits, J. "Liberated Africans and the History of Lagos Colony to 1886". Unpublished. D. Phil Thesis. Oxford, 1960.

Hewett. J. F. *European Settlements on the West Coast of Africa* (London, 1862).

Hinderer, Anna. *Seventeen Years in Yoruba Country, Memoirs of the Wife of David Hinderer Compiled by her Friends* (London, 1872).

Johnson, T. S. *The Story of a Mission. The Sierra Leone Church. First Daughter of CMS* (London, SPCK, 1953).

Kalu Ogbu ed. *The Nigerian Story* (Ibadan, Day Star 1976).

Kerrow, J. M. *History of Foreign Missions of the Session and United Presbyterian Church* (1869).

Kimble, D. *A Political History of Ghana. The Rise of Gold Coast Nationalism, 1850-1928* (Oxford, 1963).

Labouret, H., *Encyclopedia of Islam.* Vol. III (London).

Latourette, S. K. *The Expansion of Christianity*, 4 Vols. (Harper & Row).

Lucas, J. O. *History of St. Paul's Church Breadfruit, Lagos* (Lagos, 1954).

MacFarlan D. *Calabar: the Church of Scotland Mission 1846-1946* (London, 1946).

Major, R. H. *The Discoveries of Prince Henry the Navigator and their Results*, 2nd ed.(*1877*).

Manuel F. N. "A Brief History of the A.M.E. Zion Church, West Africa", (Private Manuscript, Cape Coast).

Marshall, James, Sir, *Reminiscences of West Africa and its Mission* (1865).

Mays, B. E. and Nicholson, J. W. *The Negro's Church* (New York: Institute of Social and Religious Research, 1933).

Methodist Hymn Book.

Mobley, Harris W. *The Ghanaians Image of the Missionary* (London, E. J. Brill, 1970).

Muller, Car. *A Hundred Years of Moravian Missions* (Herrenhut, 1931).

Page, J. *The Black Bishop, Samuel Adjai Crowther* (London, 1900).

Pascoe, C. F. *Two Hundred Years of the SPG*, Vol.I (1901).

Pierson, Donald, *Negroes in Brazil* (Chicago, 1942).

Porter A. T. *Creoldom: A Study of Development of Freeton Society* (Oxford, 1963).

Prickett, Barbara, *Island Base* (Meth. Church Gambia, n.d.).

Proceedings of the Church Missionary Society (1854, 1855, 1856, 1857, 1908).

Reindorf, Carl Christian, *The History of the Gold Coast and Asante* (Accra, 1960).

Sadler, G. W. *A Century in Nigeria (Baptist)* (Nashville, U.S.A., 1950).

Schon, J. F., and Crowther, S. A., *Journal of an Expedition up the Niger in 1841* (London, 1843).

Scottish Mission Records

Shropshire, D. W. T. *The Church and Primitive Peoples* (London, SPCK. 1938).

S.M.A. *100 Years of Missionary Achievement* (Cork, 1956).

Smith, E. W. *The Christian Missions in Africa* (International Missionary Council, *1926*).

Smith, J. N. *The Presbyterian Church of Ghana 1835-1960.* (Accra, Waterville 1966).

Staudenraus, P. J. *The African Colonization Movement, 1816-1865* (New York: Columbia University Press, 1961).

Thomas T. *An Account of Two Missionary Voyages, Re-print* (1937).
Townsend Henry, *Memoirs of Henry Townsend* (London, 1887).
Tupper H. *Foreign Missions of Southern Baptist Convention* (Richmond Va., USA, 1880).
Venn, Henry, *Memoirs of Henry Venn by William Knight* (London, 1880)
Waddell, Hope M. *Twenty-Nine Years in the West Indies and Central Africa* (London, 1863).
Wand, J. W. C. *A History of the Modern Church from 1500* (London, 1952).
Walker, Deaville F. *The Romance of the Black River* (Lon. CMS. 1930).
Ward, W. E. F. *A History of Ghana* (London, 1967).
Warren, Max, *Social History and Christian Mission* (London, 1967).
Westermann, D. *Africa and Christianity* (OUP, 1937).
Wiegrabe, P. *Ewe Mission Nutinya1847-1936* (St. Louis., U.S.A. 1936).
Williams, H. J. "An Outline of the Early Beginning of the United Brethren Church, Now United Methodist Church in Sierra Leone." (Mimeographed, Freetown, 1972).
Wiltgen, F. M. *Gold Coast Mission History 1471-1880* (Illinois, 1956).
Woodson C. G. *The African Background Outlined* (Washington DC., The Association for the Study of Negro Life and History Inc., 1936).

NEWS PAPERS

The Gold Coast Aboriginees.
The Gold Coast Leader.
The Gold Coast Methodist Times.

JOURNAL

Ghana Bulletin of Theology

REVIEW

International Review of Missions

INDEX

Ababio, John, 90
Abolition Movement, the, 115
African Methodist Episcopal (AME) Zion
  Church 143-151, in Liberia, 143-145,
  in the Gold Coast (Ghana), 145-151
Agbeti, J. K., 90n-91n
Aggrey, 147-148
Ahuma, Samuel Richard Brew Attoh,
  146, Samuel Solomon Attoh, 146
Ajayi, J. F. A., viii, 97n
Akolatse, Chief, 107
Akropong, 63, 65-68, Seminary, 157
Alvazez, T. E., 31
Amissang, George Amile, 105
Amu, E., 165
Andoh, Nana, 103
Ansre, G. B., 82n, 84n, 85n
Antonio, Padre, 97
Archibong II, Chief, 76
Arthur, Frank, 148-151
Ashanti, John, 104
Ayandele, 162n, 163-164n, E.A., viii

Baëta, C. G., viii
Bane, M. J., ix, 97n, 99n
Barrerius, Jesuit Father, 4
Bartels, F. L., viii, 54n, 56n
Basel Mission, 47, Trading Factory, 70
Basel Missionaries, Pioneers, 63
Bathurst, Mr., 24
Beckles, E. A., 29-30
Beecroft, Consul, 36
Beetham, T. A. viii
Berlin Missionary Seminary, 21
Bickersteth, Edward, 23-24
Biggs, Wilfred W., 15
Blyth, G., 73
Bonnat, Mr., 103-104
Borghero, Francesco, Fr., 96-97
Bossman, William, 5
Bowen, John, 39
Brazilian Immigrants, 97
Bremen Mission, first seven African
  Pastors ordained, 91
Bresillac, Melchior deMarion, 93-95
Brunton, Henry, 21n
Buergi, 92, Ernest, 158
Bultman, Luer, 81
Burns, A., 37
Butscher, 24, Leopold, 22

Capitein, 6, Jacobus Elisha Johannes, 6
Cartwright, Andrew, Rev., 143-144
Cason, Walter, 113-115
Caulker, Chief, 131, family, 132-133
Cauthen, Baker, J. and others, 122n,
  124n, 126n, 130n
Chaplains, 5-10
Cheetham, H., 30
Christaller, Johnson Gottlieb, 68-69
Church Missionary Society (CMS), 19-23,
  28, 32
Clapham Sect, 16
Clark, Kitson, G., viiin
Clarke, Rufus and Wife Training School,
  134
Coke, Dr., 49
Cole, E. T., Rev., 31
Countess of Huntingdon's Connexion, 20
Cranmer, Thomas, 14
Crowther, 35, Samuel Ajayi, 37, 44
Curtis, Mr., 22

d'Azambuja, Don Diogo, 3
Debrunner, Hans, viii, 143, 146n-147n
deGraft, William, 54-55, 59-60
Deism, 15
Der, Benedict, 58n, 110n
deRichelieu, Major, 62
Desai, Ram, 162n, 166n-167n
Descartes, 15
Deserving African Boys, 6
Du Bois, W. E. W., 143
Dunwell, Joseph, 55
During, 24
Dzani, 85
Dzelukofe, 88, 107

Eannes, Gil, 4
Egyir-Asaam, Kobina Fynn, Rev., 145-
  148
Erasmus, in Rome, 13
Esien Esien, Ukpabio, 77
Euthanasia of Mission, 28
Evangelical Revival, 10, 15
Eyo iii, 76

Falconbridge, 19
Flato, Karl, 81
Forbes, R. N. Commander, 36
Fourah Bay College, 26
Freeman, Thomas Birch, 56-57, 59-60,
  81, 147, Jr., 151